The Radical Mind

STUDIES IN US RELIGION, POLITICS, AND LAW

Leslie C. Griffin

Laura R. Olson

Tisa Wenger

Series Editors

The Radical Mind

The Origins of Right-Wing Catholic and Protestant Coalition Building

Chelsea Ebin

University Press of Kansas

Published by the University Press of Kansas (Lawrence, Kansas 66045), which
was organized by the Kansas Board of Regents and is operated and funded by
Emporia State University, Fort Hays State University, Kansas State University,
Pittsburg State University, the University of Kansas, and Wichita State University.

This book will be made open access within three years of publication thanks to Path to
Open, a program developed in partnership between JSTOR, the American Council of
Learned Societies (ACLS), University of Michigan Press, and The University of North
Carolina Press to bring about equitable access and impact for the entire scholarly
community, including authors, researchers, libraries, and university presses around the
world. Learn more at https://about.jstor.org/path-to-open/.

Library of Congress Cataloging-in-Publication Data

Names: Ebin, Chelsea, author.
Title: The radical mind : the origins of right-wing Catholic and Protestant
  coalition building / Chelsea Ebin.
Description: Lawrence : University Press of Kansas, 2024. | Series: Studies
  in US religion, politics, and law | Includes bibliographical references
  and index.
Identifiers: LCCN 2023050814 (print) | LCCN 2023050815 (ebook)
  ISBN 9780700636990 (cloth)
  ISBN 9780700637010 (ebook)
Subjects: LCSH: Religious right—United States. | Catholic
  Church—Relations—Protestant churches. | Christian conservatism—United
  States. | Christianity and politics—United States. | Weyrich, Paul M. |
  Falwell, Jerry
Classification: LCC BR516 .E36 2024 (print) | LCC BR516 (ebook) | DDC
  261.70973—dc23/eng/20240109
LC record available at https://lccn.loc.gov/2023050814.
LC ebook record available at https://lccn.loc.gov/2023050815.

British Library Cataloguing-in-Publication Data is available.

Cover photograph: Joel Avery (all rights reserved).
Instagram: @wait.for.steady.light

Chapter 2: Paul Weyrich: 1968 and the Roots of a (Catholic) Radical was originally
published in *American Catholic Studies*, Vol. 131, No. 3 (Fall 2020), and is reprinted with
permission.

For my families, birth and chosen

Falwell, looking toward the press table, said it all: "The media had better understand that in another context we would be shedding blood. But our commitment to the family has brought those of us of differing religious views and backgrounds together to fight a just cause . . . to fight for the family."

—Paul Weyrich

CONTENTS

PREFACE

A Roman Catholic [John F. Kennedy Jr.] is rushing toward the White House. The next President of the United States may owe allegiance to an alien potentate. Italian Pope John heads the vast RC [Roman Catholic] octopus that drains the resources of nations around the earth.

—Masonic anti-Catholic flier

Breaking the barriers between evangelical leaders and Catholics was key. There were years of anti-Catholic feeling in the fundamentalist community. But I had more in common with some in terms of belief in the Lord and fundamentals of the faith than I did with some liberal Catholics. I worked on Catholics to support evangelical candidates and evangelicals to support Catholic candidates.

—Paul Weyrich

I frequently—and somewhat apocryphally—say that I have Sarah Palin to thank for planting the seed for this book. In 2009 I was deep in the weeds of Catholic natural law theory, with the intent of examining its influence on constitutional interpretation and Supreme Court decision-making. Then my partner sent me a clip of Palin talking about inalienable rights in a way that conjured the natural law and asked me to explain why Palin, a self-identified charismatic evangelical, was using language traditionally associated with Catholic thought. I had no ready answer to explain what looked like a crossover of Catholic doctrine into evangelical political discourse. So, I began digging and found that Palin employed a conservative who was raised Catholic as her primary speechwriter during her failed run for vice president in 2008. I then read her autobiography, *Going Rogue*, and it struck me that Palin's rhetoric seemed to gesture toward ideas and language I associated with the Catholic tradition of natural law.[1]

But this only raised more questions, the most perplexing of which was: When—and how—had conservative Catholics and Protestants become political bedfellows on the American right? If they had converged, as I began to think was the case, what had motivated their union? Moreover, how was a coalition between the two built and mobilized? Were they brought together by a reactionary backlash to progressive rights? Or were conservative Catholics and Protestants united by a shared vision of what the future could hold and a collective desire to transform American politics that transcended doctrinal differences and identity-based hostilities toward one another? These are the questions that came to animate this book.

To understand why the seeming fact of Catholic and Protestant convergence struck me as pivotal for American political development, it is important to recognize that for much of the nation's history, Protestant hostility toward Catholics was commonplace. American Christianity has historically been a house divided, with the lines separating American Catholics and Protestants starkly drawn. From the time of the country's founding, American Catholics were viewed with suspicion and hostility.[2] "Nativism, notably anti-Catholicism, had been part of American politics and culture as early as the Jacksonian period," according to historians writing to the US Supreme Court. In the late nineteenth century, anti-Catholic and anti-immigrant "nativist fears coalesced into a drive against what was then called 'race suicide.' The 'race suicide' alarmists worried that women of 'good stock'—prosperous, white, and Protestant—were not having enough children to maintain the political and social supremacy of their group."[3] Catholics were, in short, perceived as a threat to the dominance of White Protestants in the United States. Colonial anti-Papist sentiments merged in the nineteenth century with Malthusian fears of overpopulation to produce a nativistic, anti-immigrant strain in American politics that would endure well into the twentieth century. American Catholics (often first- and second-generation immigrants) were frequently cast as the enemy within, even as they fought to be more fully included in the body politic.

The process of incorporation into the polity demanded that American Catholics prove their racial and religious belonging. By the dawn of the twentieth century, as Tisa Wenger has shown, American Catholics capitalized on the colonization of the Philippines to demonstrate their "Americanness" and to assert their place—as Christians—at the top of a religious and racial hierarchy alongside White Protestants.[4] And yet, as the twentieth century progressed, American Catholics continued to occupy a liminal space. When faced with a common enemy, such as the specter of communism[5] or the Supreme Court's ban on school prayer,[6] Catholics and

Protestants oscillated between seeing one another as allies and as enemies. This ambivalent relationship broke down in 1960, as the United States considered the election of its first Catholic president. Anti-Catholicism returned to the forefront of American politics with the National Association of Evangelicals (NAE) baldly stating, "Whereas separation of church and state is the historic American principle, be it resolved that the NAE states its belief: That due to the political-religious nature of the Roman Catholic Church we doubt a Roman Catholic president could or would resist fully the pressures of the ecclesiastical hierarchy."[7] Fear-mongering headlines and anti-Catholic propaganda flyers containing sentiments such as that reflected in the first epigraph abounded. And yet, over the past fifty years, Catholics and Protestants have increasingly come to see themselves as comrades in God's army.

By the early 1980s, the Moral Majority, the most publicly recognizable institution representing the right-wing conservative Christian movement known as the New Christian Right (NCR), claimed to represent conservative Catholics alongside its majority evangelical and fundamentalist Protestant base. A decade later, this easing of hostility and suspicion was reflected in a joint ecumenical proclamation titled Evangelicals and Catholics Together, which held:

> As Christ is one, so the Christian mission is one. That one mission can be and should be advanced in diverse ways. Legitimate diversity, however, should not be confused with existing divisions between Christians that obscure the one Christ and hinder the one mission. There is a necessary connection between the visible unity of Christians and the mission of the one Christ.[8]

The convergence of Protestants and Catholics is particularly striking among those who identify as conservative. Increasingly, conservative Christians have set aside their denominational differences to work together, in the process coming to politically resemble one another and share in the collective belief that they are being threatened.

As recently as the 1960s, this would have been unthinkable given the high levels of animosity between Catholics and Protestants and the distinctly drawn lines of demarcation separating their faith practices. And yet, the perceived threat of Catholicism has been replaced by a set of simultaneously generalized but totalizing beliefs surrounding an imagined assault on American Christianity—and American Whiteness—writ large. In 2023 it is not uncommon to hear conservative Christians talk about how, as a group, they are "under attack." Narratives of victimization abound as conservative Catholics and Protestants alike voice fears of an existential threat to an American way of life that they believe is intrinsically tied up with Christianity.[9] This book seeks to explain how conservative Protestants and Catholics, antagonists for much of US history, formed a political coalition and came to share in the belief that they have a common identity and that their—and the country's—traditions are under attack.

Puzzled by the prevalence of a Catholic-inflected natural law discourse on the evangelical right,[10] I turned to the archives. I set out to uncover the origins and, by extension, the implications of what on its face appears to be a most unlikely alliance of conservative Catholics and Protestants. Pursuing this line of inquiry led me to adopt an "actor-centered view of institutional change" as I homed in on the work of a group of conservative Catholic "political entrepreneurs"[11] who were active in creating the New Right in the early 1970s.

While the Christian Right of the 1980s promoted itself as an explicitly religious coalition of the "moral," the New Right of the 1970s was an ostensibly secular movement aimed at promoting conservative political actors and advancing conservatism as a governing political ideology.[12] Mobilizing in response to President Richard Nixon's real and perceived failures to toe the conservative line, these hardline conservative activists began floating the idea of challenging his reelection. The journalist Kevin Phillips coined the term "New Right" to describe conservatives who sought to organize a pseudo-populist, radical insurgency to reorient the American political system and forge more right-leaning conservative coalitions that breached party lines. On its face, the New Right was centrally concerned with electoral politics, focusing much of its resources and attention on the election of "real" conservatives and congressional lobbying efforts. But behind the scenes, many of the movement's key leaders were devout Catholics who were conservative in both their politics and faith and deeply committed to so-called social issues. Moreover, while the New Right was a nonhierarchical, horizontally structured movement, it nonetheless was helmed by several political entrepreneurs, including Paul Weyrich, and Connaught Marshner, who left a deeply Catholic imprint on the ostensibly secular movement, directed its ideological and institutional development, and spearheaded the formation of a coalition with White conservative Protestants (CPs).

While existing literature on the Christian Right credits the political activist Paul Weyrich and other members of the New Right with helping to create the Christian Right,[13] this scholarship is not attendant to the influence of Catholic theology on Weyrich and his collaborators or on the development of key Christian Right discourses. But, I argue, it is difficult, if not impossible, to understand the New Right without taking into account the deep Catholicism of its leaders. By examining the importance and influence of conservative Catholics on the formation of the New Christian Right, this book tells a familiar story in an unfamiliar way. Exploring the relationship between Catholic New Right (CNR) activists and conservative Protestant religious-political brokers not only helps us to better understand the Christian Right; it also sheds light on how an enduring coalition of conservative Catholics and Protestants emerged and was mobilized. In doing so, it draws attention not only to the nuts and bolts of how the coalition was built and the mobilization strategies it pioneered but also to the ways in which new ideas and identities were produced as a result of the convergence of conservative Catholic and Protestant political elites.

In order to gain insight into the development of the political ideology and strategies adopted by CNR activists, my research has largely focused on primary texts written by the actors themselves. Over the course of seven years, I consulted the following archival collections: the Jerry Falwell and Moral Majority Archives at Liberty University; the Paul Weyrich Scrapbooks at the Library of Congress; the Paul Weyrich Papers at the American Heritage Center at the University of Wyoming, Laramie; the Jimmy Carter Papers at the Jimmy Carter Library; the Sara Diamond Collection at the Bancroft Library, University of California, Berkeley; and the William Martin Religious Right collection at the Woodson Research Center at Rice University. I also reviewed all issues of *Conservative Digest* and *The New Right Report* in the period under investigation (most issues are located in the Rare Book and Manuscript Library at Columbia University; however, I supplemented these holdings with those held at the New York Public Library and, in a few cases, with volumes available via interlibrary loans). These archival collections include institutional memos, speeches, policy papers, and public-facing writings by the actors under investigation as well as extensive news coverage of the New Right and the Christian Right. The Paul Weyrich Scrapbook collection is a particularly rich source of material, as Weyrich obsessively cataloged news coverage of his work. Together, these documents form the backbone of my research. Additional material comes from media accounts and texts written by activists and journalists during the period under investigation and books written by CNR and Christian Right actors.[14] These texts provide crucial insight into both how the movements were understood by the actors themselves and how they were received by their political opponents, both liberal and conservative.

The archives also informed—and expanded—the time frame for this study. Initially, I anticipated focusing on the period beginning with Nixon's reelection in 1972, as the New Right formed in response to Nixon's perceived failure to be a "true" conservative, and ending with Ronald Reagan's election in 1980, a victory that was initially heralded as the dawning of a new day by the New Right and Christian Right alike. The data led me to reconsider my understanding of what events, and by extension years, were most relevant to the creation of a conservative Catholic and Protestant coalition, which I term the New Christian Right (NCR) to reflect the merging of composite movements.

In working my way through these archival collections, I was comforted by the knowledge that the historical arc I was constructing through primary texts broadly matched that depicted in seminal histories of the Christian Right, such as those by William Martin and Daniel K. Williams.[15] The compelling history of the Christian Right has been thoroughly and painstakingly detailed in these works, along with a host of others.[16] This project does not aim to reproduce or remake this history; rather, its baseline historical narrative overlaps to a significant degree with the excellent and comprehensive literature on the subject. While the story of conservative Catholic and Protestant convergence on the Christian Right has implications for how we think about electoral realignment and party incorporation/capture, it is not intended as an intervention in these conversations.[17] Instead, this work is interested in the production and promulgation of ideas by political and religious elites and the ways in which political elites transformed theological understandings, social relations, and institutional arrangements in order to facilitate the union of conservative Catholic and Bible-believing Protestants. It seeks to uncover the discursive mechanisms used by conservative Catholic and Protestant political entrepreneurs to reshape their relationship to one another and to the American Right. And, along the way, it also shows how the convergence of these two groups was motivated by a profound desire to transform American political culture and institutions. Such an examination leads to two key findings: (1) these groups built an enduring and influential political coalition by instrumentalizing a shared identity of victimhood to stitch together a plurality of right-wing single-issue groups;[18] and (2) that conservative Catholics and Protestants were not motivated by backlash, but rather by a proactive desire to transform the American political landscape.

This book is, in essence, a history of the ideas developed and promulgated by conservative Christian elites in the 1970s. It therefore tells only one part of a much bigger story about the rise of a right-wing Christian movement in the twentieth century and its impact on the American electorate and American political institutions. But it is an important part of the story. To understand the ideas, institutions, and processes that underpinned the convergence of conservative Catholics and Protestants is to come to understand the radicality of the New Christian Right in the twenty-first century.

Acknowledgments

This book was many years in the making, giving me ample time to rack up a host of debts of gratitude. I owe the best and brightest insights of this work to conversations with Ricky Price, Jack Vimo, and Howell Williams. They patiently read every single draft and helped me develop my analysis and hone my writing from the very beginning to the very end. Without the work of archivists, this project would, quite simply, not exist. It also would not exist without the support of James Miller, David Plotke, Mark Larrimore, and Randall Balmer, who shepherded it through its first incarnation at the New School for Social Research, and David Congdon, my editor at the University Press of Kansas (UPK), who championed its transformation into this book. Thanks are also due to the entire team at UPK and to Joel Avery for allowing me to use the incredible photograph that graces the cover of this book.

Archival research and academic writing can be a lonely endeavor during the best of times, but this was all the more the case during the COVID-19 pandemic. I am, therefore, particularly grateful to the intellectual communities that helped foster this work during the pandemic, including the members of the 2021 American Examples working group, the Far-Right Analysis Network (formerly CARR), and the incredible community of scholars, journalists, and advocates who make up the Institute for Research on Male Supremacism (IRMS). In the final stretches of putting together this manuscript, as we reemerged from pandemic lockdowns, Shana Sippy talked through so many of its core ideas with me and provided daily writing encouragement as we labored side by side in the Lexington Writer's Room. I am so very grateful for Shana's support and friendship throughout this process and beyond. Thanks are also owed to the folks who made the Writer's Room such an accessible, welcoming, and productive space. I feel very fortunate to have been able to write the final draft of the book there.

My thanks go to the countless scholars who provided feedback on chapter drafts at a host of conferences and the external reviewers of this manuscript as well as related articles. In particular, I owe a real debt to Joseph Lowndes, for his generous feedback and for the inspiration his work has given me. Likewise, I am indebted to Carol Mason, whose scholarship has been formative for me and has inspired my work. Chapter 2 owes much to the editor of the *American Catholic Studies* journal, Thomas Rzeznik, who helped me work through the thornier aspects of Catholic theology discussed in it. This work also benefited from being workshopped in a number of writing groups, and special thanks go to Emily Carian, Meredith Pruden, Anastasia Todd, Karrieann Soto Vega, and Elizabeth Williams for their insightful and interdisciplinary feedback. Any and all errors and omissions are mine alone.

Additionally, I am thankful to the New School for Social Research, the American Heritage Center, and the Faculty Development Committee at Centre College for providing research and travel funding that supported my research.

Many acknowledgments would end here, but I want to take this opportunity to recognize that it took a veritable village to produce this work. I am a working-class academic who followed a nontraditional path to college and beyond, working my way through undergrad and large parts of grad school as a hairstylist. Early on, unfamiliar with the hidden curriculum of academia, I looked to the acknowledgments section of books in my discipline for clues as to how a successful monograph was made. Instead, I found the acknowledgments read more like academic pedigrees than road maps to producing scholarly work. Rarely did I find acknowledgment of the financial challenges attendant to the production of scholarly work or recognition of the difficulties of laboring under a system of precarity. More often than not, I was left with the impression that only those who followed a "traditional" path published in academia. Having taken many circuitous turns to get to this place, I do not feel qualified to share a road map, but I can, in some small way, try not to present the journey as one that was seamlessly facilitated by only elite institutions and people. While I've been fortunate to receive the support of both, I want to also acknowledge that this book would not have been possible without the encouragement, help, and support (both personal and financial) of my friends, family (both chosen and birth), and community. It also would not have been possible had I not worked many long hours both inside and outside of the academy to pay the bills.

In roughly chronological order, I owe a profound debt of gratitude to the following people: the Wallen/Loya/Ebin family for their love and for teaching me how to read and encouraging me to always be critical of existing power arrangements; Penny Anderson, Sean Brookins, Heather Howard, and Melissa McGrogan for believing in me from the time I was a punk-rock teenager, and supporting my dreams of going to cosmetology school and getting a PhD with equal measures of encouragement and enthusiasm; Ronnie Lipschutz and Vanita Seth for seeing past my working-class insecurities and cultivating my scholarly potential; and all of the salon clients who tipped a little extra to help me cover the cost of tuition and textbooks while I was completing my undergraduate degree at the University of California, Santa Cruz.

I would never have survived the move to New York and the transition to graduate school without the love and friendship of Hilary Davis and Neshani Jani. Likewise, I would not have made it without the monthly care packages my sister, Raven Loya, mailed me and the MetroCard she paid for, or the political theory books my mom, Judi Ebin, found for me by scouring library sales before the start of each semester. During those very lean years, Kate Eichhorn and Mark Larrimore took a chance on me as an early graduate student, providing me with administrative and teaching experience at the New School as well as a paycheck that kept a roof over my head. While I left the New School with a staggering amount of student loan debt, it was worth every cent because I would not have otherwise come to be in community with Luis Herran Avila, Biko Koenig, Desiree LaVecchia, Ricky Price, Margarita Velasco, Howell Williams, Jack Vimo, and so many others.

I began finding my financial and academic footing while working at Columbia University's Institute for Religion, Culture, and Public Life, where Mark C. Taylor helped me to learn the habitus of academia and sharpened my editorial skills, and Emily Brennan encouraged me to pursue this topic when it was just a twinkle in my eye while also becoming a lifelong friend. Later, Bene Coopersmith and Scott Pfaffman made it possible for me to open my own tiny salon in the Record Shop, which afforded me the security and flexibility to conduct the research for this book. Raven Loya, Jivani Chandiramani, and an American Express credit card provided the seed funding to get my little shop, The Walk-In, off the ground. But it would never have happened without the incredible friendship of Sara Edwards and Matt Rubendall, whose friendship and generosity in all areas of life knows no bounds.

Post-graduate school—in Florida—Daniel Griffin, Benjamin Hudson, Kristy Lewis, Marta Lyons, Giovanna McClenachan, Gab Reisman, Roisin Stanbrook, and Maridath Wilson kept me sane and fed while I was teaching a four-four course load and trying to get on the tenure track. A special shout-out goes to Alison Reeve at Rollins College for being my rock, to Maura Wittkop for her research assistance on a separate but related work, and to St. Matt's for providing a safe space. From my time at Centre College, I am particularly grateful for the friendship, comradery, and commiseration that Dina Badie, Amy Frederick, Megs Gendreau, and Shana Sippy provided and for the students who inspired me to keep researching, writing, and teaching about the American Right. Thanks also to Joshua Sto. Domingo, for many great conversations and help in checking the citations for this book.

Through it all, I have received unconditional love and support from my many families (both birth and chosen), my partner, Jack, and the furry creatures with whom we share our home. It is to them that I owe my greatest debt of gratitude.

A Note on Terminology

Defining the terms used in this book is not an altogether straightforward task. There is considerable slippage between and among the groups and identities—both religious and political—that this book attends to. This is all the more the case because this work seeks to track the movement and convergence of conservative Catholic and Protestant elites and their collective political mobilization. Thus, both the religious identities and political groups under investigation are necessarily in flux. The problem of naming is compounded, in part, by the institutional murkiness that characterizes organizations associated with what I term the New Christian Right. This murkiness was often intentional as the proliferation of overlapping institutions and coalitions served to obscure the role of Catholic New Right elites while emphasizing the importance of the conservative Protestant grassroots base. But it also stems from the difficulty of ascribing a collective identity on the basis of both religious beliefs and practices and political ideology, all of which are necessarily varied and subject to (re)interpretation and contestation over time.

There is a further danger in naming and studying these groups as I have, which the religion scholar L. Benjamin Rolsky points to: scholars of the New Christian Right are participants in the making of the movement and "have also contributed to the formation of the subject itself—the evangelical."[1] This danger is reflective of a number of "theoretical barriers" to the study of evangelicalism, chief among them the tendency among scholars of both religion and the right to view evangelicalism as "passe" and retrograde.[2] Thus, many scholars approach the study of conservative Protestants from a pathologizing perspective that seeks to answer some variation of the question, "What is wrong with conservative Christians?" This work begins from a different starting point. It began not by asking what was *bad* about the politics of conservative Christians but rather what it was that made conservative Christians so very *good* at politics. The answer I found lies in the coalition-building strategies and mobilization techniques pioneered by Catholic New Right and conservative Protestant political elites. In this way, I hope this work manages to neither produce nor pathologize its subject of analysis.

Setting these difficulties and dangers aside, it is nonetheless necessary to provide some baseline definitions for the descriptive terms I most frequently use to talk about conservative Christians and their associated political movements in the United States from the late 1960s through the early 1980s. They are as follows:

1. Conservative Catholic: refers to a particular subset of Catholics who both espouse orthodox religious beliefs and hew to traditionalist political positions. These Catholics may also be referred to as "traditionalist Catholics" or "Catholic Integralists." Conservative Catholics hold socially conservative attitudes on sex, gender, and family, and are frequently critical of the reforms initiated by the Second Vatican Council.

2. Conservative Protestant (CP)/Bible-believing Protestant: these terms are used interchangeably to refer to White evangelical and fundamentalist Protestants who share both a conservative religious and political outlook. My use of the term intentionally excludes mainline Protestants with conservative political viewpoints, evangelicals who identify as politically progressive, and Protestants of color. Doctrinal differences exist between fundamentalist and evangelical Protestants, as well as within these two groups. Following Susan Friend Harding's usage, both groups can be broadly termed "Bible-believing," that is, they are Protestants who adhere to the belief that the Bible is the literal word of God. While these two groups have frequently acted in conjunction, there nonetheless is a distinction between their belief systems. I, therefore, also frequently refer to "Evangelicals/fundamentalists" to avoid the danger of collapsing the two groups.

3. Evangelical Protestant: refers to a broad and diverse group of Protestant denominations and churches that share a central set of beliefs. I define the group according to the guidelines produced by the National Association of Evangelicals, which identifies four primary characteristics: "Conversionism: the belief that lives need to be transformed through a 'born-again' experience and a lifelong process of following Jesus; Activism: the expression and demonstration of the gospel in missionary and social reform efforts; Biblicism: a high regard for and obedience to the Bible as the

ultimate authority; Crucicentrism: a stress on the sacrifice of Jesus Christ on the cross as making possible the redemption of humanity."[3]

4. Fundamentalist Protestant: refers to a specific subset of conservative Protestants, who initially organized in response to a series of twelve pamphlets titled *The Fundamentals*, which were published between 1910 and 1915. By and large, fundamentalists seek to revive traditional Christian viewpoints and reject modernism. Broadly speaking, we might say that while all fundamentalists are evangelical, not all evangelicals are fundamentalists.

5. New Right and Catholic New Right (CNR): the New Right can briefly be summarized as a self-identified insurgent and radical political movement that formed in the early 1970s with the intent of advancing "true" conservatism. Comprised of a network of over-lapping political brokers and conservative institutions, the New Right sought to force the Republican Party to adopt more conservative positions while also disrupting the two-party system through the creation of a broad-based conservative coalition that would cleave across traditional Republican and Democratic party lines. While the New Right is generally regarded as a secular movement, it was deeply informed by the conservative Catholic views held by many of the movement's leaders. I term this group of activists, which included Paul M. Weyrich, Connaught Marshner, and Richard Viguerie, the Catholic New Right. While I do so in order to avoid making overly broad generalizations about the New Right, in most instances there is little distinction between the views and strategies adopted by the CNR and those taken up by the New Right as a whole.

6. Christian Right and New Christian Right: I use the term Christian Right to refer to politically and socially conservative Christians broadly. When referring to the Christian Right movement that originated in the late 1970s and 1980s with the help of the New Right, I use the term New Christian Right (NCR). This sociopolitical movement was formed with the aim of injecting "Judeo-Christian" values and beliefs into American political institutions, laws, and public discourse. While marketed as a conservative "Judeo-Christian" coalition of Jews, Latter-Day Saints, Catholics, and Protestants, the NCR base was predominantly composed of conservative Protestants. There is much to be said about the place of conservative Jews and Latter-Day Saints in the NCR, and this book focuses more narrowly on the influence of conservative Catholics and the relationship between conservative Catholics and Protestants. While evangelical and

fundamentalist Protestant faith leaders tended to utilize the more ecumenical moniker of the "Religious Right"—in order to lay claim to the Old Testament and to appear inclusive of conservative Jews—I find "Christian Right" to be a more accurate and apt name for the groups this book examines.

ABBREVIATIONS

CNR	Catholic New Right
CTM	Catholic Traditionalist Movement
CUF	Catholics United for Faith
CSFC	Committee for the Survival of a Free Congress
CP	Conservative Protestant
EOE	Economic Opportunity Extension Act
ERA	Equal Rights Amendment
ESEA	Elementary and Secondary Education Act
FLSE	Family Life and Sex Education
FPA	Family Protection ACT
FPAB	Family Policy Advisory Board
NCR	New Christian Right
RAVCO	Richard A. Viguerie Company
SEC	Security and Exchange Commission
SBC	Southern Baptist Convention
SALT	Strategic Arms Limitation Treaty
USCCB	United States Conference of Catholic Bishops
WHCF	White House Conference on Families

INTRODUCTION

Beverly LaHaye (BLH): We were getting word through the international news system that Anita Bryant was speaking out on the homosexual movement in Dade County, Florida. And we would read of cases where she was getting accosted or she would get pie thrown in her face. And I remember, as Tim and I were travelling through France, he said somebody should be doing something about that. . . .

Tim LaHaye (TLH): I kept saying why don't the Ministers stand. . . . Why does a woman have to stand up and get the abuse of these homosexuals? Because in our country the church has always been the conscience of America. . . .

BLH: Well, I believe when we first came back into the country and we went to a big conference in the city and Anita Bryant was to be one of the speakers and we visually

TLH: Yes

BLH: We visually saw with our own eyes

TLH: Discrimination.

BLH: The homosexuals lined up outside of the auditorium trying to block the entrance and trying to get to her and we began to realize that something had to change in America. They were trying to silence her voice.[1]

In the United States, the first few years of the 2020s have been defined by a resurgence of so-called culture war issues. These contestations—over issues like abortion, transgender health care, bathroom access, youth sports, LGBTQ+ public accommodation, the recognition of structural racism and gender-based discrimination, and the value of diversity—are being pushed by Republican legislators at the state and national levels and taken up by a Supreme Court that is dominated by a conservative Catholic majority. While battles over social issues were already at the forefront of domestic politics, a frontier was breached on June 24, 2022, when the Supreme Court of the United States handed down a decision in *Dobbs v. Jackson Women's Health Organization* overturning the constitutional right to abortion established by the Court's landmark decision *Roe v. Wade* forty-nine years earlier. In the twelve months following the Court's decision, a truly stunning number of bills were introduced in state legislatures that promote a Christian Right agenda for restricting reproductive autonomy. Republican-led state legislatures passed laws ranging from those that make virtually all abortions illegal (North Dakota) to those restricting access to abortion to the first six or twelve weeks of pregnancy (Florida and North Carolina, respectively). Other restrictions have taken the form of laws intended to control access to information about abortion (Texas) and the criminalization of "abortion trafficking" (Idaho).[2]

This has been accompanied by a wave of anti-transgender legislation as, according to the Trans Legislation Tracker, seventy-nine anti-trans bills were passed in the first six months of 2023.[3] State legislatures have voted to prohibit trans youth from accessing gender-affirming health care, ban trans youth from participating in sports, and limit bathroom access for trans people in public education and governmental facilities.[4] Additional laws censoring discussions of LGBTQ+ people and issues (colloquially referred to as "Don't Say Gay" laws) have been passed in at least ten states.[5] These join a bevy of legislative acts aimed at restricting discussions of systemic racism, White supremacy, and racial oppression in US history. Most of these laws explicitly take aim at Critical Race Theory (CRT).[6] While CRT is a theoretical framework for analyzing how White supremacy structures legal, political, and social institutions that is most often taught in graduate schools, it has come to stand in for any teaching that acknowledges racism (and, increasingly, sexism or homophobia). In this way, CRT has become an empty signifier that functions like the concept of "secular humanism" did in the 1980s.[7] The intended effect of Don't Say Gay and anti-CRT laws is to erase the historical and continued existence of systemic oppression and deny the structural and institutional causes of inequality. They also serve the Christian Right project of defining the United States as a White, Christian republic where "men are men, and women are women."

But the Christian Right agenda in 2024 is not limited to "culture war" issues; it also extends to the economic realm and to the institution of democracy itself. This is reflected in the conservative push to rollback COVID-era social welfare benefits[8] and debt ceiling negotiations, which resulted in the introduction of new work requirements for food aid benefits that will increase food insecurity and hunger for many Americans.[9] This is to say nothing of the threat to democracy posed by conservative Christians who, along with other right-wing supporters of President Donald J. Trump, stormed the Capitol on January 6, 2020, and who have continued to promulgate the "Big Lie" and baselessly assert that Trump won the 2020 presidential election.[10] These affronts against democracy have been accompanied by continued assaults on the democratic process itself, with new bills intended to restrict voting introduced at a record-breaking pace.[11]

It would not be possible to pursue this agenda without the support of a Supreme Court that was remade with the seating of three new justices during Trump's single term as president. Right-wing Christians have been aided by a federal judiciary that was transformed by Trump appointees.[12] Put plainly, with Trump's help, the Christian Right effectively captured the American judiciary.[13] It is no surprise, then, that while antidiscrimination, reproductive, and LGBTQ+ rights have fared poorly in the courts over the past several years, Christians seeking to assert their rights have been received warmly. In decisions on school prayer and government funding for (Christian) religious organizations, the conservative majority of the Supreme Court has, in effect, rewritten the religion clauses contained in the First Amendment of the US Constitution in order to ascribe the status of most favored freedom to the Free Exercise clause.[14]

The Court has also begun carving out exemptions for religious believers from compliance with nondiscrimination law as it applies to LGBTQ+ individuals. The restraint the Court exercised in its 2018 decision in *Masterpiece Cakeshop, Ltd. v. Colorado Civil Rights Commission* was nowhere to be found in the majority opinion for *303 Creative, LLC. v. Elenis* in 2023. In ruling that a Christian website designer could not be compelled to not discriminate against same-sex couples seeking wedding websites, the Court used the Free Speech clause of the First Amendment to override public accommodation protections for LGBTQ+ people. Following this precedent, the right of Christians to practice their faith is likely to increasingly supersede the rights of others in all areas of life. This extends to a host of rights, including but not limited to the right not to be discriminated against in places of public accommodation, bodily autonomy, sexual freedom, marriage equality, health care, and so on. I do not think it is an overstatement to say we are hurtling toward a legal framework that will systematically disadvantage religious minorities, Black, Indigenous [and] people of color (BIPOC), queer and trans people, and women. In short, the Court's recent First Amendment decisions seemingly seek to promote and institutionalize Christian supremacy in the law.

How do we explain the seeming gains of the Christian Right and the morally super-charged domestic political landscape of the early 2020s?

One popular explanation asserts that the United States is simply experiencing a Christian Right backlash. The backlash thesis can be applied in more and less sympathetic ways. A sympathetic reading goes something like this: After forty-nine years of abortion access, two decades of increased acceptance—both socially and legally—for LGBTQ+ people, and the 2020 protests in support of Black lives, which were accompanied by demands for a national reckoning with the effects of White supremacy, conservative White Christians are the real victims of discrimination. As victims, conservative Christians are acting in self-defense, reacting to progressive gains and trying to return the nation to an earlier status quo when forced pregnancy was the norm, queer people were closeted, and people of color were more effectively oppressed. A less sympathetic reading promotes the idea that conservative Christians are dinosaurs, holding on to retrograde beliefs and trying to resurrect a past that belongs to the ash heap of history. In this telling, the current wave of Christian Right opposition to progressive gains is just the last gasp of a dying breed, and the legislative and judicial backlash will not prevail in the long run.

I believe both of these accounts are wrong. Conservative Christians are neither victims nor reprobate representatives of a bygone era. They are sophisticated and modern political actors. Moreover, their assaults on the rights and freedoms of women, people of color, LGBTQ+ people, social welfare benefits, and democratic institutions do not merely seek to return the country to its recent past. Rather, they represent a desire to make the sociopolitical landscape of the country anew. Taken together, attempts to strip historically marginalized and underrepresented groups of rights and recognition, undermine the social welfare state, and erode democratic procedures and safeguards signal a profound rejection of American political norms. The legislative agenda of the Christian Right actively promotes the supremacy and domination of White, cisgender, Christian men over all facets of life in the United States. It is, at its core, an illiberal and antidemocratic agenda.

This is not a book about the contemporary Christian Right or its agenda for the next decade and beyond. Rather it is a book about the actions and ideas of conservative Catholic and Protestant political elites over roughly two decades, spanning the early/mid-1960s to the early/mid-1980s. In doing so, it aims to help us understand how we got to this point in time.

In the following chapters, I excavate the foundations for this current moment by examining how a coalition between conservative Catholics and Bible-believing Protestants was created and the ideas and beliefs that drove their convergence and shaped their vision for American politics. In the process, I illustrate not only how the Christian Right came to embrace supremacist politics, but also how it obscured its desire to remake American democracy and society as a desire to conserve the past.

I use the archives to tell a complex narrative about the political convergence of Catholic New Right (CNR) activists and White conservative Protestant (CP) religious elites and the corresponding production of new ideas and strategies that were informed by conservative Catholic beliefs. Along the way, I find that the New Christian Right (NCR) coalition they built was premised on manufactured narratives of the past and centered on an artificial identity of victimhood. By problematizing the discourse of victimhood and the backlash narrative that right-wing Christians promoted from the 1960s to 1980s, I show how the NCR coalition produced a fundamentally illiberal politics that was premised on the "rights" of the family and motivated by the desire to radically transform American social and political institutions. Doing so enables us to view conservative Christian political actors as not merely reactive but *proactive*, their aim not merely conservation but *creation*. It is in this way that this book about the past helps us to make sense of the present and, perhaps, even future political aims of the Christian Right.

Methodological Approach: Taking Ideas Seriously

In order to explain how the NCR coalition was built and mobilized in the 1970s and understand its continued impact and legacy, I utilize Vivien

Schmidt's "discursive institutionalism" methodological framework.[15] To understand large-scale political ruptures and transformations, Schmidt explains, "we need to engage in a contextualized analysis of the substantive content of agents' ideas and their interactive processes of discourse."[16] Discursive institutionalist methodologies, therefore, share a commitment to: (1) taking "ideas and discourse seriously," (2) placing "ideas and discourse in institutional context," (3) applying a constructivist lens to understanding how meaning is made; and (4) having "a more dynamic view of change, in which ideas and discourse overcome obstacles" that other forms of institutionalist analysis may view as intractable.[17] As applied here, discursive institutionalism contributes to the American political development scholarship on the right by helping to elucidate the importance of ideas in shaping large-scale institutional changes sought and accomplished by the New and Christian Rights over the course of two decades.[18]

Taking up Schmidt's call to think seriously about ideas and discourse, I employ a discursive institutionalist framework to interrogate the complex set of religious, social, and political discourses that were central to the creation of the NCR coalition. For example, as shown in chapter 4, Bible-believing political entrepreneurs (such as Jerry Falwell and Francis Schaeffer) rationalized their work with nonfundamentalists in terms of "co-belligerency," which functioned as a sort of fundamentalist doctrine for single-issue coalition-building with those outside of the fundamentalist fold.[19] Following Schmidt's classification, this coalition work might be described in terms of the production of a "coordinative discourse," which "consists of the individuals and groups at the center of policy construction who are involved in the creation, elaboration, and justification of policy and programmatic ideas." Schmidt further explains, "These are the policy actors—the civil servants, elected officials, experts, organized interests, and activists, among others—who seek to coordinate agreement among themselves on policy ideas."[20] Thus, as a coordinative discourse, the doctrine of co-belligerency facilitated agreement between fundamentalist, evangelical, and Catholic political elites on policy matters like abortion.

However, political entrepreneurs need to not only produce policies but also sell them. This public, or communicative, discourse "consists of the individuals and groups involved in the presentation, deliberation, and legitimation of political ideas to the general public," who work to "communicate the policy ideas and programs developed in the coordinative discourse to the public for discussion and deliberation."[21] And so, while co-belligerency produced ecumenical agreement on matters of policy, the concept also functioned as a means of rationalizing ecumenicism to fundamentalist Protestants. Without this common ground, the Protestant grassroots would likely have expressed hostility to those from outside of their own faith tradition. Applying the aforementioned terms from Schmidt's work allows us to identify how the NCR coalition was built and how it mobilized on two fronts: on one hand, elites rhetorically constructed a new political past, present, and future—generating a saleable communicative discourse. On the other hand, movement activists built organizations and institutions to sustain an electoral and policy coalition, thereby producing a coordinative discourse that helped reshape the American political landscape.

The developments taking place within the New Right and Christian Right between 1965 and 1985 were part of a broader political change to the American right in the twentieth century. The mobilization of conservative White Christians corresponded with the movement of White Southern voters away from alignment with the Democratic Party and toward the Republican Party, and it was part and parcel of a right-ward shift in American political discourse that began with Barry Goldwater and continues to the present.[22] On one hand, conservative White Christians drove these trends. On the other hand, conservative White Christians were responding to outside social, economic, and political transformations. While attentive to a variety of the institutional factors that informed this push and pull, my primary concern is with the ideational constructions and discursive practices that produced conservative White Christians as a unified and influential political force.

For the most part, discursive institutionalism operates in the background of this book, serving as an analytical framework that informs the questions posed by this study. However, the terms "coordinative discourse" and "communicative discourse" are used fairly regularly, as they help capture the ways in which conservative Christian elites produced and operationalized new ways of thinking. For example, in chapter 1, I explore how the communicative discourse of backlash, premised on a narrative of conservative Christian victimization and reactionary self-defense, helped to obscure the radicality of Christian Right social policies and legitimize the movement's claims to represent the true (i.e., traditional) body politic. Later, in chapter 5, I turn to the convergence of CNR and CP political entrepreneurs to demonstrate how the NCR coalition was formed on the basis of a communicative discourse of the "traditional family" and a coordinative discourse comprised of New Right and Christian Right single-issue groups as well as broader-based right-wing organizations, which hinged on the advancement of "pro-family" policies and the election of "pro-family" politicians. Taken together, the communicative and coordinative discourses—which is to say, the ideas—of the CNR and the CP right are shown to form the foundation for the creation of a radical and proactive political movement that sought to alter the American political landscape.

Foundational Concepts and Recurrent Themes

From the outset, my interest in conservative Christian politics was motivated by the sense that the Christian Right was, to put it simply, good at politics. I wanted to uncover what it was that made the movement so efficacious and the coalition of conservative Catholics and Protestants so enduring. The desire to understand what the NCR got right rather than what the movement got wrong led me to focus my attention on the coalition-building and mobilizing strategies employed by both CNR and CP political entrepreneurs. Digging into the nuts and bolts of the coalition unearthed more at work than just novel fundraising and media strategies or the promotion of hot-button single issues. (This is not, by any means, to suggest that the NCR's innovations in these arenas were not important; they were.) I found that the convergence of conservative Catholics and Protestants was also driven by the cultivation of an ideology of victimhood and the adoption of prefiguration as a future-oriented political strategy. Understanding the NCR as a prefigurative and forward-looking movement helped to bring its ultimate aims and aspirations into clearer focus. The goal of the movement is not to capture some share of the pluralist pie, but rather to disrupt and replace the existing system in its entirety. Rather than viewing the NCR simply as one of many movements competing within the framework of a rights-based and pluralist system, I came to view it as fundamentally illiberal and antipluralist, grounded in a deep and abiding ideological commitdfc, Christian, and male supremacism. While these themes—of victimhood, prefiguration, and supremacism—are explored throughout the book, I will next briefly sketch how each operates within and is operationalized by the NCR.

The Ideology of Victimhood

In 1977 Miami-Dade County passed a gay rights ordinance offering a modicum of employment and housing protections to gay and lesbian residents of the county. *Conservative Digest*, a monthly magazine published by Richard Viguerie, described it as a "pro-homosexual ordinance" that "banned discrimination in employment and housing based on a person's 'affectional or sexual preference,' and thus, among other things, denied schools the right to prohibit an admitted homosexual from teaching sex education or biology."[23] In response, the singer Anita Bryant launched the "Save Our Children" campaign to repeal the ordinance. Bryant's campaign portrayed lesbian and gay people as a contagion, likely to infect children with immoral and deviant sexualities, and as a pedophiliac threat to children. Moreover, as the historian Gillian Frank explains, "A strong emphasis on child protection ran through white conservative opposition to both racial and sexual minorities that helped legitimize and popularize conservative ideas and activism."[24] The Save Our Children campaign simultaneously appropriated the language of "civil rights" for parents and capitalized on White supremacist arguments against school desegregation on the grounds of these newfound "parental rights." And yet, even as the campaign drew on the supposed supremacy of the rights of (White) parents, it also posited that not only were children the victims of a homosexual agenda, so too were their parents. This logic is aptly demonstrated by the opening to this introduction, drawn from an interview transcript in the William Martin Religious Right collection with the Christian Right pastor and political entrepreneur Tim LaHaye and his wife, Beverly LaHaye, founder of the antifeminist Concerned Women for America organization. In the interview, the LaHayes explain that Bryant and, by extension, Christians are the real victims of discrimination.

Of course, the Christian rhetoric of victimhood has deep roots in the theological foundations and early history of the faith, and the foundational narratives of persecution and martyrdom. Victimization is, in many ways, necessary to the faith: without the crucifixion of Christ, there is no salvation. But early narratives of Christian martyrdom taught that the persecuted faithful would be rewarded in the afterlife, and victimization should be met with a stoic resolve and acceptance.[25] The message for twentieth-century conservative Christians was quite different. New and Christian Right political entrepreneurs, including the LaHayes, translated a radical coordinative discourse, which aimed at revolutionizing American policymaking via single issue networks, into a communicative discourse defined by victimhood and grounded on the right to self-defense. Oppressors were rhetorically transfigured into victims, and acts of aggression metamorphosed into acts of righteous self-defense and community protection.

To better understand this communicative discourse, I borrow from the sociologist Mitch Berbrier's understanding of "the ideology of victimhood."[26] In his constructivist study of how White supremacists adopt an identity of victimhood, Berbrier identifies "five interrelated victim themes: 1) that whites are victims of discrimination, 2) that their rights are being abrogated, 3) that they are stigmatized if they express 'pride,' 4) that they are being psychologically affected through the loss of self-esteem, and 5) that the end product of all of this is the elimination of 'the white race.'"[27] The first three themes have to do with how White supremacists define their status as victims; the latter two identify the perceived harms they experience.[28]

We can identify variations on these themes in the communicative discourse of the NCR. Paraphrasing closely from Berbrier, the conservative Christian ideology of victimhood is reflected as follows: (1) Christians are victims of discrimination; (2) their religious and parental rights are being violated; and (3) they are shamed for defending their socially conservative religious beliefs. While the alleged perpetrators have changed over time from "secular humanists" to "cultural Marxists," since the 1970s the victims have remained constant: White Christians are an oppressed and persecuted majority.

We might add to these first three themes a belief in Christians' entitlement to dictate the social and political organization of the United States. As reflected in countless publications and speeches, and evidenced by recent scholarship on Christian nationalism,[29] conservative Christians assert an originary position in relation to the founding of the nation-state. The belief that America was once and always should be a Christian nation bolsters an ideology of victimhood as anything perceived to challenge Christian supremacism is perceived as an assault.

In terms of harm, the Christian ideology of victimhood operationalizes the threat of two complementary dangers: (1) the erosion of Christian morality in the social and political spheres endangers the individual salvation of all Christians, and (2) "the end product" is the death of God and the replacement of Christians with Godless homosexuals, secular humanists, cultural Marxists, and Muslims. Within the Christian Right, religious and racial identities and supremacist beliefs are overlapping and intersecting. Often unsaid, but always implied, is the threat of racial replacement. It is, therefore, neither possible nor desirable to fully distinguish between how White supremacists and Christian supremacists utilize these themes.

A key purpose of the communicative discourse of victimhood is the obscuration of the radicality and theocratic bent of conservative Christian political activism behind a smokescreen of self-defense. But, perhaps even more important, the ideology of victimhood is used to bring Christians into the conservative political fold and to produce a shared identity. An ideology of victimhood serves to knit together single-issue groups who otherwise may not readily find commonality. Berbrier identifies the powerful affective purpose of victim ideology, which "can serve the function of a recruiting strategy: to give meaning and purpose to feelings of anger on the part of embittered and frustrated people." This strategy is intended "explicitly to develop the consciousness of whites as whites, understanding whites as a class of victimized persons."[30] As we see in the following chapters, while Protestants and Catholics historically viewed one another as antagonists, throughout the 1970s single-issue politics, which were predicated on a fundamental friend-enemy distinction, helped forge a common identity of victimhood. By the late 1970s and into the early 1980s, single issues were brought under the umbrella of "pro-family" politics, which further cemented the convergence of conservative Catholic and Protestant thought and identities.

Over the past forty years, the rhetoric of Christian victimhood has spread, becoming the steady drumbeat of contemporary right-wing discourse, cropping up everywhere from former president Trump's Twitter feed to Tucker Carlson's monologues on Fox News.[31] It comes as little surprise, then, that in the aftermath of *Dobbs*, a decision that was an unequivocal win for the Christian Right, conservative Christian think tanks focused not on the threat the Court's decision posed to people who can experience pregnancy but on the threat to Christians. For example, six days after the Dobbs decision was handed down, the International Christian Concern published an article warning of a wave of "violent attacks" against Christian pro-life organizations.[32] A few months later, in September 2022, the Religious Freedom Institute published a report titled "Religious Pro-Life Americans under Attack: A Threat Assessment of Post-*Dobbs* America."[33] Just as the anti-gay activist Anita Bryant claimed to be a victim of homosexuals, in post-*Dobbs* America, the "real" victims are Christians, not those who are denied abortion care. (This is the same logic at play in *303 Creative, LLC. v. Elenis*, mentioned earlier, which effectively held that Christians are harmed when they are denied the right to harm LGBTQ+ people.)

And yet, at the same time, conservative Christians have increasingly embraced what Bradley Onishi terms the "Christian nation myth," believing the "country was built for and by Christians."[34] In June 2022 the writer and journalist Katherine Stewart attended the Road to Majority Policy Conference, where she observed an uptick in violent rhetoric, an overt embrace of "the theology of dominionism—that is, the belief that 'right-thinking' Christians have a biblically derived mandate to take control of all aspects of government and society," and enthusiasm about the "legal arsenal" produced by recent Supreme Court decisions.[35]

By applying a discursive institutionalist framework to the period under investigation and focusing on the coalition-building strategies and mobilizing tactics pioneered by the CNR and adopted by the NCR, we can better understand the Christian Right's simultaneous and contradictory claims to represent the nation's (moral, religious, and racial) majority and its defensive posturing as a victimized and persecuted minority. Of particular note, this book illuminates the role of NCR political entrepreneurs in cultivating a future-oriented politics through the construction of an imagined past.

Prefiguration and Prefigurative Traditionalism

As suggested by the communicative discourse of victimhood, and as detailed in chapter 1, New Right and Christian Right political entrepreneurs certainly took advantage of openings in the political opportunity structure generated by progressive social movements and landmark Supreme Court decisions. But these movements were not solely backlash-driven, and they were not solely composed of reactionary victims seeking to protect themselves. Rather, these movements sought to transform politics. Thus, it makes sense that the political entrepreneur Paul Weyrich recognized and proclaimed the radicality of the New Right, asserting it was "radical . . . in the same way that FDR's young brain trust was radical—committed to sweeping changes and not to preserving the status quo."[36] Likewise, CP political leaders sought to remake the political world in their—or, perhaps, God's—own image. As the Reverend Jerry Falwell put it, "I said you and the media like we in the ministry are the leaders, you shape opinion, you set lifestyles. And, I say, as leaders, you and I have the responsibility not to present life the way it is, but the way it ought to be."[37] While claiming to be provoked by progressive action and motivated by the desire to conserve old ways of being, conservative Christian activists sought to redefine the very meanings associated with the "traditional." Put another way, they worked to bring about a future political world that was premised on an imagined return to a past (i.e., the traditional), which was, in turn, being actively manufactured in the present. Applying concepts from Schmidt's work on discursive institutionalism to the study of the NCR makes it possible to identify how the movement articulated and manifested, or *prefigured*, the most radical, transformative, and forward-looking aspects of its agenda.

Taking the work of the critical theorist Carl Boggs, who first articulated an understanding of political prefiguration, as my starting point, I term this practice *prefigurative traditionalism*.[38] In his writing on workers' councils, Boggs explained, "By 'prefigurative' I mean the embodiment, within the ongoing political practice of a movement, of those forms of social relations, decision-making, culture, and human experience that are the ultimate goal."[39] Put plainly, prefiguration tries to bring about sociopolitical change by intentionally living as if the change has already occurred.

The practice of prefiguration is most commonly associated with leftist political movements,[40] as it seeks to advance a future-oriented emancipatory politics through the active embodiment of alternative forms of social relations and political practices.[41] Some leftist movements, including workers councils, Students for a Democratic Society, and Occupy Wall Street, have sought to prefigure a more democratic, more just society by forming communities that operate on the basis of horizontalism, egalitarianism, and via deliberative democratic processes. On its face, conservatism necessarily runs counter to prefiguration as it looks back in time as a means of hewing to the traditional. Understood in this way, conservative movements are viewed as reactionary while progressive or leftist movements are credited with being generative and proactive. But superimposing this dichotomous understanding of right and left onto conservative movements only serves to obscure the radicality of the right and leads to a misrecognition of the capacities and capabilities of right-wing movements.

To ascribe prefigurative practices to the New Right and NCR is also, to some degree, to take the movements at their word. The New Right self-consciously and proudly claimed it had adopted its organizing strategies from the New Left.[42] While the New Right's discourse of "learning from the left" should be problematized as a strategy for deflecting attention away from the movement's own radical agenda, there is also truth to it: the New Right did promote single issues, build organizations, adopt media strategies, and craft coalitions using a model borrowed from the left in the 1960s and early 1970s. These coordinative strategies facilitated the New Right's successful transformation of socially conservative single issues into a cohesive political identity that was expansive enough to anchor a coalition of conservative Catholics and Protestants, mobilize a large grassroots base, and achieve incorporation into the Republican Party. But conservative Christians also *prefigured* a new political world. On one hand, New Right and later NCR elites justified the transformative social policies they put forward on the grounds of "returning" the country to a "traditional" that was given meaning, or manufactured, in the present. On the other hand, grassroots actors sought to create "traditional" social relations through localized political campaigns that targeted education. In shaping school curricula, the grassroots also prefigured a set of social relations predicated on a conservative Christian worldview (see chapter 4 for more on this).

Conservative Catholic and Protestant activists did not merely aim to halt progressive religious, social, and political reforms. Instead, they built on both conservative traditions *and* modern institutional changes to define a new conservatism that was articulated in the language of Christian morality and through the institution of the family. CNR activists then sought to implement this new traditionalism through legislation and public policy initiatives. At the same time, rightist family policy discourse aimed to define the conditions under which women and children lived, thereby manifesting the social outcomes sought by CNR family policy initiatives.

Prefigurative traditionalism enabled social conservatives to advance policies—targeting the family, women, and children—and campaigns—focused on childcare, diversity and sex education in school curricula, divorce, abortion, pornography, homosexuality, and taxation—that would transform American social and political life through the imposition of certain types of social relations from the top down. Simultaneously, the movement advanced a communicative discourse premised on a fabricated past, wherein American society was organized and functioned according to Christian precepts, in order to assert their present was being threatened and to justify the future implementation of policies that collapsed the distinction between church and state. Along the way, the conservative Christian grassroots was encouraged to embody *new* "traditional" social relations in their families and schools that synchronously reproduced and redefined White, male, and Christian supremacist power relations. For example, by embodying what it meant to be a new "traditional" wife,[43] conservative Christian women prefigured social relations that injected the idea of a past patriarchal traditionalism into their present-day institutional context. Put another way, as employed by the NCR, prefiguration took the form of calling into being a new political world through the active construction of "tradition" that never was and only could be brought into being through its present and future-oriented practice.

Prefigurative traditionalism is necessarily tied up with a communicative discourse of victimhood. For the NCR, casting political opponents as an existential threat to a past Christian way of life sustains the movement's belief that it is entitled to dictate the form and content of social relations. At the same time, the claim that one is defending an established way of being—the "traditional"—encourages the belief that Christians are victims who are being harmed by agents of social change. It further supports the discourse of harm by associating the "traditional" with the Christian community so that the promotion of new or alternative "traditions" becomes synonymous with Christian replacement. Recognizing certain practices as forms of prefigurative traditionalism helps us to further identify: (1) how the embodiment of certain sets of social relations provides community members with the affective benefit of belonging; and (2) how communicative and coordinative discourses work together to promote a radical and future-oriented agenda.

Supremacism and Illiberalism

While the emergence of the NCR coalition is an expression of pluralist democracy, it is a mistake to assume the movement embraces the system that created it. Both the ideology of victimhood and prefigurative traditionalism work in the service of advancing a political worldview that is premised on supremacism and is, by logical extension, necessarily illiberal. Supremacism functions as both an ideological embrace of inequality, which ascribes hierarchical rankings to difference and views difference as fundamental and natural, and an institutionalized system of oppression. Supremacist politics are, therefore, informed by one group's belief in its inherent superiority and by the desire to institutionalize the capacity to dominate and subjugate. As I explore in more detail in chapter 1, three overlapping and co-constitutive supremacisms inform the political ideology and aspirations of the NCR: Christian supremacism, male supremacism, and White supremacism.

My understanding of Christian supremacism is in line with the framework of Christian nationalism as explained by Andrew Whitehead and Samuel Perry, who define it as "an ideology that idealizes and advocates a fusion of American civic life with a particular type of Christian identity and culture."[44] But in labeling this ideology Christian supremacism, I hope to make explicit that it is a belief system that asserts the superiority of (some) Christians and that expressly promotes the domination and subjugation of those who are not recognized as (the right kind of) Christian Americans.

Much as Christian supremacism extends beyond the confines of religious identity to encompass national identity, the ideology of White supremacy extends far beyond the creation and maintenance of a racial hierarchy. As Loretta Ross explains, "The fact that race relations in the United States are usually presented as a Black/white model disguises the complexity of color, the brutality of class, and the importance of religion and sexual identity in the construction and practice of white supremacy."[45] Thus, while White supremacism takes a belief in White racial superiority as its starting point, it is institutionally and ideologically tied up with other forms of supremacism. This is not to reduce Christian and White supremacism to being one and the same, but rather to say they are interlocking systems of oppression.

Male supremacism functions in tandem with both Christian and White supremacism. The NCR also seeks to institutionalize the domination of cisgender men over women and prescribe a set of rigid gender roles and identities on to American society. A male supremacist system, as I have written elsewhere, is defined as "a cultural, political, economic and social system in which cisgender men disproportionately control status, power, and resources, and women, trans men, and nonbinary people are subordinated. Such systems are underpinned by an ideology of male supremacism: the belief in cisgender men's superiority and right to dominate and control others."[46] NCR social policy reflects the movement's attempt to use the power of the state to create structural conditions premised on a belief in patriarchal traditionalism and gender essentialism. These ideologies are premised on a particular interpretation of Christianity that fuses male and Christian supremacism.

From opposing sex education curricula to advocating for school prayer, from opposition to abortion to the belief that the family is the basic unit of society, these supremacisms are seen to inform and structure the political

aims of the NCR. The movement sought—and continues to seek—to harness the coercive capacity of the state to impose a particular set of social
relations that are predicated on a normative model of the "good" White,
heteronormative and cisgendered, patriarchal, Christian family. In doing
so, it also aims to institutionalize inequality and systems of domination
and control. While often expressed in the liberal rhetoric of "rights," that
is, parental rights or the rights of the preborn, supremacist politics are fundamentally illiberal, if we take liberalism to be, at baseline, predicated on
a belief in the primacy of the individual as a free, equal, and rights-bearing
subject. Thus, the political system the NCR seeks to prefigure should be
understood as one that is in competition with and opposed to that of a
liberal pluralist democracy. The epilogue takes up the project of detailing the illiberalism of CNR thinkers and the NCR movement, but earlier
discussions of fundamentalist Protestantism, secular humanism, and the
discourses of "parental rights" and "pro-family" politics also gesture toward
a fundamental rejection of liberal principles by conservative Christians.

Chapter Overview

This book is concerned with the influence of the Catholic New Right on
the development of the New Christian Right over time. But it is also concerned with the construction of political time itself or, to put it another
way, with the temporal discourse of the past as it pertains to the manufacturing of the future in the present. Chapter 1 dives into a discussion of
the temporal politics of conservative Christians by way of exploring the
discourse of backlash as an explanatory frame for the mobilization of the
NCR. I highlight several landmark Supreme Court decisions that are cited
in support of the backlash thesis, which holds that conservatives were reactionary agents who were mobilized by opposition to progressive political
gains. While these cases are shown to have created openings in the political
opportunity structure that conservative actors capitalized on, I advance the
claim that we should not understand the development of the NCR in terms
of backlash. Rather, I contend we should interrogate how the discourse of
backlash advances an ideology of victimhood through the construction of
an imagined past and, in so doing, obscures the radicality of right-wing
Christian activism. Problematizing the discourse of backlash feels particularly salient given its continued use as an explanatory frame for contemporary Christian Right assaults on the rights of historically marginalized

and underrepresented groups. Thus, while chapter 1 looks back in time to problematize Christian Right origin stories that center backlash, its central intervention is a timely one.

On the whole, I seek to shift our attention away from looking for external events or actors to blame for motivating the NCR and instead direct our attention inwards toward the movement's internal coordinative and communicative discourses and the processes by which the movement was built by elites. As later chapters show, internal changes and developments within both American Catholicism and Protestantism facilitated the emergence of conservative Christian political entrepreneurs, and both the CNR and CPs utilized openings in the political opportunity structure to pioneer new coalition strategies and forged enduring alliances between conservative Catholics and Protestants—that is, produced coordinative discourses—while using the communicative discourse of "pro-family" politics to advance a political platform premised on the ideologies of White supremacism, male supremacism, and Christian supremacism.

This work challenges traditional understandings of the New Right as a secular movement by highlighting the deep influence Catholicism had on the architects of the movement. Chapter 2 grounds this rereading of the New Right in a close examination of the early religious and political formation of one of the New Right's founders, Paul Weyrich. The chapter focuses on how the transformation of the Catholic Church in the 1960s shaped and informed Weyrich's conservative worldview, making it possible for him to identify as a "conservative Catholic." His religious beliefs are examined with an eye to his development of the "pro-family" political platform—later adopted by the NCR and the Republican Party—and the production of a conservative ideology that would carve out space for a new kind of state: one that could use the family and social welfare provision in the service of social regulation and to advance White, male, and Christian supremacism.

Weyrich was not the only conservative Catholic helming the New Right, and chapter 3 broadens our focus to include the work of two of Weyrich's conservative Catholic collaborators, Connaught (Connie) Marshner and Richard Viguerie. Throughout the early and mid-1970s, these CNR political entrepreneurs spearheaded the organizational and institutional growth of the conservative movement by building ad hoc single-issue coalitions, which enabled the movement to retain its relatively fluid and horizontal structure. Chapter 3 examines the emergence of the New Right as an insurgent right-wing movement, focusing on its organizational and ideational development. Highlighting the work of Marshner, the chapter locates the origins of the "pro-family" platform in the social conservatism of CNR activists and their reconceptualization of conservatism and the "traditional." The single-issue strategy employed by the CNR is also shown to have encouraged the cultivation of an ideology of victimhood, which would be key to the convergence of New Right and CP positions at the end of the 1970s and into the early 1980s.

Pivoting to zero in on developments within White conservative Protestantism, chapter 4 examines institutional and theological changes within American fundamentalism. Around the same time that Weyrich was struggling to carve out space for a hyphenated conservative-Catholic identity, a struggle ensued within fundamentalism over how to reconcile a century-old conflict over the faith group's place in secular society. Cultivating an identity of victimhood in response to the perceived threat of "secular humanism," the fundamentalist grassroots is shown to have launched head-first into localized political activism. And so, while the New Right was building a sentinel of think tanks and political action committees to support its conservative movement, fundamentalist and evangelical Protestants were building the foundations for a socially conservative grassroots army, ready to do battle over school prayer, sex education, women's and gay rights, desegregation, and abortion. Propelled by the actions of the grassroots base, Reverend Falwell can be seen to have adopted a new theological position that favored robust political engagement. Chapter 4, then, surveys not only the fundamentalist and evangelical religious landscape but also Falwell's development into a political entrepreneur responsible for launching the Moral Majority. Tracing parallel organizational developments on the part of fundamentalist Protestants illuminates the proactive and independent character of the Protestant right wing as well as the conditions that led CP elites to embrace the help of their CNR counterparts. Together, chapters 3 and 4 demonstrate how, as the political organizing strategies of the New Right and White CPs began to parallel one another in the mid-late 1970s, both groups recognized the limitations of their individual movements and saw the potential to fulfill mutual political needs in one another.

Chapter 5 focuses on the period when CNR and CP elites converged under the auspices of a shared "pro-family" politics. Their union was made possible by both groups pivoting from single-interest issue coalitions—built around issues like abortion, education, religious freedom, and gun rights—to adopt an umbrella coalition strategy by unifying these same is-sues under the catchall of "pro-family" politics. Robert O. Self has expertly detailed how "views on gender, sexuality, and family made the conserva-tive coalition that coalesced around Ronald Reagan in the 1980s possi-ble."[47] Rather than retell this history, the chapter focuses more narrowly on explicating how conservative Christian political entrepreneurs seized on a political opening created by the Carter administration's White House Conference on Families (WHCF) to cast Christians as victims of the lib-eral state and secular humanism. It also demonstrates how, by couching their political agenda in terms of a "backlash" against progressive attacks on the family, conservative Christian actors manufactured new fears to help mobilize the grassroots and obscure the proactive and prefigurative nature of their political ideology.

While New Right political brokers have long been credited with sup-porting the NCR at its inception, their contribution to the movement was neither limited to secular political organizing and institutional support nor one-sided. On one hand, the New Right helped create the NCR as a be-hemoth social movement by providing CPs with institutional and ideolog-ical support, and, on the other hand, CPs provided the former group with the grassroots base and electoral support it needed to realize its conserva-tive agenda. But CNR activists did not stop at providing the institutional and intellectual know-how necessary for their Protestant counterparts to launch a successful sociopolitical movement. They also produced a com-municative discourse premised on victimhood and oriented around the ideological umbrella of the "traditional family," which was filtered through the lens of conservative Catholicism.

By seeing the production of coordinative and communicative discourses as integrally linked throughout the book, we can identify how the NCR's success depended on a two-part mobilization: CNR and CP political en-trepreneurs built an electoral coalition of White Christians premised on a shared identity of victimhood and a program of socially conservative policy proposals that sought to enshrine religious norms and beliefs into law. At the same time, a new political past, present, and future was rhetorically constructed and shared by elites—thereby generating a saleable commu-nicative discourse of backlash and rhetoric of persecution that continues to be used to frame a proactive assault on liberal democracy in terms of self-defense.

Primarily drafted by CNR thinkers, the move to talking about "pro-family" politics enabled the NCR to put forward a broad, national political agenda, which would be incorporated into the Republican Party's platform under President Reagan and obscured the radicality of centering the family as the basic unit of social and political organization. But, while both the NCR and the CNR initially heralded Reagan as a symbol of the dawning of a new conservative day in America, the celebration of Reagan's election was short-lived. CNR and NCR activists quickly soured on the new president when he failed to appoint a sufficient number of staffers drawn from their ranks. Their collective frustration waxed and waned over the course of Reagan's first term, with opposition to Reagan mounting when he was perceived to backburner social issues in favor of advancing his economic agenda and receding when the president promoted conservative Christian policy issues, such as mandatory school prayer. When measured on the basis of independent social issue policies, like prohibiting gay rights or mandating school prayer, or its influence on the culture writ large, the NCR has met with both spectacular loses and wins.

Over the course of my time spent in the archives, I came to view this back-and-forth as reflective of both the influence and precarity of the CNR and the NCR in national politics in the 1980s. I further came to the conclusion that scholarly conversations about the relative success and influence of these groups tend to miss the mark when they uncritically accept the "culture war" framing promoted by the NCR. Rather than embrace the twinned narratives of backlash and culture war, with their attendant claims to seek a "return" to the past, the epilogue makes the case that NCR and CNR elites have, in many ways, succeeded at prefiguring a new politics, premised on supremacism and dependent on a shared ideology of victimhood. By reconceptualizing attitudes to political organizing within and between conservative Catholics and Protestants, CNR and NCR elites sought to both codify and embody particular forms of gender, sex, and family relations. But the ultimate goal of both conservative Catholics and Protestants has been the legislation of Christian morality. In short, the NCR seeks to build a new, modern "city upon a hill." The epilogue takes the program laid out in *Cultural Conservatism: Toward a New National Agenda*, a book co-authored by Connie Marshner's husband William Marshner and published by Weyrich's Free Congress Research and Education Foundation, as a starting point. By taking seriously the agenda put forward by the CNR in 1985–1986, I sketch the contours of a radical right-wing Christian agenda that reflects the convergence of conservative Catholic and Protestant thought and seeks to use the coercive power of the state to create a new political system, premised on the principle of subsidiarity and intended to reshape society and the state in the image of a cultural conservative communitarianism. In sum, I argue that if we measure the NCR based on its broader and much more radical agenda to redefine the past, transform social relations in the present, and advance the country toward an illiberal future, it has been—*and continues to be*—a remarkable success.

I

―・―

Problematizing Backlash

What galvanized the Christian community was not abortion, was not school prayer, was not the ERA. You'll read in all kinds of textbooks that those issues galvanized the Christian community. Not so. I am living witness to that because I was trying to get those people interested because of those issues and I utterly failed. The reason is because in the mind of the evangelical Christian of the time was the notion: . . . What we want to do is lead our lives the way that we want to lead them; we'll teach our children the truth and so we don't need to worry about those kinds of issues. And the same with school prayer: "Fine, we'll form our own schools." Many people took their kids out of public schools, formed Christian schools, that was a great period of growth for Christian schools. And so, well we don't need school prayer. And the ERA [Equal Rights Amendment], you know many believed that this ran contrary to the biblical view of the family. But as long as they were free to preach what they wanted they really didn't care about public policy. What changed their mind was Jimmy Carter's intervention against the Christian schools, trying to deny them tax-exempt status on the basis of so called de facto segregation. In other words it wasn't that they had a policy that wouldn't accept minorities, it was simply that they didn't have many minorities, because their churches with whom they were associated also didn't have them. And Carter's view was that this meant that they were in fact segregated. And that they should go out and find a quota depending upon the level of minorities in the community and they should have those people in that school. That so enraged the Christian community and they looked upon it as interference from government and suddenly it dawned on them that they were not going to able to be left alone to teach their children as they pleased. That they were going to be interfered with on the part of the federal government, and it was at that moment that conservatives made the linkage between their opposition to government interference and the interests of the evangelical movement which now saw itself on the defensive and under attack by the government. That was what galvanized the Christian community.

—Paul Weyrich, interview[1]

What motivates the Christian Right—or the American Right as a whole, for that matter? The prevailing wisdom since the publication of Thomas and Mary Edsall's groundbreaking book *Chain Reaction* has been that the right is motivated in response to the left. Writing in 1991, the Edsalls explained that conservative polarization and electoral realignment were the result of "the collision of race with taxes with two additional forces [rights and reform] over the past twenty-five years that created a *chain reaction*, a reaction forcing a realignment of the presidential electorate."[2] Subsequently, and stemming in large part from their work, two theses have very nearly acquired the force of dogma among scholars and pundits of American politics: (1) A national electoral realignment occurred in the late 1960s and through the 1970s as Southern White voters migrated to the Republican Party, and (2) this realignment was caused by a backlash to civil rights gains and motivated by the desire to conserve institutionalized forms of White supremacy.

The backlash thesis proposed by the Edsalls is a compelling one, in no small measure because it provides a causal explanation for developments in American politics: action creates reaction, and progressive change produces conservative retrenchment. It is common for scholars and pundits alike to speak of the right in terms of its reactionary nature and to expect that the right is dependent on the actions of the left to determine its next steps. As such, the right is often described as a "counterrevolutionary" or "countercultural" movement.[3] Daniel Martinez HoSang summed up the power of backlash accounts in 2010, writing, "Today, backlash remains the framework of choice to describe public support for measures banning services to immigrants, opposing affirmative action programs, and demanding harsher sentences for criminal offenders."[4] While this remains the case a little over a decade later, we might also add that it is the framework of choice for explaining widespread attacks on reproductive autonomy, the erosion of LGBTQ+ rights, and the erasure of Black history in America. Over and over again, we are told that the right is driven by the left, right-wing mobilization is a response to left-wing wins, and one step forward will be met by one step backward.

Taking a more sweeping historical and philosophical view of conservatism, Corey Robin has similarly found that the right is the product of "reactionaries," constructed through and by a call-and-response relationship with progressivism. It is "forged in response to challenges from below" by those seeking liberation, and it "stems from a genuine conviction that a world thus emancipated will be ugly, brutish, base, and dull."[5] Conservatism, Robin finds, is a "backlash politics," defined in relation to "a specific reaction to a specific movement of emancipation."[6] At the same time, Robin cautions against viewing conservatism as merely reflexive, asserting instead that it is an "idea-driven praxis" that "begins from a position of principle," which centers on a right to rule *over*. This does not, however, undermine the central contention that conservatism is always reactionary, as evidenced for Robin by the fact that "the conservative has consistently affirmed that his is a knowledge produced in reaction to the left."[7]

But what if conservatism aims not to conserve a past order, but rather to produce a new one? What if the right, or at least a faction of it, is not reactionary, but rather proactive? What if it is not motivated by backlash, but by a desire to transform political and social institutions rather than restore them to a previous state?

In positing, as I do, that the Christian Right is proactive, it is tempting to make a strawman out of Robin's reactionary conservative. But to do so would be disingenuous. There are many points on which I agree with Robin's understanding of conservatism: at the root, it is an "idea-driven praxis" committed to the production of hierarchy.[8] This understanding is also shared by other scholars of the right, including Cas Mudde, who draws on Norberto Bobbio in writing, "The key distinction between the left and right [rests] on the basis of their view on (in)equality: the *left* considers the key inequalities between people to be artificial and negative, which should be overcome by an active state, whereas the *right* believes that inequalities between people are natural and positive, and should either be defended or left alone by the state."[9] Conservatism is also, as Robin writes, "a deliberate, conscious effort to preserve or recall 'those forms of experience which can no longer be had in an authentic way,'" and so transforms "items of lived experience [into] incidents of an ideology."[10] In this, I find an expression of the relationship between conservatism and the past that accords with what I have termed the practice of prefigurative traditionalism. But, while Robin may see these traits as evidence of the reactionary character of conservatism, I believe that, at least within the Christian Right, they point to its productive capacity and future-oriented ideology. Christian conservatives have not only reacted and responded to progressive gains; they have also sought to produce a new and different political future. They are not merely reactionary. They are visionary.

I am not alone in finding backlash to be a deficient framework, and other political scientists have similarly pointed out its shortcomings. For example, HoSang highlights the danger of treating racial attitudes on the right and left as monolithic and backlash as a natural reaction, as "scholars treat the white backlash that ensued as a fait accompli rather than the contingent outcome of historically specific events, claims, and struggles."[11] Likewise, Joseph Lowndes explains that backlash cannot adequately "explain how that [racial] political identification became linked to others, such as social or economic conservatism, in a coherent political rhetoric." Moreover, while backlash may account for some aspects of the right's motivation, it "cannot tell us how that rhetoric was translated into effective political strategies by the Republican Party."[12] In short, the backlash framework flattens the relationship between historically contingent institutional and ideological forces and fails to take into consideration the production of the very ideas and identities that it ostensibly motivates. Thus, while perhaps accounting for some portion of the right's motivation, backlash may conceal rather more than it illuminates.

But perhaps the real utility of backlash lies in its ability to obscure and deflect. On the one hand, it can flatten history, masking ideological commitments and hiding institutional structures. On the other hand, it can be used to rhetorically shift the responsibility of right-wing activism onto the left. In these ways, backlash functions as a script that constructs (and reconstructs) a particular historical narrative and related set of identities to shape our knowledge of both events and actors. While many scholars utilize the concept of "scripts," particularly in relation to gender, my usage is most directly informed by Natalia Molina's formulation of the concept in *How Race Is Made in America: Immigration, Citizenship, and the Historical Power of Racial Scripts*. In this work, Molina identifies three primary ways in which racial scripts operate: (1) "They highlight how racialized groups are acted upon by a range of principals, from institutional actors to ordinary citizens." (2) Racial scripts help us to "see different racial projects operating at the same time, affecting different groups simultaneously." And (3) "Racialized groups put forth their own scripts, *counterscripts* that offer alternatives or directly challenge dominant racial scripts."[13] To conceive of backlash as a script is to resist the temptation to think of backlash as purely causal, and instead to think of it as a socially and politically constructed discursive framework that has material and tangible effects not only on how we understand our political world but also on how we exist in it. In a similar fashion to racial scripts, multiple backlash scripts may operate at the same time, and they may impact "different groups simultaneously." Moreover, they can be countered, as is the case when one group seeks to invert the causal narrative and/or the identities imposed by a backlash script. If the explanatory framework of backlash works to obscure historical, institutional, and ideological forces, examining backlash scripts—or backlash discourses—aims to do the inverse, focusing our attention on the range of actors, ideas, and institutions that help mobilize and produce a political backlash.

Continuing to think along these lines, we might conceive of the existence of victimhood scripts, which operate alongside and in conjunction with backlash scripts. On the one hand, backlash discourses help to reinforce the ideology of victimhood by alleging the left has perpetrated an assault against the right. On the other hand, the ideology of victimhood reinforces the narrative of backlash as the right constructs its motivations in terms of self-defense. Together, these scripts help camouflage the forward-looking and supremacist aims of the movement. In conjunction with the ideology of victimhood, backlash discourse helps to erase existing institutional and power structures while simultaneously facilitating the construction of new identities and the production of new ideologies.

To be clear, I am making a distinction between the phenomenon of backlash, which can and does occur in some contexts, and the concept of backlash as an analytical framework for rationalizing the politics of the right. While the former describes a causal relationship between events, the latter helps construct our knowledge of the logic and discourse of the right, how and why right-wing mobilizations take place, and what it is the right seeks to accomplish. More often than not, this latter process (of knowledge production) is enabled by the ascription of causality, as the right's motivations are understood to be in response, or reaction, to actions undertaken by the left. It is this—the narrative of causality that backlash scripts promote—that I believe should be problematized if we are to develop a more complex and accurate understanding of the political motivations that drive the Christian Right.

To complicate our understanding of backlash as an explanatory framework for the mobilization of Christian conservatives, I reconsider the impact of key Supreme Court cases concerning school prayer, reproductive autonomy, and desegregation on the formation of the New Christian Right (NCR). In doing so, I show how the Court's landmark decisions served as catalysts for right-wing Christian activism but not necessarily in the ways we commonly assume. Rather than view conservative Christian mobilization as a straightforward response to these decisions (i.e., in terms of a causal backlash framework), I find it was the discourse of backlash (i.e., the narrative that the right is motivated by the left) that aided in the movement's development by serving to manufacture an imagined past through the production of a "before" and an "after."

Furthermore, the discourse of backlash is shown to flatten the dynamic and often conflictual relationship between Catholics and Protestants. In doing so, backlash scripts render invisible the strategic processes and institutional arrangements that eventually allowed for the convergence of Catholics and Protestants on the right. Viewing the process of conservative Christian political mobilization through the application of a backlash framework masks the Christian Right's future-oriented ideology and obscures the movement's proactive strategies during the period under investigation. Thus, instead of understanding the Christian Right as a purely reactive movement, I propose we examine it as a radical and revolutionary movement that uses the discourse of backlash to obscure how it seeks to capitalize on openings in the political opportunity structure—understood broadly as the "features of the political environment that influence movement emergence and success"[14]— to implement a new agenda of its own design.

Origin Stories

Central to the Christian Right origin story is the concept of backlash. To dive into the beginnings of the Catholic New Right (CNR) and NCR is to become immersed in a story of conservative Christians under attack, forced to adopt a defensive posture by an oppressive and aggressive left. The idea that the NCR formed in response and opposition to progressive gains has been picked up by scholars and activists of the movement alike. The details vary, as there is disagreement and uncertainty over precisely which progressive issue—secularism, racial equality, abortion, gay rights—catalyzed the mobilization of conservative Christians, but its basic contours are consistent: the left articulated a radical agenda that demanded the invention of new rights and would necessarily result in the fundamental reorganization of society and the destruction of traditional practices, values, and rights. It was aided and abetted by the Supreme Court, which failed to accurately uphold the Constitution, and issued landmark decisions that recognized and affirmed the demands of the left. As the true representatives and defenders of the nation, conservative Christians were forced to take action to defend the nation against leftist revolutionaries who sought nothing less than the destruction of White Christianity.[15]

While the New Right and NCR focused much of their collective efforts on influencing congressional and presidential elections in the late 1970s and 1980s, it was the Supreme Court that came to stand in for the evils of a too strong and too distant government run amok in the 1960s. As Frederick S. Lane explains, "During much of that time [the 1960s], the Court was under the leadership of Chief Justice Earl Warren, whose name became an epithet among religious conservatives."[16] Warren had, of course, overseen the Court during the brief window, commonly referred to as the "rights revolution," in which it rapidly and profoundly expanded Americans' individual and civil rights. Nominated by Nixon to replace the liberal Warren upon his retirement, Chief Justice Warren Burger was confirmed in 1969 amid the expectation that he would be a "strict constructionist."[17] And yet, while Burger succeeded in pulling the Court to the right over the course of his seventeen years on the bench,[18] the Court nonetheless continued to issue decisions on sexuality[19] and gender[20] that riled and provoked conservatives. The structure of the Court does not in and of itself afford a high degree of political access, but the dependence of the Court's composition on the office of the president makes it relatively open to outside influence. Thus, open revolt against the Court's decisions created an opportunity for conservative activists to both decry federal abuses of power while simultaneously promoting the election of a conservative president who could rectify the imbalance.

A host of different explanations have been offered as to what precise Supreme Court decision and corresponding issue motivated religious conservatives to mobilize politically. Some suggest that the 1973 *Roe v. Wade* decision, which legalized abortion across the nation, galvanized American Christians and spurred them to take up political action in the hopes of stemming the tide of "feticide" suddenly sweeping the country.[21] Others maintain that race, rather than abortion, was the driving force behind White conservative Protestants' (CP) reentry into American political life. Focusing on the 1971 *Green v. Connally* decision, religion scholar Randall Balmer has argued that opposition to the civil rights movement and a deep desire to maintain segregated educational institutions led evangelicals to political organizing.[22] The political scientist Daniel Schlozman's analysis of the movement follows in Balmer's footsteps, but takes it one step further, arguing that the Internal Revenue Service's targeting of Christian schools, known as segregation or "seg" academies, was the key opening seized upon by Weyrich and other New Right activists to entice Bible-believing Christians into politics.[23] A third group, which includes Falwell biographer Michael Sean Winters, has attempted to split the difference and assert that abortion, desegregation, and Supreme Court decisions prohibiting prayer in public schools (*Engel v. Vitale*, 1962; *School District of Abington Township, Pennsylvania v. Schempp*, 1963) all forced Bible-believing Christians to take action.[24] Each of these explanatory frameworks understands the origins of the NCR in terms of backlash, or "the resistance of those in power to attempts to change the status quo."[25]

There are other equally important backlash-oriented origin stories attached to the NCR, most notably one that centers on opposition to gay rights, which is largely omitted from this discussion. This is, in part, because the presumed backlash to gay rights does not focus on a Supreme Court decision and so takes a slightly different narrative form. But it is also because there is little mention of anti-gay activism in New Right archives until the mid-1980s, which does not fit with the other, earlier, backlash discourses discussed below. I have no doubt that Weyrich and other CNR activists, including Connie Marshner and Richard Viguerie, were opposed to advances in gay rights on both religious and political grounds early on; however, the issue did not seem to capture their collective imagination in the same way as other single issues, like school prayer, abortion, and school desegregation during the period under investigation. Perhaps CNR activists did not regularly single out gay rights in the 1970s because their opposition was rolled into their promotion of other "pro-family" single issues. Or perhaps it was because the CNR was simply late to the anti-gay game. By the mid-1980s, Weyrich perceived AIDS as an electoral issue, and he expressed anti-gay attitudes even as he recognized that punching down was not a smart political strategy. Identifying HIV/AIDS as a "new issue for the right wing," a 1985 article captures this sentiment:

> The problem, says a conservative pollster, is distinguishing between fear and hate. It's one thing to try to respond to the public's legitimate fear of AIDS, another to use the issue to vent hatred of homosexuals. Nothing wrong with playing on fear, the consultant adds, so long as hatred is stifled. The public often recoils at a hate campaign. Naturally, everyone involved denies hating gays. "I'm not for gay bashing," says Weyrich. "I have compassion for those people who've gotten themselves into a reprobate mind-set. But we have a community welfare problem . . . and it's the homosexual community and its life-style that has made this a public health hazard."[26]

This is not to say that the gay rights backlash narrative did not have traction with White conservative Protestants earlier on. It certainly did, as exemplified by Anita Bryant's Save Our Children campaign, which took resistance to the passage of a gay rights ordinance in Orange County, Florida, as its starting point.[27] Additionally, as Gillian Frank has shown, opposition to gay rights, much like school prayer, was inherently tied up with White supremacist attitudes and was central to the development of the discourse of "parental rights."[28] The narrative of anti-gay backlash was very effective at helping to further the victimhood script, framing White Christian parents as innocent victims whose rights were being taken away not only by gays and lesbians but also by a host of feminist and BIPOC perpetrators.

What all of these Christian Right discourses of backlash have in common is that they reduce politics to a Manichean duality, splitting the world into defenders and aggressors, victims and perpetrators, good and evil. "The concept of backlash tends to suggest a unidirectional flow of action," Didi Herman explains, and "has both a clear perpetrator and a clear victim." When applied to the dynamic between the NCR and the gay and lesbian rights movement, Herman further shows how the unidirectional flow can be reversed, and the roles assigned to either group flipped. In one formulation, "The perpetrators are the attackers, the members of a regressive bloc calling for a halt to perceived changes in sexual relations. The lesbian and gay movement is the victim—fighting for equality, it finds itself confronting

reactionary forces that, in the name of tradition, are set on denying change."
But in another formulation, "Demands for lesbian and gay equality are an
attack upon the hegemony of heterosexual culture; that is, they constitute
a reaction against the imposition of a particular construction of normalcy.
In this sense, the lesbian and gay movement is the counterforce, the backlash, and the Christian Right merely the establishment."[29] Backlash scripts
can accommodate such contradictory interpretations because they take as
their starting point the discursive construction of a mythical "before" that
is challenged by progressive social and/or political changes. If the before is
the point in time when the gay and lesbian rights movement has secured
a rights ordinance in Orange County, lesbians and gays are the victim of
Anita Bryant's campaign to legalize discrimination. But, if the before is a
point in time when lesbian and gay individuals were denied basic protections, then White conservative Christians are the victims of a radical queer
insurgency.

While backlash discourse is open to either party occupying the role of
either victim or perpetrator, more often than not, the mantle of victimhood
is claimed by the party that can lay claim to the "traditional." This is, in
part, because we associate conservatism with "traditional" morals and values and, in part, because American political culture is resistant to change.
And so, while either party can theoretically claim injury and the moral high
ground, the party that can claim it is "conserving" the past is more likely to
prevail in casting itself in the role of victim. Davina Cooper connects the
impulse to favor the party that can claim it is motivated by conservation to
"liberal discourse and its dislike of radical change. . . . Liberals may dislike
what is happening, they may feel that the backlash is going too far, but
they see it as inevitable, even necessary, if a more acceptable equilibrium is
to be attained."[30] Thus, in the US context, the group seen as advocating for
change is systematically delegitimized and cast as the responsible agent for
harm that may befall it. (In practice, this often takes the form of apologist
arguments that recognize the validity of rights-based claims while simultaneously alleging marginalized groups are to blame for their continued
oppression because they have asked for too much, too quickly.) The discourse of backlash, then, serves to justify the actions of the NCR in terms
of self-defense and a "return" to the past, while reinforcing an identity of
(White Christian male) victimhood. In the process, it obscures the power
of the powerful, masking the supremacist nature and the radicality of the
movement's aims. In short, regardless of its perceived cause—whether

women, Black people, or gays and lesbians—the discourse of backlash always provides a strategic benefit to those on the right.

To say that the discourse of backlash helped to produce the NCR is neither to say that the movement was wholly the result of backlash nor to suggest it was not motivated by external events. Rather, it is to assert the importance of the *idea* of a backlash and its significance for the construction of the NCR's coordinative and communicative discourses by serving three primary purposes. The narrative of backlash: (1) gives support to the ideology of victimhood by helping to articulate the roles of victim and perpetrator, casting the agents of change in the role of aggressor and assigning a defensive posture to those who are resistant to it; (2) temporalizes, creating a before and an after; and (3) obscures the politics of the NCR, both in terms of the mechanics (e.g., resources, institutional access, mobilization) of the movement and the radicality of its agenda.

School Prayer

One of the common (and pernicious) elements of Christian Right backlash scripts is the belief that conservative Christians were missing in action, slumbering through seismic waves of cultural and political change in the 1960s. As Tim LaHaye put it in the 1990s,

> Ever since probably 1962, when the court decision was passed that outlawed prayer in the school and then in 1963, [when] they kicked the bible out of the schools . . . it just seemed that there was one relentless attack after another before the Supreme Court, trying to secularize our country and Christians were sound asleep. They were still back in the '40s and '50s, [thinking] that we were one nation under God while the whole message of God was [being] taken from the public sector of life.[31]

Regardless of the cause of their stupor (which changes depending on the narrator), in this story, conservative Christians were somehow unaware of the threats they faced and the potent influence they could collectively exert on American politics. That is, until they reached a critical juncture[32]—more often than not a Supreme Court decision—and conservative Christians were jolted awake and into action. As we saw in the introduction, for LaHaye, this did not occur until the late 1970s, when he witnessed Anita Bryant become a "victim" of gay discrimination and realized he needed to "Wake up the Christian community." For most Christian

Right mythologists, including Jerry Falwell, the supposed critical juncture was the Court's ruling on abortion. There are some, however, for whom the opening salvo in the battle for America's eternal soul began in the early 1960s with the Court's decisions on school prayer. While backlash to school prayer is a less popular origin myth than abortion, it plays a critical part in retrospectively framing conservative Christians as innocent and unsuspecting victims of an activist Court. As such, it crucially helps reinforce a shared identity of victimhood among conservative Christians by papering over the ways in which denominational identities and antipathies informed complex and contradictory responses to the Court's ruling.

In 1962, in *Engel v. Vitale*, the Supreme Court was asked to determine whether students could be subjected to the daily recitation of a school prayer that was composed by state officials.[33] In a 6–1 decision, the Court responded with a resounding no, holding that "Under [the First] Amendment's prohibition against governmental establishment of religion, as reinforced by the provisions of the Fourteenth Amendment, government in this country, be it state or federal, is without power to prescribe by law any particular form of prayer which is to be used as an official prayer in carrying on any program of governmentally sponsored religious activity."[34] The following year, in 1963, the Court cited *Engel* in a subsequent school prayer case, *School District of Abington Township, Pennsylvania v. Schempp* (consolidated with *Murray v. Curlett*), finding mandatory devotional readings in public schools unconstitutional. Together, the court's decisions in *Engel* and *Abington* created a clear legal prohibition against state-mandated prayer in public schools,[35] and added several feet to the proverbial wall separating the state from the church.

Even though a majority of the American public supported prayer in public schools,[36] the *Engel* decision was met with mixed responses. Following the decision, President John F. Kennedy issued a public statement that tried to strike a careful balance, seeking to quell public dissent without undermining support for the Supreme Court: "We have a very easy remedy here, and that is to pray ourselves. We can pray a good deal more at home and attend our churches with fidelity, and emphasize the true meaning of prayer in the lives of our children."[37] But not everyone was appeased by the suggestion that they could simply move religion into the private sphere. "The reaction to the cases was immediate and intense," explains Michael D. Waggoner, a professor of religion and education, as it was "sensationalized by the media as kicking God out of the public school." But "among America's Christian leaders," Waggoner continues, "the response was surprisingly mixed. Some conservatives like Billy Graham and Cardinal Francis Spellman, along with the more liberal Episcopal Bishop James A. Pike, decried the decisions. Others, including the National Association of Evangelicals, applauded the Court for appropriately separating the state from the affairs of the church."[38]

Assessing one side of the Protestant spectrum, the historian Angela Lahr has documented fierce condemnation of the school prayer decisions by CPs who "placed [the decision] within the apocalyptic Cold War paradigm."[39] Borrowing from Cold War discourses and interpreting the decision as part of a cosmic battle, Lahr explains, CPs viewed the Court's actions in terms of a war against God. While not the beginning of conservative Protestant hostility to government institutions, the heightened animosity engendered by the school prayer decisions certainly made CPs more receptive to the anti-statist message expressed by fusionist conservatives in the early 1960s.[40] Thus, for some CPs, the decision sparked a foray into political activism as they mobilized to propose constitutional amendments to reintroduce school prayer.[41] In short, while some were outraged, the response of the faithful to the Court's decisions on religious disestablishment was varied and factionalized in the 1960s.

But for many Protestants, opposition to the decision was tempered by anti-Catholic bias.[42] The constitutional law scholar Douglas Laycock notes that in the early 1960s, "a fundamentalist press published a five-hundred-page hate tract proposing that Catholics be barred from teaching in public schools or holding high office. The book described Catholicism as a 'totalitarian system' that threatened American freedoms and was more dangerous than Communism because 'it covers its real nature with a cloak of religion.'"[43] Thus, despite a gradual thawing in relations between Catholics and Protestants spurred by anticommunism and a shared rejection of secularism,[44] some Protestants grudgingly supported the decision on the grounds that it would keep Catholics from corrupting their children in public schools.

Even though the Court's school prayer decisions did not provoke a broad-based backlash, school prayer was viewed as a mobilizing tool by some right-wing activists. "As early as 1962," Paul Weyrich claimed that he was trying "to get the Republican party to go on record supporting those people who wanted to repeal the school prayer decision of the Supreme Court." But he could not gain traction on the issue. Rather, Weyrich recalled, "the then Republic chairman thought I was crazy in the state of Wisconsin for calling him and suggesting that he make a statement on that." Instead of getting on board with the issue, the chairman reportedly asked Weyrich: "Why would we want to involve ourselves in that, that's crazy. Are you out of your mind?"[45] By the mid-1970s, the New Right was receiving pushback from establishment conservatives as it began to systematically operationalize so-called Red Flag issues, that is, morally charged social issues, including school prayer. An article in *The Nation* from 1977 highlights establishment conservatives' frustration with the New Right's victim-baiting, quoting Daniel Joy, legal counsel to Sen. James L. Buckley, as saying, "The Viguerie people address only those issues which tend to stir up hostilities among lower-middle-class whites." Later in the article, Joy gripes, "They have no ideology at all. . . . They consistently ignore the substantive issues and emphasize only the peripheral ones—gun control, busing, prayer in the schools—which feed the gnawing suspicion among a good many lower-middle-class Americans that somehow, somewhere, something is oppressing them."[46] Conservative concern over the New Right's use of single issues, including prayer, was echoed the following year by Rep. Phil Crane (R-IL), when he asserted, "Those are the issues that are short-term. . . . You can catch the blue-collar people on busing, prayer in school, abortion and some other questions. The thing is not just to catch them for a short while on one or two issues but to keep them."[47] But Republican squeamishness around the instrumentalization of school prayer did not live out the decade.

In 1979 the New Right darling Sen. Jesse Helms (R-NC) "offered an amendment [to a bill that would create a Department of Education] that said the Supreme Court should be stripped of jurisdiction to review any state or local law permitting voluntary prayers in schools and other public buildings."[48] By 1982 school prayer had become a mainstream GOP issue, as reflected by President Reagan's endorsement of a constitutional amendment to "return" prayer to the public schools.[49] "Succumbing to strong pressures from the right-wing Christian fundamentalists and political conservatives to bring prayer back into the public schools," the *Christian Science Monitor* reported, "Mr. Reagan has officially endorsed the framing of a constitutional amendment to accomplish this."[50] School prayer had become a signature issue for the GOP, and the New Right was instrumental in focusing Reagan's attention on it.

It only took twenty years for school prayer to be effectively mainstreamed as a bona fide conservative issue and for there to be a "backlash" against it. For school prayer to appeal to a broader conservative Christian base, the CNR produced a coordinative discourse that knitted together a diverse and overlapping set of right-wing organizations and issues (discussed in more detail in chapter 3), and a communicative discourse that made school prayer more saleable as an issue. To do the latter, the CNR downplayed the radicality of attempts to legislatively mandate school prayer or enshrine it in the US Constitution, shrouding their actions in terms of conservative self-defense and reactionaryism. Weyrich and his fellow CNR activists were instrumental in promoting this backlash narrative as they constructed a communicative discourse that justified proactive action in terms of "return" to the "traditional" and promoted a shared identity of Christian victimhood.

For New Right and Christian Right political entrepreneurs, the Court's decisions in *Engel* and *Abington* were used to draw a bright red temporal line in the sand, demarcating American political time into a Christian "before" and a secular "after." The temporal framing of the political problem of school prayer can be seen in the language used by Reagan's White House. Messaging coming from the Reagan administration promoted the amendment as a return to tradition, dismissed concerns about the coercive effects of state-sponsored prayer, and promoted the idea that America was and always had been a Christian nation. A question-and-answer memo, presumably intended for the press, asserted: "The Lord's Prayer and the Ten Commandments are reflections of our Judaeo-Christian heritage that could not fairly be described as instruments for the imposition of narrow sectarian dogmas on school children."[51] A 1983 message to Congress urging passage of the amendment went further, hinting that America was intended to be a Christian state: "One hundred fifty years ago, Alexis de Tocqueville found that all Americans believed that religious faith was indispensable to the maintenance of their republican institutions. Today, I join with the people of this Nation in acknowledging this basic truth, that our liberty springs from and depends upon an abiding faith in God."[52] While Reagan's language stops short of identifying Christian Americans as victims, the New Right exercised far less restraint.

New Right publications like *The Family Protection Report* and *Conservative Digest* strongly implied that Christians, conservatives, and American society writ large were in need of "protection" from, in no particular order, communists, liberals, feminists, homosexuals, civil rights advocates, and secular humanists. An extreme articulation of this rhetoric can be seen in a report that was mailed to Phyllis Schlafly in 1979 by a group calling itself "Citizens for God and Country," urging her and Weyrich's organization, the Committee for the Survival of a Free Congress, to oppose the Family Protection Act for not going far enough to protect White Christians.[53] The introduction to the report details perceived attacks on Christianity by American Jews, noting, "Again, we see the Jews in the IRS [Internal Revenue Service] challenging the right of Christian schools to remain all White and continue to receive federal tax exemption." It goes on to blame Jews for having "prayer outlawed in the public schools because of 'separation of church and state,'" before stridently proclaiming Christians are victims: "The attack on Christianity goes on and on and NO major Christian denomination or so-called 'Christian' LEADER makes any protest. While Christianity is attacked and Christians look for someone to speak on their behalf, pictures of the smiling fools calling themselves ministers and priests appear in Jewish publications receiving awards from the enemies of Christ!" Additional explicit references to the "attack" on "White Christians" by Jews and implicit references to the threat posed by desegregation set up a stark warning: "White Christians are becoming "SECOND-CLASS CITIZENS in their own country," and that they will soon be a "MINORITY."[54] While the antisemitism reflected in the Citizens for God and Country report is not reflective of New Right publications, New Right political entrepreneurs used the issue of school prayer to promote the same underlying message: White Christians were under attack and needed to defend what was rightfully and originally theirs.

Contestation over the place of religion in American public education neither began nor ended with the Supreme Court's school prayer decisions in 1962 and 1963. But the Court's school prayer decisions and the varied and changing responses to them are instructive for several reasons. First, they demonstrate how lingering Protestant hostility to Catholics undermined political coalition-building between these groups in the early and mid-1960s, which, in turn, underscores the importance of the institutional changes within both Catholicism and Bible-believing Protestantism that are examined in later chapters.[55] Second, the ongoing development of school prayer as a mobilizing issue for conservative Christians and its adoption by the Republican Party under Reagan demonstrates the utility of backlash discourse in framing school prayer as an issue. By claiming that those who represent the country's true "heritage," that is, White Christians, were under attack, the New Right reinforced the narrative that conservative Christians were victims and any political action on their part was, necessarily, defensive. This, in turn, highlights the ways in which backlash discourse played a key role in the temporalization of politics through the active manufacturing of a before (when White Christians were free to impose prayer on public school children) and an after (when the dominance of White Christians was threatened by the Court), a process that can also be seen to be at work in the backlash framing of abortion opposition.

Abortion

The discourse of backlash is premised on the idea that political time can be carved up into a "before" and an "after." For the Christian Right, backlash becomes a temporal framework that explains the mobilization of right-wing Christians in terms of a motivation to "return" to the country to a "before" time when White, male, and/or Christian supremacy was unchallenged. Within this temporal construction, the problems facing the American body politic do not stem from inequality or the failure to uphold individual rights and democratic processes. Rather, America's social and political problems are the result of too much change, undertaken too fast and illegitimately. As Davina Cooper explains in an article challenging the backlash framework, "Backlash suggests that rapid progress is undesirable because it generates acute fear and defensive responses; it is the populist, intuitive reaction of those who feel that democracy is not functioning."[56] Conservative Christian backlash scripts suggest that the political system is not corrupted by systemic inequality and disenfranchisement, but rather by attempts to make it more inclusive and representative. As part of this process, backlash discourse conjures a moral past—a traditional—in the present. This imagined traditional order then becomes the ground on which a hierarchical and unequal future can be manifested.

Never mind that conservative Christians have always taken issue with both the past and present of American social and political life. Drawing on a detailed exploration of conservative Protestants' cultural discontent with "sexual immorality" as reflected by the evangelical publication *Christianity Today*, Didi Herman problematizes this aspect of backlash, explaining: "While some Christian Right activists do idealize a mythical past, a cursory glance at their literature shows that they were *never* happy with the status quo and have no wish to return to it (e.g., their vehemence against immorality was as strong in the 1950s as it is now, even though they idealize this earlier period).''[57] While Herman's work focuses on conservative Protestants, we might likewise assume the same for Catholics, who found themselves the object of Protestant discrimination for much of America's history. In other words, any construction of an idealized past is necessarily historically suspect. But by framing the origins of the NCR in terms of backlash, the movement justifies its political aims in terms of the preservation of the past. Perhaps nowhere is this clearer than in the backlash discourse surrounding abortion.

The Supreme Court's decision in *Roe v. Wade* (1973), which recognized abortion access as a constitutionally protected right for forty-nine years, is more often than not credited with being the spark that lit the Christian Right's fire and polarized voters on matters pertaining to reproductive autonomy. Thanks in large part to Christian Right activism, positions on the legality of abortion are now widely seen as a litmus test issue for Republican and Democratic political candidates and voters alike. In 2019 the last pro-abortion rights Republican representatives retired from the House, making the House Republican caucus united in its opposition to abortion,[58] and in 2023 over a quarter of voters reported that they would not vote for a candidate who does not share their position on abortion.[59] But abortion has not always been a key issue for CPs or the Republican Party, and its politicization did not immediately follow the Supreme Court's decision to legalize abortion in 1973.[60]

Unlike the Catholic Church, which prohibits birth control and abortion on the grounds that both violate the "seamless garment" of life that stretches from conception to death,[61] the majority of Protestant denominations embraced family planning beginning in the 1930s and 1940s. As a result, the landmark Supreme Court decision legalizing access to birth control, *Griswold v. Connecticut* (1963), was not met with generalized opprobrium from Protestant churches. Prior to and in the immediate period following the *Roe* decision, there was even support among some Protestant religious leaders for expanding access to therapeutic abortion.[62] In 1971, Southern Baptist Convention (SBC) delegates voted to support abortion legislation in cases of "rape, incest, and clear fetal deformity," and when necessary to preserve the "emotional, mental, physical health" of the mother. The SBC reaffirmed this commitment in 1974. Along these lines, the National Association of Evangelicals (NAE) initially supported therapeutic abortion for the health and well-being of the mother, while condemning the *Roe* decision for legalizing abortion on demand.[63] This flies in the face of the contemporary public perception that conservative Christians were politicized by their unequivocal opposition to abortion, or what the religion scholar Randall Balmer has termed the "abortion myth."[64] In reality, abortion was regarded by many Protestants as a "Catholic issue," and anti-Catholic sentiment led many Protestants to view anti-abortion attitudes with suspicion and hostility.

In part deriving from theological differences, elite Protestant support for abortion access was also driven by anti-Catholicism. As Mark Rozell explains, "So deep was the contention [between Protestants and Catholics] that, prior to the landmark abortion decision of the U.S. Supreme Court in Roe v. Wade (1973), evangelicals and Southern Baptists often led opposition to state proposals to restrict abortion rights because Catholic-led organizations such as the National Right to Life Committee (NRTL) were promoting such legislation."[65] But a sea change was coming in terms of Protestant attitudes toward abortion (and Catholics). In 1976 the SBC reversed its position, and limited support for abortion to those cases when a woman's life was in mortal danger. By 1980 the SBC adopted a resolution endorsing "appropriate legislation and/or a constitutional amendment prohibiting abortion except to save the life of the mother."[66]

While a whole-scale Protestant backlash did not immediately follow the *Roe* decision, the discourse of backlash was used by religious elites to encourage Protestants to embrace opposition to abortion as a defining issue. In particular, the fundamentalist theologian Francis Schaeffer is frequently credited with transforming White conservative Protestant attitudes toward abortion over the course of the mid-to-late-1970s and into the early 1980s. Writing with Dr. C. Everett Koop, who would later be named surgeon general by Ronald Reagan, Schaeffer's 1979 book and 1979 film series, *Whatever Happened to the Human Race?*, are cited as having fueled the Protestant anti-abortion movement.[67]

Whatever Happened to the Human Race? embraced backlash discourse and promoted the idea that political time could be divided into a before and an after: "First, the whole concept of law has changed. When a Christian consensus existed, it gave a base for law. Instead of this, we now live under arbitrary, or sociological, law."[68] In the "before" time, society and law reflected Christian beliefs and were governed by Christian morality. In the "after," Christianity has been shunted aside, and Christians are "faced today with a flood of personal cruelty." In the past, this was not the case, as "the

Christian consensus gave great freedoms without leading to chaos—because society in general functioned within the values given in the Bible, especially the unique value of human life." But in the present, "humanism has taken over, the former freedoms run riot, and individuals, acting on what they are taught, increasingly practice their cruelties without restraint."[69] The threat of cruelty to Christians stems, first and foremost, from the Court's decision in *Roe*, which marks a rupture:

> Of all the subjects relating to the erosion of the sanctity of human life, abortion is the keystone. It is the first and crucial issue that has been overwhelming in changing attitudes toward the value of life in general. The Supreme Court of the United States on January 22, 1973, in deciding Roe v. Wade and Doe v. Bolton declared that a new personal right or liberty existed in the Constitution—the right of a woman to procure an abortion at any time. The right of privacy was given a completely new interpretation.[70]

For Schaeffer and Koop, *Roe* is used to symbolize entry into a new era, which is characterized by a fundamental disregard for human life that they term "secular humanism."

In a post-*Roe* world, they suggest, anyone may be killed at any time, and Christians must, therefore, fear for their lives and the lives of those they love. Foreshadowing the anti-abortion movement's cooptation of civil rights discourse,[71] Schaeffer and Koop proceed to draw a line between the dehumanization of slavery and abortion: "In our day, quite rightly, there has been great protest because society in the past viewed the black slave as a nonperson. Now, by an arbitrary absolute brought into the humanist flow, the law in similar fashion declares millions of unborn babies of every color of skin to be nonpersons."[72] Schaeffer and Koop, unsurprisingly, fail to address how the Christian and moral "before" sanctioned abject and inhumane cruelty toward enslaved people. The past can be constructed and reconstructed as necessary to assert a tradition of Christian supremacy and warn of a future of Christian victimhood. It follows, then, that there is no choice but for Christians to defend themselves from the assault of a secular humanist society that permits the slaughter of the unborn.

Other CP activists also promoted the narrative that the transformation of evangelical and fundamentalist Protestant attitudes was driven by a backlash against the Court's decision in *Roe*. In his autobiography, *Strength for the Journey*, Jerry Falwell claims that the *Roe* decision was, in and of itself, responsible for his recognition that abortion needed to be opposed and his politicization as he came to realize that "to stop the legalizing of death by abortion, opponents of the *Roe v. Wade* decision were protesting in the streets." As Falwell's biographer, Michael Sean Winters, notes, "But in the short term Falwell did nothing specific to overturn *Roe* beyond preaching about the 'national sin' on the *Old-Time Gospel Hour* and on his many trips to other churches and during his rallies with his Liberty Baptist College singers."[73] While Falwell had referred to abortion as a "national sin" in the mid-1970s, he gave his first sermon dedicated exclusively to abortion in 1978.[74] And so, in order for the backlash narrative to carry water, Falwell had to explain the six-year gap between the Court's decision and the formation of the Moral Majority. He did so by maintaining that the decision to join the anti-abortion movement was a difficult one for him: "For the first time in my life I felt God leading me to join them. But such a step was entirely against my nature."[75]

While Falwell's first overt dalliance with politics was in 1976 when he organized a series of "I Love America" rallies focused broadly on "moral decay," he did not launch an explicitly political campaign until 1978, when the "Clean Up America" morality campaign took aim at porn, abortion, and homosexuality.[76] Falwell's abortion story, discussed in more detail in chapter 4, helps to rewrite his past excoriation of religious leaders for their participation in the civil rights movement by providing a veneer of moralism for his own entry into politics. As we also see in chapter 4, in the mid-late 1970s it was Schaeffer's theory of co-belligerents, which held that interdenominational rifts could be overlooked when done in the service of pursuing a greater political good, that enabled Reverend Falwell to instrumentalize abortion as a tool for forming political coalitions with other Christians and Jews in the late 1970s.[77]

Even if Falwell's six-year gap undermines the abortion backlash narrative and instead points to a different Christian Right origin story (discussed below), it is fair to say the *Roe* decision created an opening in the political opportunity structure. Fundamentalists like Schaeffer and Falwell, along with New Right activists like Paul Weyrich, Richard Viguerie, and Connaught Marshner, capitalized on this opening to begin brokering coalitions between Bible-believing Christians, who represented a large portion of the nation's population, and conservative Catholics, who already had sophisticated theological and institutional tools at their disposal. The temporalized politics of abortion facilitated the process of coalition-building by both providing a moral justification for ecumenism and by providing an explanatory framework for Christians to view themselves as victims.

Opposing abortion rights was one way in which CPs processed their discomfort with expanding women's rights and changes in American gender and sexual relations. Likewise, resistance to the changes wrought by the sexual revolution and women's rights movements motivated some conservative Christians to take political action, as the historian Kristen Kobes DuMez explained in a 2022 interview with NPR:

> But what happens in the 1970s is, first of all, with the passing of Roe v. Wade, you see a spike in the number of abortions. And that causes many Americans, not just evangelicals, to kind of rethink is this what we wanted? But I think more importantly, you have the rise of second-wave feminism and, in conservative, white, evangelical spaces, a real backlash against feminism. And over the course of that decade, abortion becomes linked to feminism. And so you see the sentiment start to shift so that in 1979, when political activist Paul Weyrich identifies abortion as a potential to really mobilize conservative evangelicals politically, to help build the Moral Majority, then it is a very effective mechanism for doing so. And from 1979 on, that's when you see a real kind of shrinking of space within conservative evangelicalism to have any view on abortion that isn't strictly and staunchly pro-life, life begins at conception.[78]

Du Mez is right to expand the frame to include evangelical opposition to feminism as a result of an entrenched belief in patriarchal traditionalism and the supremacy of men over women. But even this expanded narrative of backlash against legal abortion suffers from both chronological discrepancies and explanatory deficiencies. If the primary motivator for Christian Right mobilization was opposition to women's emancipation, it is not immediately clear why backlash would have followed from the Court's decision on abortion and not an earlier decision legalizing access to contraception.[79] Why does the legalization of birth control not possess a starring role in the origin story of the Christian Right in the 1970s? The short answer is that while conservative Catholics vehemently opposed both the *Griswold* and *Roe* decisions and had organized against contraception and abortion access *prior* to the Court's decisions, these were perceived as Catholic issues, and neither birth control nor abortion was seen as a political issue for CPs from the mid-1960s through the mid-1970s. For there to be a backlash against abortion, CPs had to both be convinced that it was an issue worth mobilizing around and overcome their antipathy to Catholics.

Even with this more nuanced account in mind, the very framework of backlash is misleading when applied to abortion. There was never a "before" time when the US legal system was premised on Christian morality, and all life was valued and protected. Access to safe and legal abortion was not a slippery slope that would lead to American collapse or Christian persecution. Conservative Christians were neither victims of a humanist coup nor were they merely seeking to hold the line against social change. Rather, in the time before, during, and after the feminist movement and the legalization of contraception and abortion that created new opportunities for women, fundamentalist and evangelical Protestants had a clearly articulated political theology in respect to women and their place in society.[80] Their beliefs about male patriarchy and female submission, which would be translated into social policy via the "pro-family" political platform, were not reactionary sentiments formed in response to the legalization of birth control or abortion. Rather, as theological precepts, these ideas preceded the social changes they were ostensibly formed in response to. Moreover, in a move that seemingly ran counter to the conservative Cold War ethos of demanding *less* government, anti-abortionists demanded *more* government control over women's bodies. New Right political entrepreneurs, therefore, had to redefine conservatism and promote a new activist vision for American government. They did so through the creation of a "pro-family" platform, which advocated for limiting government intervention into the male-dominated family while simultaneously subordinating the rights of women to those of the unborn child. As the foundation for a new political ideology, which sought to impose Christian sexual and gender norms, this political platform represented a radical break from the liberal tradition in America.

Desegregation

Paul Weyrich was emphatic that evangelicals were politically motivated by backlash, just not backlash against the issues Christian Right activists tended to highlight. According to Weyrich, the "real" issue was not school prayer or abortion but the desegregation of public schools. In Weyrich's hands, this became not an issue of racial equality, but one of government interference with the rights of Christian parents to educate their children as they saw fit. The religion scholar Randall Balmer has made a forceful and compelling argument that "protecting segregated schools" was the real motivation behind the emergence of the NCR.[81] According to Balmer, Weyrich had been "trying out different issues, hoping one might pique evangelical interest: pornography, prayer in schools, the proposed Equal Rights Amendment to the Constitution, even abortion" for years before the IRS began using tax-exemption policies to enforce *Brown v. Board of Education's* prohibition on segregation.[82] Recounting a meeting of New and Christian Right activists he attended in November 1990, Balmer writes,

> In the initial session, someone made passing reference to the standard narrative that the *Roe v. Wade* decision of 1973 had served as the catalyst for the Religious Right. I tuned in. Weyrich forcefully disputed that assumption, recounting that ever since Barry Goldwater's run for the presidency in 1964, he had been trying to enlist evangelicals in conservative political causes, but it was the tax exemption for religious schools that finally caught the attention of the evangelical leaders. Abortion, he said, had nothing to do with it.[83]

Weyrich's reported downplaying of the centrality of abortion should not be taken at face value, given that opposition to abortion was a genuinely held position for segments of the evangelical and fundamentalist Protestant grassroots base.[84] But Weyrich's claim is nonetheless instructive for what it tells us about CP leaders and the issues that did and did not capture their political imaginations. While the Bible-believing Christian grassroots may have been receptive to other issues, such as school prayer and abortion, in the 1970s the leadership was not initially motivated by these issues. They were, however, motivated by racism.

According to the desegregation backlash narrative, what spurred CPs into action was a chain of events set in motion by the 1954 *Brown v. Board* decision holding that the doctrine of "separate but equal" could not be sustained and ordering the desegregation of public schools. As Gerald Rosenberg has shown, while the Court's decision initially had a limited impact on school desegregation, after 1964, its rulings were bolstered by congressional legislation and executive action, which resulted in more meaningful action.[85] Title VI of the 1964 Civil Rights Act (CRA) restricted federal funding to segregated schools, while the 1965 Elementary and Secondary Education Act (ESEA) made a large pot of funds available to schools that served low-income students if they were desegregated.[86] The Department of Health, Education, and Welfare (HEW) was tasked with enforcing Title VI, and after a slow start, "by the end of the Johnson administration, HEW had come to officially require complete desegregation as a requirement for receiving federal funds under Title VI."[87] In response to the federal government's push to desegregate public education, there was a proliferation of all-White private primary and secondary schools across the South, commonly referred to as "seg academies." [88]

Created as part of a White supremacist strategy to resist integration, segregated private schools took both secular and religious forms, and received active state support as "many Southern state governments encouraged [the] establishment of private schools, enacting legislation mandating or allowing the closing of public schools to resist desegregation or providing state tax credits and tuition grants to students attending private schools."[89] Drawing additional support from advocates for school prayer and those who opposed sex education curricula, the number of all-White Christian schools quickly surpassed that of secular segregation academies. The legal scholar Olatunde C. A. Johnson explains, "Yet racial beliefs and religion became intermingled in the mission and founding concepts of some of the religious schools, leading some observers to claim that 'Christian schools and segregation academies are almost synonymous.'"[90] Thus, by the 1970s, Southern segregation academies were largely religious schools.

The private nature of seg academies presented the government with an enforcement challenge, as they did not receive federal funding or operate in a public capacity and so fell outside of the scope of Title VI enforcement. A 1973 article in the *Journal of Negro Education* highlighted the importance of the private/public distinction for seg academies: "The idea of private property is essential to the case of the white segregationist. As one said, 'The n—s can come on public property, but, by damn, they can't come on private property unless we let them. And we ain't going to let them.'"[91] If the federal government was to pursue desegregation in education, it needed to find a different way to target the seg academies. And so, in the early 1970s, during the Nixon administration, the IRS began holding that segregated private religious schools were not entitled to tax-exempt status.[92] The IRS policy did not threaten segregation academies with closure; rather, it sought to encourage desegregation by targeting these school's bottom line by requiring them to pay taxes.

In 1971 the IRS policy was challenged and upheld by the DC District Court in *Green v. Connally*. Nonetheless, Bob Jones University, a bastion

of hardline Baptist fundamentalism in South Carolina, refused to desegregate on the grounds that being forced to do so would violate the school's
religious beliefs. The IRS issued repeated warnings to the school before
revoking its tax-exempt status in 1976, prompting a series of court battles
that eventually found their way to the Supreme Court in 1982.[93]

Sensing an opportunity to rally conservative religious leaders around a
political cause, "Falwell and Weyrich quickly sought to shift the grounds
of the [seg academy] debate," Balmer explains, "framing their opposition
[to school desegregation] in terms of religious freedom rather than in defense of racial segregation."[94] Both men jumped at the opportunity to lay
claim to the narrative that the federal government's intervention into the
business of seg academies was stripping Bible-believing Christians of their
religious freedom and impinging on their familial rights. By denying White
Christian parents the "right" to choose how and with whom their children
would be educated, the government was attacking both God and the family. Framed in this way, White Christian segregationists became the true
victims of a secular and hostile government. In this way, both backlash and
victimhood scripts were operationalized in the defense of seg academies.

This discourse rang true for some White Catholics as well, even though
the desegregation of Catholic schools—and White Catholic opposition to
desegregation—followed a somewhat different pattern. The existence of
private parochial schools long predated the Court's decision in *Brown v.
Board of Education*, and the official stance of the Catholic Church in America was to oppose segregation. The United States Conference of Catholic
Bishops (USCCB) repeatedly issued statements in support of recognizing
the political, religious, and social equality of Black Americans, beginning
in 1943.[95] In 1963 the USCCB reiterated its opposition to segregation, asserting, "These truths [the fundamental equality of the races] being understood, no Catholic with a good Christian conscience can fail to recognize
the rights of all citizens to vote. Moreover, we must provide for all equal
opportunity for employment, full participation in our public and private
educational facilities, proper housing, and adequate welfare assistance
when needed."[96] But not all White Catholics were swayed by pastoral letters calling for racial justice and harmony, and some flatly rejected the integration of parochial schools. "Many Southern Catholic school officials have
refused to allow their schools to enroll pupils fleeing from integrated public
schools," a 1970 article in the *New York Times* reported. "However, some
have accepted the fleeing whites and have thus served the same purpose as

do private schools set up to maintain segregation."[97] In the North, many White Catholics, particularly those in urban areas, simply picked up and moved. In his 1977 dissertation, James Charles Moses set out to examine parochial school desegregation, but instead discovered a process of "reseg-regation," or "as one anonymous cynic put it, the process of change in school population from 'the first black in to the last white out.'"[98]

White Catholics, like their White Protestant counterparts, framed their disagreements with desegregation using the language of "religious freedom." A December 1974 survey administered by the Boston Archdi-ocesan School Office found that "half of [affected principals and pastors] also expressed serious dissatisfaction and a belief that the policy violated the natural right of Catholic parents to send their children to Catholic schools."[99] American discourses of religious freedom, such as this one, have historically been weaponized in the service of promoting and maintaining White supremacy, as Tisa Wenger has detailed. "The dominant voices in the culture," Wenger writes, "linked racial whiteness, Protestant Christian-ity, and American national identity not only to freedom in general but often to this [religious] freedom in particular."[100] Initially excluded from the top of the American racial-religious hierarchy, White American Catholics used the imperial aspirations of the United States and the discourse of religious freedom to assert their place alongside their Protestant counterparts.[101] For both Protestants and Catholics, then, the discourse of religious free-dom has long been one that serves to uphold the dominance and suprem-acy of both Whiteness and Christianity.

Drawing on Wenger's analysis, it is not difficult to see how the discourse of religious freedom was weaponized in the service of maintaining segre-gated schools and helped to bridge the CP and Catholic divide. For White Protestants and Catholics alike, "religious freedom" served to simultane-ously gesture toward and obscure the White supremacist beliefs that un-derpinned segregation. It also, crucially, helped to rewrite history and create a new past for conservative Christians to seek a return to. Throughout the 1970s, the American consensus shifted (at least superficially) to condemn segregation and racial inequality, making calls to return to a Jim Crow past politically untenable. But conservative Christians *could* demand a return to the time when "religious freedom" was upheld. As a result, the discourse functioned as a more socially acceptable justificatory schema for conserva-tive base-building than did pure, unadulterated racism. While opposition to desegregation informed the coordinative discourse that brought CNR and CP leaders together, "parental rights" and "religious freedom" became linchpins of the NCR's communicative discourse. Moreover, the narrative of backlash—whether to school prayer, abortion, or the revocation of tax-exempt status to seg academies—accommodated a host of issues concerning gender, sex, and reproduction that helped to reinforce an identity of Christian victimhood.

Supremacist Politics

Conservative Christians' opposition to these landmark decisions reflects three arenas of supremacist politics (Christian, male, and White) pursued by the NCR. As we have seen in this chapter, both elite and grassroots conservative Catholics and Protestants were mobilized, to some degree or another, by a desire to shape: (1) the place of (a Christian) God in the public sphere, which corresponds to Christian supremacism; (2) sexual and reproductive behavior, which corresponds to male supremacism; and (3) the racial terrain on which social relations in the United States are formed, which corresponds to White supremacism. These supremacist ideologies should be understood as necessarily intertwined. To illustrate their co-constitutive nature, we can take school prayer as an example.

The aim of school prayer mobilizations has never been to advance a pluralist conception of religious freedom and religious equality.[102] The aim has been to define public spaces as Christian spaces and to utilize public education to produce future generations of (White) Christian Americans. The mobilization around seg academies highlights the interdependent relationship between White supremacism and Christian supremacism, as the "right" of parents to have their children pray in school was collapsed with their "right" to maintain racially exclusionary, all-White spaces in the public sphere. As Anthea Butler has powerfully shown, racism courses throughout the history of American evangelicalism, and the ideology of White supremacy provides a clear throughline from one moment in evangelicalism's history to the next.[103] Additionally, the claim that parents have a "right" to determine how and where their children are educated also implicates male supremacism as it serves to define the structure of the family in terms that are delimitated by patriarchal traditionalism and White supremacism, or what anthropologist Sophie Bjork-James has termed "white sexual politics."[104]

Each of these supremacist belief systems are grounded in history, function in the present, and look to the future. The NCR agenda is one that is forward-looking and motivated by a belief that White Christian cisgender men are entitled to positions of dominance, a vision of the form American social relations *should* take, and a desire to harness the coercive capacity of the state in the service of making the nation anew. As Didi Herman explains, "the Christian Right has a comprehensive, progressive future vision: it is, I would argue, a paradigmatic movement for social change having neither more nor less to do with backlash than do the feminist and gay rights movements."[105] We need to look no further than to a recent spate of Supreme Court decisions—dismantling the separation of church and state (*Kennedy v. Bremerton* 2022; *Carson v. Makin* 2022; *303 Creative, LLC v. Elenis* 2023) and overturning legal access to abortion and undermining the right to privacy (*Dobbs v. Jackson Women's Health Organization* 2022)—to see the successful realization of the NCR's agenda for social change in the present.

But we would be mistaken to read the Court's most recent decisions as a return to the past or even the preservation of the status quo. The White male Christian supremacism of the early 2020s is neither synonymous with nor seeks a return to its antecedent form in the 1920s (or 1820s or 1720s, for that matter). To experience the creeping criminalization of abortion in an era of digital government surveillance is different from experiencing it in an era without phones that track our every movement and apps that record menstrual cycles. To be denied the right of reproductive choice in the context of late-stage capitalism and its attendant labor demands is different from being denied access to abortion in an era when (White) women were largely denied employment opportunities outside of the home. To exist in 2022 without the right to bodily autonomy is different from living in a world where a constitutional right to privacy has not yet been articulated and has not yet transformed our social, economic, and political institutions.

The political future the NCR works to manifest—that is, its motivation—is one that has been obscured by backlash discourse, as the movement's advancement of intersecting and overlapping supremacist ideologies is framed as a "return" rather than the production of a new set of social relations and corresponding political institutions. Put differently, the NCR works to shape the future through the successful implementation of a coordinative discourse (i.e., the shaping of legislation and judicial decision-making) that is justified by a communicative discourse that promises a "return" to an imagined and falsified past. In these ways, the discourse of backlash works in the service of supremacist politics.

Concluding Thoughts

This chapter has largely focused on three central backlash narratives that form part of the NCR origin story. Each has some kernel of truth to it, but, following Davina Cooper's lead, I believe "the concept of backlash fails (1) to sufficiently account for the production of resources and (2) to sufficiently account for the production of motivation."[106] Conservative Catholics and Protestants reacted to progressive changes in the American political land-scape and the Court's decisions, but their responses were neither uniform nor immediate, and it is an overstatement to credit the Court with ignit-ing the spark of the Christian Right revolution. This is not to deny the reactionary impulse found among Christian conservatives, nor to dispute that the Supreme Court was instrumental in helping mobilize Christian conservatives. On one hand, many conservative Christians genuinely were angered by the changes augured by the Court's rulings. On the other hand, decisions affecting school prayer, abortion, and school desegregation both created and reflected new institutional arrangements, which, in turn, al-lowed for the mobilization of resources in new and different ways and by new and different actors. But to credit the NCR's origins to backlash is to flatten and obscure the unique institutional and historical develop-ments, and concomitant political work in the form of institution-building, resource mobilization, and collective identity formation, that went into mobilizing the NCR. Moreover, to call it backlash is to misrecognize the movement's fundamental aims.

As we have seen, opposition to the Court's decisions helped conser-vative Christians demarcate a "before" and an "after," and, in the process, construct a temporal politics that weaponized the "traditional." At the same time, framing the movement's mobilization in terms of "backlash" served to shift the responsibility for right-wing mobilization onto the left by casting the right as a defensive movement. In doing so, it helped reinforce an ideol-ogy and identity of victimhood among conservative White Christians. The victimhood script, in turn, helped to obscure the supremacist politics of a movement that sought to advance—not merely maintain—male, White, and Christian dominance and replace a liberal and pluralist democratic order with the politics of an illiberal and coercive cultural conservativism. Interrogating NCR origin stories that center on backlash helps us to move away from an understanding of the movement as reactionary and move toward an understanding of it as proactive and engaged in a radical and revolutionary project to make the country anew.

This is not to say that conservative Christians were not motivated by and mobilized in response to external factors and sociopolitical transformations. Racial backlash certainly loomed large as a motivator for conservative Christian political mobilization, but it was by no means the sole reason conservative Christians sought to reorient American politics. Conservative Christians were also acutely aware of the rising tides of secularism, the sexual revolution, and the gay rights and women's rights movements, and CNR and CP political entrepreneurs seized on landmark Supreme Court decisions on matters like school desegregation, school prayer, birth control, and abortion. To borrow from the language of social movement theory, the Court's decisions served as critical junctures insofar as they provided new opportunities for the mobilization of conservative Christians. But they should be read in relation to other, related openings in the political opportunity structure that were capitalized on by both political entrepreneurs and grassroots activists. Thus, as we see in the following chapters, in addition to trading on racist attitudes and opposition to desegregation and mobilizing conservative religious identifications pertaining to gender, sexuality, and the family, the NCR coalition was developed in relation to religious and political institutional transformations that included Vatican II, the Watergate scandal, campaign finance reform, and the development of new electoral strategies. The production of new ideas that stemmed from the convergence of conservative Catholic and Protestant religious beliefs and sociocultural practices should be understood as historically and institutionally contingent. The conservative agenda the CNR promoted, and CPs embraced, was developed to radically transform American politics— not to stem the tide of change or return to some mythical "originary" position. Thus, the NCR was driven not solely by the force of negative reaction, but also by the productive creation of new coalition-building strategies and the development of new social policies that were uniquely influenced by conservative Catholic thought.

Given its utility as an explanatory frame, its widespread usage, and "its naturalized, interpretive implications,"[107] I recognize that there will likely be resistance to eschewing the discourse of backlash when thinking about the NCR and the political right more generally. But to disavow the discourse of backlash is not to disavow history. Rather, it is to avow a more institutionally grounded understanding of historical developments and to encourage a more honest reckoning with the Right's political aims. Opposition to the aforementioned judicial rulings and resistance to the sexual revolution, the civil rights and women's rights movements, and the rising tide of secularism certainly contributed to the mobilization of conservative Christians. But backlash discourse has served to obscure the ways in which the NCR agenda was proactive, not reactive; progressive, not regressive. CNR and CP elites did not simply seek to hold the line against the turbulence of social change. Much like their progressive antagonists, they sought to radically transform it. Paul Weyrich said as much: "We don't accept the status quo, we want to change it. . . . They did not carry the battle into the streets; we do."[108]

2

———•••———

PAUL WEYRICH

1968 and the Roots
of a (Catholic) Radical

The social gospel tells us to change man's environment and that will change the world. The real gospel tells us to reform man first, so that a reformed man can change the world. But the citizens of our Nation have few beacons of truth upon whom they can rely. Only the truth can make us free, and the truth must be based on the commandments and the moral law. So, even though we deal with "politics and issues," our real task is a moral one.

—Paul Weyrich

There was a time, not so very long ago, when Paul M. Weyrich was one of the patron saints of American conservatives in Washington, DC, honored at galas and at least one roast, which focused more on lambasting Ronald Reagan for being a weak conservative than on poking fun at Weyrich himself.[1] Weyrich was a "political entrepreneur," who made transformative contributions to the American political landscape while never holding elected office himself.[2] He not only fulfilled the primary characteristics of a political entrepreneur; he excelled at them. As one of the key architects of the New Right, he was part of an insurgent political movement that ushered in a new brand of self-proclaimed "radical conservatism" during the 1970s and early 1980s. As demonstrated in chapter 3, he spurred the creation of a number of right-wing organizations, including the Heritage

Foundation, Committee for the Survival of a Free Congress (CSFC), and the American Legislative Exchange Council (ALEC); supported the candidacies of conservatives in both the Democratic and Republican parties; and forged new ad hoc single-issue coalitions. Over the course of a decade, Weyrich and other leaders of the New Right—including Richard Viguerie, Howard Phillips, and John Terry Dolan[3]—pioneered novel strategies, implemented new direct mail technologies, and laid the institutional and ideological foundations for the conservative revolution that would come to be personified by Reagan's presidency and the culture wars of the 1980s.

Weyrich's role as a political entrepreneur extended to and was informed by the emergence of a new Catholic conservatism, which in turn shaped the political formation of the New Christian Right (NCR). Weyrich did not just broker an enduring alliance among conservative Christians; he also infused the politics of the New Right, and later the NCR, with a distinctively Catholic sensibility that was incorporated into the socially conservative policy agendas of both movements. While much has been written about the relationship between the New and Christian Rights,[4] much less attention has been dedicated to understanding the influence of conservative Catholic thought on the formation of both movements. Weyrich offers an opportunity to explore that connection.

Evidence suggests that Weyrich had a knotty relationship with the Catholic Church. As a young man, he rejected ecumenical reforms ushered in by the Second Vatican Council in the 1960s. And yet within a decade, he would reach out to welcome Protestants into a conservative religious alliance, a move that suggests the explicitly political nature of the alliance he forged. He combined a deep personal faith with a desire to promote moral values in the public sphere through political activism, as indicated by this chapter's epigraph and his assertion that political issues are, in fact, moral issues. Yet the origins of Weyrich's conservative development are rarely, if ever, addressed, which has led the Catholic dimensions of the New Right and the NCR to be overlooked. This chapter seeks to remedy the aforementioned omission by addressing the impact on Weyrich of institutional and doctrinal changes within the Catholic Church in the United States in the 1960s, and by exploring how these transformations shaped and informed his conservative worldview and made it possible for him to identify as a "conservative Catholic." I examine his religious beliefs with an eye to the production of a conservative ideology that seeks to carve out space for a new kind of state—one that would be dramatically limited in terms of social welfare provision and vastly expanded in terms of social regulation.

As subsequent chapters show, Weyrich helped secure a place for conservative Catholicism in American politics through his contributions to the development of a pro-family political platform (explored in detail in chapter 5),[5] which drew heavily on Catholic thought, and through the institutional and ideological support he provided for the Christian Right. Examining his personal relationship to Catholicism helps explicate how his religiosity informed not only his own political views but also the politics of the American Right more broadly. As a political conservative, Weyrich was certainly responsive to the revolutionary movements convulsing secular America in 1968, including growing opposition to the Vietnam War, student protests, and the increasing visibility of the civil rights movement, but it was a series of changes taking place within Catholicism that freed him to develop a new brand of religious conservativism that operated outside the traditional confines of both the Church and the Republican Party. In addition to his more straightforward work as a political broker within the New Right, Weyrich was also a religious entrepreneur, carving out a new political identity for conservative Catholicism and producing new political coalitions and ideologies among conservative Christians.

Weyrich was a complicated man, an ideologue and an instrumentalist, a political pugilist and a militant religious believer. Making sense of him poses a particular set of difficulties. Weyrich cast himself in a contradictory set of roles, as he cultivated an image as both radical and traditionalist. Likewise, he claimed to simultaneously be an undercover strategist, working behind the scenes, and a primary mover of history. Not one for humility, Weyrich obsessively documented his own life in a series of scrapbooks that are now housed at the Library of Congress.[6] Within this archive, as if to underscore his importance, Weyrich's name is underlined in every article that mentions him. A danger lies in relying on these materials, as they record a story Weyrich himself wanted to tell. Rather than take either Weyrich's statements about himself or the documents he archived at face value, they need to be read skeptically, with an eye for the complications and inconsistencies inherent in his biography. Doing so enables us to interrogate some of his most basic and oft-recited claims about his relationship to ecumenical coalition-building and coalition strategies. At the same time, the point of this endeavor is not to excavate a truer narrative about Weyrich, but rather to come to a better understanding of how he was shaped by and shaped (conservative) Catholicism.

The Apple Doesn't Fall Far from the Tree

When he arrived in the District of Columbia in the late 1960s, with his trademark severe side-part and thick, horn-rimmed glasses, Paul Weyrich's conservative worldview was already in place. Born in Racine, Wisconsin, in 1942, Weyrich came of age during the height of the Cold War in Senator Eugene McCarthy's home state. While anticommunist sentiment coursed across the United States and much of the nation was swept up in the second Red Scare throughout the 1950s, Weyrich's politics and piety were first born in the home. Baptized at Holy Name Parish in Racine, Weyrich was raised in the Catholic Church.[7] A strong student, he received top academic honors in the state and participated in the debate club in the extemporaneous reading category. He exhibited a precocious interest in mass transit, which would become a lifelong obsession, forming a railway club and hosting picnics to educate people about and raise awareness of the importance of trains. He was also involved early on with the local branch of the Young Republicans club, first joining as a teenager, and was an active and engaged member during his time at the University of Wisconsin, Racine. He briefly worked on Philip Kuehn's failed gubernatorial campaign in 1962 and was a vocal supporter of Barry Goldwater in 1962 and 1963.[8] In June 1963 he resigned his membership in the Young Republicans club as a result of an acrimonious relationship with the club's leadership that began when Weyrich vigorously opposed the club's resolution not to endorse any political candidates for office. The following month, having completed his sophomore year, Weyrich dropped out of college and married Joyce Smigun at St. Patrick's Roman Catholic Church. While Weyrich showed signs of becoming a conservative activist early on, much of his time during this period was invested in building his career as a journalist, working first as a manager of a local radio station before moving into print and television news reporting, and starting his family (his first child was born in the late spring of 1964).[9]

From the beginning, for Weyrich, faith, family, and politics were deeply intertwined. In a 2005 interview Weyrich recalled that his father, Ignatius Weyrich, a German immigrant and devout Catholic, "used to say, in America they say you shouldn't talk religion and politics. But one determines your temporal life, and the other determines your eternal life. What else is there to talk about?"[10] Given Weyrich's lifelong devotion to the twin subjects, it was clearly a lesson he took to heart.

Throughout his life, Weyrich mythologized his father as a paragon of conservative ideals. In a 1969 editorial extolling his father's virtues for the Catholic newspaper *The Wanderer*, Weyrich held up his father as a patriarchal model:

> When his family needed a few things that his small hospital wages would not buy ... such as an automobile ... he didn't strike or blame Society. He got a second part-time job and purchased those things ... with cash ... because he never believed in credit and he likes to practice what he preaches. He is not, it must be said, the typical American father. He was no "pa" to his son. Indeed, his son's earliest recollections of him do not bring to mind fairy tales and baseball games, but rather lengthy sermons on the folly of the New Deal and the fallacies of U.S. foreign policy.[11]

In Paul Weyrich's imagination, his father represented the American conservative man *par excellence*. He personified the key tenets of one variant of Cold War political ideology: a belief in self-reliance, rugged individualism, frugality, and fiscal responsibility, coupled with a distaste for organized labor, social welfare programs, and political dovishness.[12]

From his depiction of his father, his involvement in the Young Republicans, and the local Racine Republican Party, we can paint a picture of what conservatism meant to Weyrich in the 1960s: he understood the ideology as being in line with fusionist thought, as a political orientation predicated on the tenets of limited government, fiscal responsibility, free market capitalism, obedience to law and order, and conformity to "traditional" social norms. This version of conservativism had its origins in the early 1960s, when the conservative publication *National Review*, under the editorial review of the devout Catholic William Buckley Jr. and the ex-communist Frank Meyer, had attempted to paper over a growing rift between libertarians and traditionalists.[13] Rejecting President Dwight Eisenhower's brand of "moderate Republicanism," Meyer's "fusionism" bridged Lockean libertarianism with Burkean traditionalism. At the core of the principles articulated by Meyer was a belief in the fundamental and expansive "freedom of the person," which was accompanied by a radical shrinking of the state.[14] In short, for Meyer, man left alone to exercise his freedom and rationality in the absence of all state and institutional interference would necessarily arrive at virtue because of the existence of an "organic moral order."[15] As the 1960s unfolded, law and order became the conservative linchpin that would hold the disparate elements of fusionism together. Espoused in race-baiting terms by presidential hopeful Barry Goldwater and others, the convergence of traditionalism and libertarianism came to be framed as the individual's inherent and natural right to be free from the reckless and top-down imposition of equal rights for all by the federal government.

The traditionalism espoused by fusionism was not synonymous with the social conservatism that would subsequently arise from the New Right and Christian Right. The emphasis on traditional morality in fusionism certainly paved the way for the later conservative Christian political movement, but fusionist moralism was held in check by its libertarian impulses. For Weyrich and other social conservatives, by the late 1970s this conservative ideology would morph to encompass a much more radical and rigid social conservative emphasis on the place of family and religion in government while also adopting a more flexible attitude toward the idea of limited government and free market capitalism as the New Right flirted with "lunch bucket issues" and made populist appeals to the working class.[16]

While informed by the dominant conservative ideology of his time, Weyrich was also strongly committed to his faith. The personal importance of religion for Weyrich is evident when he eulogizes his father for his "strong faith . . . for when the false prophets of the social gospel and the anti-Catholic Catholics became commonplace in the Church, he stood up against them." Every time a liberal priest "uttered a false or unorthodox statement," Weyrich's father would stand to deliver his own layman's sermon on orthodox Catholic teachings.[17] Weyrich's writing conjures images of his orderly, clean-cut father standing in the darkened aisle of his church to challenge a horde of young and unwashed, longhaired priests, defending the one, true church in his German-accented English against the heresy of "the social gospel and the anti-Catholic Catholics," the spread of which both Weyrich and his father interpreted as being indicative of the liberal decline of the Catholic Church.

Weyrich's treatment of his father speaks to his understanding of how the family should be organized and function in society. For Weyrich, his father, representative of the model patriarch, is not only the head of the family unit but is also the conduit through which the family interacts with the rest of society. In other words, the father is responsible for the spiritual and material welfare of the domestic sphere; he takes individual responsibility for providing for the family. In this conception of the well-ordered Catholic family, there is no need for the state to provide social welfare programs, and it is not difficult to extrapolate how state-run programs, like public education, could be seen as intruding on the purview of the patriarch to instruct his progeny on religion and the "folly of the New Deal and fallacies of U.S. foreign policy" as he wished.[18]

The veneration of his father as a strong patriarch suggests Weyrich followed a traditionalist Catholic understanding of the family as a religious institution in and of itself. In 1930, in response to the liberalization of Protestant attitudes toward birth control, Pope Pius XI issued an encyclical on Christian marriage, *Casti Connubii*, which held that marriage is an institution ordained by God, reasserted "the primacy of the husband with regard to the wife and children, the ready subjection of the wife and her willing obedience," and affirmed the Catholic ban on birth control and the primary aim of marriage as being the production of offspring.[19] It was seemingly met with wide support by the Catholic hierarchy and laity alike. "The wide publicity afforded the encyclical, coupled with its respectful reception, greatly enhanced its ability to effect change among Catholics," Leslie Woodcock Tentler explains, "Since *Casti Connubii* was near-universally regarded as conveying an infallible teaching, it seems unlikely that many priests took the instruction lightly."[20] Thus, although Weyrich's writings on morality and the family do not make direct mention of *Casti Connubii*, it can be surmised that his understanding of the sacred basis for the family was informed by the teaching, whether directly or indirectly via church instruction. As norms surrounding the American family underwent a cultural liberalization in the 1960s, Weyrich might very well have felt both his traditional understanding of the family and his faith were under attack as the Catholic Church underwent a rapid process of modernization, with the convening of the Second Vatican Council in 1962 under Pope John XXIII.

As American culture changed throughout the 1960s, so too did the culture of the Catholic Church—and while many Catholics were eager to embrace a more modern Church, traditionalists appeared to cling to the past, actively opposing Church reforms. Cleavages in Catholic identity began forming. The reforms introduced by the Second Vatican Council, which ran from 1962 to 1965, transformed the rituals and practices of the Catholic Church, including the introduction of vernacular masses, changes to the liturgy, and a fundamental shift in how the Church approached church-state and ecumenical relations. As the Catholic priest and theologian Joseph Komonchak has argued, viewed separately, "none of these changes was revolutionary, but many of them had more dramatic psychological and sociological consequences than the word *reform* suggests. The everyday self-consciousness of Catholics was altered, as were the ordinary processes of the church's internal activity and its action in the world."[21] In short, the Catholic Church underwent an institutional transformation that radically altered its members' everyday experience of their faith. In *The American Catholic Revolution*, Mark Massa highlights the profound impact of these transformations on the Catholic laity, especially in Catholic self-understanding:

> For the first time in their history, ordinary Catholics now addressed how "relevant" their religious symbols and worship should be. For the first time in the lives of many adult Catholics, questions of what eucharist and prayer actually meant were presented as real, live issues that could be debated in print and at public meetings. The forces of modernity, so long held at bay outside the strong fortress of the Church, now pounded at the door and demanded attention. Quite suddenly Catholics came to utilize new prefixes in describing each other. "Liberal" and "conservative," "progressive" and "traditionalist" now appeared before the noun *Catholic* to describe how people stood on the liturgical reforms. Such prefixes were largely unknown in the pre–Vatican II world, where "lapsed" was the only adjective added to define divisions within the faith community.[22]

The openness of such divisions was a new development in the post–Vatican II church. Writing in 1995, religion scholars Mary Jo Weaver and R. Scott Appleby noted, "Thirty years ago, nearly *all* American Catholics were 'fundamentalists' in the sense that we were shaped by a post-Tridentine mentality, marked by practices judged by the culture to be esoteric, and devoted to supernaturalism."[23] In other words, in the early 1960s, one was not a conservative or a liberal Catholic; one was simply Catholic.

The combined impact of Vatican II and *Humanae Vitae*—Pope Paul VI's encyclical on birth control—along with social transformations taking place in the United States, made it possible for American Catholics to develop hyphenated identities, becoming liberal-, feminist-, social justice–, or anti-war Catholics. But in creating space for the reform-minded to question the absolute authority of the Church, it also made it possible for traditionalists to challenge the hierarchy. And so, just as progressive identities proliferated, so too did conservative, Tridentine, orthodox, and separatist identities. Thus, Vatican II opened the door for Weyrich to fuse his conservative political and Catholic identities, and to become a conservative Catholic.

For those Catholics committed to preserving what they viewed as Church orthodoxy, the need to adopt and speak from the position of a sectarian conservative Catholic identity was both necessary and emblematic of the troubles plaguing the Church. This tension was highlighted by Weyrich himself in a 1969 editorial in *The Wanderer*, when he wrote, "If the time has indeed come for Catholics to 'tell it like it is,' our criticism and questions must always be responsible, charitable and accomplished in such a manner so as not to damage the Magisterium. Indeed, the matter about which we speak must be grave, and the Church must be in danger for us to justify raising our voices."[24] Fully aware of the potential dangers and pitfalls attendant to challenging the Church, Paul Weyrich stepped into this newly created space as he assumed the mantle of conservative Catholic *and* political entrepreneur. In many ways, Weyrich's capacity to act as a political entrepreneur was made possible by the upheaval and turmoil that occurred within the Catholic Church in the 1960s. In other words, Weyrich's Catholic activism was enabled by the very changes in the Church that he sought to battle against.

The Catholic Traditionalist Movement and the Latin Mass

In 1965 the Catholic Traditionalist Movement (CTM) emerged in response to fear among some Catholics that the council's reforms were eroding the sacred identity of Catholicism by instituting changes to the mystical and hierarchical nature of the church as a result of their emphasis on ecumenism. A primary focus of CTM was the return of the traditional Latin mass, as Vatican II opened the door for the use of the vernacular. On New Year's Eve Day, 1964, the US-based CTM sent a manifesto to Pope Paul VI, as well as to "all Vatican Curia cardinals, all members of the Roman Catholic hierarchy in the U.S.A., and selected bishops in various countries," calling for, in part:

> That the centuries-sanctioned liturgical Latin form of the Mass not be banned, but, if not given full priority, at least be allowed to co-exist with the new vernacular forms, so the priests and the people be given full option and adequate opportunity to celebrate and assist at Mass in the traditional Latin form on Sundays as well as weekdays. . . . That the character of the Mass as the supreme act of worship to the most holy Trinity and

the renewal of Christ's sacrifice on Calvary through the sacerdotal media-
tion of his ordained priests be duly emphasized, and that special caution
be exercised to prevent the secondary social aspects of the Mass from being
affected by the error of homocentricity or an exaggerated concept of the
so-called lay-priesthood.[25]

To non-Catholics, the idea of worship in the vernacular is commonplace.
To American Catholics in the 1960s, hearing a non-Latin mass for the first
time on November 29, 1964, was a revolutionary act that had the effect of
personalizing, and by extension, demystifying the liturgy.

Religion scholar William D. Dinges has asserted that from the mid-
to late-1960s, Catholic traditionalists argued that changes to the liturgy
posed an imminent danger to "Catholic identity and the church's sense of
the sacred," and charged that the new liturgy was not only "the symbol of
resurgent 'modernism'" but also "contained 'heresy' and was 'invalid' because
the canon Mass had been 'mistranslated.'"[26] Dinges further explains that
during this period, "the traditionalist movement remained dependent on
crusading individuals and on localized efforts of individual Catholics."[27]
Weyrich was one of those individuals. In the archives, as early as October
1967 we find evidence of his interest in and attendance at a CTM event,
billed as a "major address entitled 'How Much More,'" by the traditionalist Reverend Gommar A. DePauw.[28] In 1968 Weyrich's name and contact
information appeared on a flier advertising "An Evening of Truth and Tradition" with the stringently traditionalist and separatist Rev. DePauw, to
be hosted by "The Emerging Catholic Laymen, Inc. in co-operation with
the Catholic Traditionalist Movement, Inc. of Greater Washington," which
would include a Latin Mass and "A revealing dissertation on what in the
name of God is happening to our Roman Catholic Church and schools."[29]

Given Weyrich's admiration for his father and his own strong faith, it
should come as no surprise that he too would take on the perceived liberalization of the Catholic Church. By the fall of 1968, Weyrich and his family
took action, petitioning to transfer from the Latin Rite of the Roman Catholic Church to the Byzantine-Slavonic Rite, a derivative of the Antiochian
Rite. The Byzantine-Slavonic Rite is comprised of the Orthodox Churches
of the East, the vast majority of which are not in communion with Rome
as a result of a schism over ecclesiastical difference and interpretation of
the liturgy dating to the eleventh century. A subgroup within the Byzantine-Slavonic Rite reunited with Rome and became known as the Eastern

Churches and Rites of the Catholic Church; the Weyrichs petitioned to one of these churches for membership. To put it another way, Weyrich remained a Catholic, but he formally expressed his frustration and displeasure with Vatican II by joining a church that continued to follow orthodox rites and rituals and delivered the liturgy in Greek.

According to the Weyrichs's letter to the Bishop, their desire to leave the Latin Rite was a result of the Catholic Church having

> introduced the new American canon into mandatory usage in most areas of this country in the fall of 1967. That canon had never been approved by Rome, in fact, it had been refused approval on three separate occasions. Since its doubtful origins were widely recognized, and since competent theologians had raised questions as to the validity of Masses using the canon, we determined to attend Mass where the canon was not in use. ... Accordingly we attended those few churches in the area where the Mass was still said in Latin, but these swiftly dwindled in number, and even where Latin was used, the Mass was often said so irreverently that it was distracting. ... The more we observed the more we became convinced that Divine Liturgy in the Byzantine Rite conveys a deep spiritual reverence that is no longer present in most services in the Latin Rite. Further, the Eastern Church appeared to us to have retained a great deal of those elements promulgated by the great early Fathers of Catholicism.[30]

This refusal of the new American vernacular mass testifies to Weyrich's radical tendencies, as he was willing to formally sever ties with the Roman Catholic Rite to register his disapproval of Vatican II. This move is characteristic of Weyrich's propensity for taking extremist positions—in regard to both his religion and politics. But it would be a mistake to understand Weyrich as a dyed-in-the-wool traditionalist, as his enthusiastic embrace of Catholic lay organizing suggests that he was certainly not opposed to all of the reforms instituted by the Second Vatican Council. Rather, Weyrich's activism suggests a sort of pick-and-choose approach to traditionalism as he embraced some of the reforms (lay activism) in order to challenge others (the transformation of the liturgy and the Church's embrace of ecumenism).

Opposition to Church and State Separation, Ecumenism, and the Civil Rights Movement

Many Catholic traditionalists, Weyrich among them, not only opposed changes to the liturgy ushered in by Vatican II but also aggressively and vehemently disagreed with the Church's new approach to politics and its ecumenical turn. *Gaudium et Spes* set new limits on the place of the Catholic Church in secular political life and asserted that the appropriate nexus of church/state interaction was located at "the moral dimension of political life." Whereas the Church had previously sought to integrate itself in state governance, according to the theologian Kenneth R. Himes, Vatican II asserted, "The political realm has a legitimate autonomy from the church. There is no desire to establish a theocracy."[31] Furthermore, Himes explains that Vatican II encouraged Catholics actively to "work with all others of goodwill to promote the common good of a society. The council documents *Unitatis Redintegratio* and *Nostra Aetate*, along with *Gaudium et Spes*, affirm this principle."[32] Alongside *Gaudium et Spes*, the declaration on religious freedom, *Dignitatis Humanae*, explicitly endorsed freedom of religion and promoted ecumenism.[33]

Taken together, these reforms were read as dramatically limiting the scope, authority, and influence of the Catholic Church in government and public life. Conservative critics alleged that "the Council abandoned the constant teaching of modern popes, particularly their condemnation of religious freedom and endorsement of the ideal of the Catholic confessional state," according to the theologian Joseph Komonchak. The Council, therefore, needed to be rejected because "it reversed the attitudes and strategy that had characterized the church since the Renaissance and Reformation and particularly since the French Revolution."[34] But for conservative Catholics, issues of morality were fundamental to politics and could not be shunted to the margins. Weyrich made clear this view in an open letter condemning Governor John A. Burns of Hawaii for signing pro-abortion legislation, wherein he likened the governor to Pontius Pilate and asserted that Burns's commitment to "never let his private political and religious convictions unduly influence his judgment as governor of the people' . . . is as wrong as [his] action on the bill." Weyrich also used the open letter as an opportunity to make the claim that American government is predicated on religious faith, writing: "As I read your remarks I could not help but think back to the men who founded America, and those through the years who made her a great nation. Had these men not been influenced by God's laws, by their religious training and by their personal political convictions, I hesitate to think of reading an American history book today."[35] Drawing on this and other writings, it is not difficult to see how Weyrich and other traditionalist Catholics could have viewed the withdraw of the Church from political life as an affront to its own teachings.

Further frustrating and motivating traditionalist Catholic activists, the adoption of an ecumenical stance was thought to challenge the place of the Catholic Church as the one, true Church. Komonchak describes how church/state and ecumenical reforms were framed along progressive-conservative lines in the late 1960s:

> The progressive interpretations of the Council work with a sharp, almost black-and-white, disjunction between the preconciliar and postconciliar church. . . . The traditionalist interpretation of Vatican II makes use of a similar disjunction between pre- and postconciliar Catholicism but reverses the appreciations. The popes from Gregory XVI to Pius XII had acutely recognized and rightly condemned the apostate and even demonic character of the liberal modernity that was thwarting Christ's right to reign over society and culture.[36]

Limiting the scope of the Catholic Church in political and public life would be tantamount to turning one's back on Jesus and ceding the world to Satan. The growing chasm between traditionalist and modernist Catholic viewpoints was not limited to the Church; it also contributed to increasingly polarized attitudes toward political and social change more broadly.

Much of Weyrich's political activism on behalf of "pro-family" policies in the 1970s and 1980s can be read as an attempt to insert Catholic morality into American politics as he first built the radical right-wing movement termed the New Right and later helped to found the largely evangelical Protestant Christian Right. But before Weyrich recruited the Fundamentalist Baptist Reverend Jerry Falwell to launch the Moral Majority, he gave frequent voice to anti-ecumenical inclinations—a fact we might find curious for a man who also claimed to have recognized as a teenager that Catholics and Protestants should be working together to advance their common causes.[37] The archival record opens a window onto Weyrich's attitudes, with one particular episode pitting Weyrich and his conservative brethren against a liberal Roman Catholic priest in the days immediately following Martin Luther King Jr.'s assassination. Revisiting it shines light not only on how Weyrich felt about Catholics fellowshipping with other Christians, but also on his distaste for the civil rights movement.[38]

The assassination of King on April 4, 1968, rocked the nation, setting off protests and riots across the country. Weyrich believed the event was cause for neither religious action, nor political protest.[39] On the night of MLK's assassination, the Reverend Richard McSorley, a Roman Catholic priest at Georgetown University, partook in an ecumenical service along with "nuns, Episcopalians, and black militants."[40] Following the service, Weyrich, who was employed at the time on Capitol Hill as an aide to the conservative senator Gordon Allott (R-CO), was the lead signatory to a petition asking that the diocese investigate and discipline Rev. McSorley for participating in an "Episcopalian 'holy communion' liturgy" and for receiving communion from the Episcopalian church "in full view of those present including other Roman Catholics and an Episcopal Bishop." McSorley was also accused of having told Weyrich "that he assisted at this Episcopal service because he believes efforts toward unification of the Roman Catholic Church with other churches are going too slowly," and that while he had "violated canon law ... he believes that 'like with any man-made laws, there comes a point when you can no longer obey them.'"[41] In short, as the country mourned and raged, Weyrich and his fellow conservative Catholics charged McSorley with violating the sanctity of the Catholic Church by joining in prayer and communion with other Christian denominations to grieve the murder of Dr. King.[42]

Weyrich castigated Rev. McSorley for embracing interdenominational ecumenism and for suggesting that the Catholic Church's laws were man-made and therefore not inviolable. (It is tempting to draw a parallel to King's taxonomy of laws in "Letter from a Birmingham Jail" here.) While it was ostensibly for his "worship of false gods" that Weyrich and others demanded that disciplinary action be taken against McSorley, we should be wary of separating either man's actions from their broader historical and political context.[43]

Opposition to "Population Control," Birth Control, Abortion, and Women's Rights

Perhaps surprisingly, Weyrich did not reject the reforms initiated by Vatican II wholesale, and his Catholic activism was not limited to the CTM or the ad hoc criticism of liberal priests who caught his attention. We also find evidence in the archives of Weyrich being closely involved with Catholics United for the Faith (CUF) at its founding in late September 1968.[44] A national nonprofit laymen's organization, CUF was described in the mid-1990s by its vice president as being dedicated to "advancing and defending the teachings of the Catholic Church through the proper implementation of the documents of the Second Vatican Council."[45] Formed in response to controversy surrounding the 1968 release of *Humanae Vitae*, CUF's "Declaration of Purpose" affirmed its members' assent to the document's teaching, and "to every truth that is taught by him [Pope Paul VI] through the Magisterium."[46] But in 1968, *Humanae Vitae* created a crisis within the Church and CUF saw itself as the Church's lay defense.

By decoupling sex from reproduction, and by shifting reproductive control into the hands of women, the recently FDA-approved birth control pill (aka the Pill) also forced Catholics to reckon head on with the Church's teaching on artificial contraception. As historian Linda Gordon has explained, for women across the nation, Protestant and Catholic, "The Pill did not so much change women's lives as enable them to make changes they longed for. Their sex was more free, their educational plans more achievable, their wage-earning more stable, their domestic labor reduced."[47] But to embrace the freedom proffered by the Pill, Catholic women also had to choose to engage, on a daily basis, in behavior the Church deemed sinful. The attendant loosening of sexual mores was met with dismay by social and religious traditionalists, who worried sexual liberation would not only erode religious norms but also rewrite social and economic relations between men and women. Further stirring the birth control waters, some progressives shared traditionalist Catholic fears that artificial contraception would be used by the government to impose top-down population control programs. While progressive concerns were focused on the potential impact of population control on people of color and poor communities, traditionalist Catholics feared their own erasure.[48] And yet, despite the misgivings of both right- and left-wing activists, broad support for the Pill was found across the political and religious spectrums of the American public as it was driven both by feminist and liberal demands for greater female autonomy and conservative Cold War fears of overpopulation in the developing world.

The arrival of the birth control pill was met with "great enthusiasm" from women, including roughly three-fifths of American Catholics, when it was introduced in 1959.[49] During the early and mid-1960s, some of this support was driven by Cold War population control debates, which "emphasized the high fertility rates of poorer and allegedly less desirable groups" and stoked Cold War fears of the proverbial barbarians at the gate, and included a domestic family planning agenda.[50] Gordon explains that support for "population control" had roots in neo-Malthusian fears of scarcity as well as in a "eugenics sensibility, notably, the distinction between the moderate, restrained 'us' and the teeming, profligate 'them.'"[51] The teeming masses were often conceived of as savages (unable to control their base desires), godless communists (aiming for world domination through copulation), and occasionally as heathen Catholics (breeding for the pope in Rome).[52] Given the long history of animosity between American Catholics and Protestants,[53] the Catholic teaching that contraception is a violation of God's law stoked Protestant antipathy by feeding the overpopulation fears of WASPs, who likely imagined their manicured lawns overrun by Catholics reproducing ad infinitum.[54]

Population restrictionists were also concerned that the Catholic Church would stymie their plans to involve the federal government in administering and promoting family planning programs, and that "behind many of the tensions within the movement lay differences over how best to address the Catholic question," as the political historian Donald Critchlow has noted.[55] On the other side, conservative Catholics, including Weyrich, warned of the rising threat of "population restrictionists," whom they feared would use the government to forcibly restrict reproduction.[56]

Leading up to *Humanae Vitae*, during the mid-1960s the majority of Catholic laity were in support of the Church liberalizing its stance on artificial birth control, and the clergy was experiencing what Leslie Woodcock Tentler has termed "a radical erosion of clerical confidence." Increasingly, liberal priests and progressive members of the laity had begun to both question the requirement of priestly celibacy and challenge the moral condemnation of artificial birth control. In a marked departure from the deference to Church authority that anchored Catholic culture, an embattled clergy faced an empowered laity that had begun to assert it too should play a role in determining what constituted a moral stance on sex and reproduction.[57] The laity's support for the Pill was affirmed by polling, as "73 percent of adult Catholics polled by a *Newsweek* survey in 1967 favored a change in the Church's stance on contraception, with the young and college educated even more apt to endorse reform."[58] Within this context, it seemed likely that the Church would amend its teaching on birth control based on recommendations issued by the Pontifical Commission on Birth Control in 1966.[59]

Counter to the widely shared expectations of many American Catholics and the broader public, the *Humanae Vitae* encyclical reaffirmed the sinfulness of artificial contraception. It was quickly met with outrage and dissent from young and well-educated Catholics, and raised suspicions that Pope Paul VI would roll back the liberalizing reforms initiated by Vatican II.[60] Almost immediately, liberal priests began challenging the encyclical by granting absolution to parishioners who confessed to using contraception without any intent of stopping the practice.[61] And, just as quickly, Weyrich and the CUF began fighting back in defense of the Church.

A central skirmish in the battle between liberal and conservative Catholics took place in Washington, DC, providing Weyrich, who was working on the Hill at the time, with a front-row invitation to the conflagration. In November 1968, at the beginning of the Catholic contraception clash, the journalist Thomas J. Fleming, writing for the *New York Times Magazine*, dove into the growing rift between liberal, dissenting clergy and the conservative archbishop of Washington, DC, Cardinal Patrick O'Boyle. He reported, "The day after the encyclical was issued, theologians at Catholic University in Washington issued a statement, which was eventually signed by more than 600 other American theologians, emphatically stating that the encyclical was 'not an infallible teaching' and concluding that 'spouses may responsibly decide according to their conscience that artificial contraception in some circumstances is permitted.'"[62] Following the release of the statement, O'Boyle asked the signatories in his diocese to issue retractions, and when they refused, he began suspending them from their religious duties. Barely a month old, CUF wasted no time in jumping into the fray to defend O'Boyle.

On November 9, 1968, the Washington, DC, newspaper *Evening Star* reported that rallies were being held in opposition to and support of O Boyle for having stripped "about 40 priests ... of some or all of their priestly ministries ... for publicly dissenting from his interpretation of the encyclical." CUF sponsored a twenty-four-hour prayer vigil with Weyrich credited as the "project chairman of the event."[63] The conflict rapidly escalated, expanding from a debate over the validity of *Humanae Vitae* to encompass deeper theological challenges to papal authority. "The suspension of a Washington Archdiocese priest this week and the impending academic trial of 17 Catholic University theology teachers for publicly disagreeing

with Patrick Cardinal O'Boyle and Pope Paul VI have shifted the emphasis of the running birth control controversy," reported the *Washington Star*.
"The nub of the issue," the article continued, "has moved beyond debating
the encyclical itself to the matter of academic freedom, formation of conscience and Catholic loyalty."[64] The priest and sociologist Andrew Greeley
went a step further, observing in 1972, "The encyclical *Humanae Vitae* was
for all practical purposes an appeal to pure authority, a pure authority the
Pope mistakenly assumed he still had."[65]

As the battle lines were drawn between supporters of the dissidents and
the hierarchy, Weyrich was at the forefront, speaking on behalf of CUF:
"We declare our loyalty to the Catholic Church, to His Holiness Pope Paul
and to His Eminence Cardinal O'Boyle. We acknowledge their authority
and accept their interpretation of divine and natural law."[66] The issue was
subsequently reframed as a matter of whether priests had the right to speak
about their own opinions and to act on their own conscience; in other
words, it became about adherence to the party line.[67]

Weyrich's involvement with CUF is indicative of how Weyrich was a
product of his time, in essence, a *modern* traditionalist. Catholics United
for the Faith—and Weyrich's involvement in the organization—highlights
a key consequence of Vatican II: the council itself encouraged the creation
of lay organizations and activism with the *Decree on the Apostolate of the
Laity (Apostolicam Actuositatem)*.[68] Much like the CUF, Weyrich himself
came to occupy seemingly contradictory positions: on one hand, he was a
conservative Catholic political entrepreneur who demanded adherence to
Church doctrine and criticized his own Church for adopting ecumenism;
on the other hand, he simultaneously disavowed the spirit of church-state
separation advanced by *Gaudium et Spes* and worked tirelessly to build an
ecumenical political coalition throughout the 1970s.

But it would be a mistake to assume Weyrich and the CUF's only dog
in the fight over *Humanae Vitae* was invested in maintaining traditional
channels of authority within the Catholic Church. The struggle over
maintaining Church authority—and adjudication of how power would
be disseminated between the Church hierarchy and liberal clergy—comprised only part of the puzzle. Weyrich and his fellow traditionalist Catholics were also developing a conservative religious identity in relation to
women's rights. In May 1969, Thomas J. Fleming covered the growing
conflict for *Redbook Magazine*. In an article titled "Can the 'Catholic Revolution' Succeed?" Fleming asserted that the skirmish was more about

the ignition of a "fermenting feminine impatience" with the patriarchy. He continued:

> The emergence of the Catholic woman as a dynamic, often angry protester is perhaps the least recognized aspect of the current revolutionary ferment. . . . Why is the emergence of a defiant woman so significant? Because in the past women have been the Church's bulwark. Men have always been rebellious against the Church's authority. But for centuries, Catholicism has successfully implanted in women's minds the Biblical teaching of St. Paul: 'Women are to keep silence and take their place with all submissiveness. [I Timothy 2].'[69]

Fleming drives at the heart of the matter: the challenge to *Humanae Vitae*, from clergy and laymen, was a clarion call for women's rights. Preserving the magisterium for Weyrich then was about preserving tradition and hierarchy in—and outside—of the Catholic Church. For the CUF and Weyrich, "tradition" likely meant patriarchy, as represented by the nuclear family and traditional gender roles and norms, and "hierarchy" extended to a husband's dominion over his wife.

Weyrich gave extensive voice to his socially conservative viewpoints as a consistent contributor to the conservative and traditionalist Catholic papers *The Wanderer* and *Eastern Catholic Life* during the late 1960s and through the 1970s. In the five years leading up to the Supreme Court's 1973 *Roe v. Wade* decision, which legalized abortion across the nation, Weyrich's writing increasingly reflected the crossover between his religious beliefs and politics.[70] Many of these writings tended to dwell on Church-related matters, such as the personal narrative he penned for *Eastern Catholic Life* on joining the Byzantine Rite or his coverage of a CUF action for *The Wanderer*,[71] but from 1970 on he began using his platform as a contributor to fight the promotion and passage of population restrictions. Weyrich was never anything but anti-choice,[72] but in the late 1960s and early 1970s, restricting access to abortion was not the most important issue for him.[73] Instead of using his column to express fear for the "lives of the unborn," Weyrich chose to focus on his concern for how lives would be impacted by "anti-family" legislation. Senator Robert Packwood (R-OR), a so-called population restrictionist, was the subject of much spilled ink for having drafted an "anti-population" bill that would deny tax breaks to families with more than three children. Even Goldwater came in for criticism for his support of Packwood's "anti-life crusade," which included lifting restrictions on abortion.[74]

Despite the fact that Weyrich was a committed and staunch opponent of abortion and that the Catholic Church hierarchy was organizing to oppose legalized abortion,[75] he remained worried about the government imposing limits on reproductive freedom. In an editorial he wrote for *The Wanderer* in praise of a large family advocacy group named Leading Families of America (LFA), Weyrich stressed the urgency of protecting Americans from population control legislation: "[LFA] did not know at the time [of its founding] that if ever in history an organization were needed to defend, honor and protect the interests of large families, it was now. ... The modern-day version of the Death Cultists, personified by several leading figures in government, industry and the Church, were to have their day. Alas, it has come to pass."[76] An article the following month, titled "Anti-Life Forces Continue Gains," noted an increase in government spending on family planning and expressed concern that "forty-three bills relating to 'population' have been introduced in the Ninety-First Congress," and "the bulk of the measures, however, relate to population restriction."[77] Reporting on a social values survey administered to high-achieving high school students, his concern was displaced onto the next generation of Catholics, whom he worried would not have the moral rectitude and fiber to stand up to government-sponsored controls on reproduction:

> The most disturbing answer of all, in the judgment of this writer, came in response to the question of whether or not these individuals would be willing to limit their future families to two children "in order to help population control." Sixty-four percent of the Catholics said Yes. ... Clearly, this makes the sixty-four percent of these Catholic leaders who are either already in or about to enter college (as well as the seventy-five percent of the national sample who answered Yes) vulnerable to the plans of the population restrictionists who have been so successful in using phony statistics and scare tactics concerning the so-called "population explosion."[78]

As long as safe abortions remained largely unobtainable and Nixon opposed legalization of the procedure,[79] Weyrich's religious beliefs (contraception is a sin) and fusionist-inspired conservative politics (government should be as limited as possible) would necessarily lead him to focus on fighting the "population restrictionists" and limiting the scope of government in order to preserve religious freedom. Moreover, with the newfound liberty granted to the laity by Vatican II, Weyrich was free both to strike out on his own and to advance a radically conservative agenda of his own making while still laying claim to represent both secular political and religious "tradition."

While the late 1960s debates over "population restrictionists" have largely faded from our political consciousness and been supplanted by new fights over access to legal abortion, there was a time when conservative Catholics were deeply concerned that the government might overstep its boundaries by regulating reproductive behavior within the family. The Catholic tradition is commonly regarded as being sympathetic to the workings of institutionalized hierarchical power and, by extension, big government. This stands in stark opposition to the anti-authoritarian attitudes of Bible-believing fundamentalists and evangelicals, whose belief in a radically personal relationship with Jesus lends itself to the anti-hierarchical nature of American Protestantism. These Bible-believing Protestant attitudes have been linked to the production of a politics that is suspicious of government and wants to limit its size and scope. That Weyrich and other like-minded individuals were concerned with limiting the scope of the federal government and fearful that if left unchecked it would impose undue burdens on the religious liberties of individuals is important because it points to a future point of political alliance between conservative Catholics and Protestants. As the dust from the overpopulation hysteria settled in the 1970s, conservative Protestant hostility toward Catholics for supposed "overbreeding" similarly dissipated, but antipathy toward and suspicion of government overreach remained for both conservative Catholics and Protestants.

Concluding Thoughts

How do we make sense of a figure like Paul Weyrich? The answer, I propose, lies in the impact of institutional and cultural transformations within the Catholic Church—what the theologian Mark S. Massa has termed the "American Catholic Revolution"—on Weyrich's understanding of what traditionalism meant and of how a traditionalist should behave. As Catholic traditionalists struggled to make sense of their need to criticize *and* defend the Church against modernization and liberalization,[80] they were also forced to wrestle with "historical consciousness," or the growing recognition that the Church exists within and is impacted by history.[81] And so, even as traditionalists cleaved to the belief that the natural law is unchanging and rejected historical consciousness, they had to contend with the inescapable reality that changes were transpiring within the Catholic Church.[82] Drawing on Massa's persuasive argument that even for those who rejected the possibility of change the 1960s had brought historical consciousness to the fore of American Catholic faith, it is possible to see how Weyrich may have come to view traditionalism as dependent on and subject to historical context.

By enraging traditionalists through an embrace of liturgical transformation and ecumenism while simultaneously opening the door to traditionalist activism and laypeople organizing, the transformation of the Catholic Church during the 1960s opened the door for Weyrich, and other conservative Catholic activists, to identify as traditionalist *and* radical, revolutionary *and* conservative. The very meaning of tradition had become open to change. Weyrich and his New Right collaborators were, in the truest sense of the term, radicals who sought to foundationally remake American political institutions and power arrangements in order to "return" the country to its "traditional" roots. That the act of conserving tradition is generally understood as antithetical to rapid and wholesale societal and political change did not trouble Weyrich, who embraced the idea that fundamental change was a requisite for getting conservativism to take root. This complex and seemingly contradictory identity was one Weyrich proudly embraced in his work with the New Right, explaining to a reporter in 1978, "We [the New Right] are different from previous generations of conservatives. We are no longer working to preserve the status quo. We are radicals, working to overturn the present power structure in this country."[83]

For all that Paul Weyrich's conservative Catholicism claimed to represent the "true" or "traditional" faith, it was also representative of a new development in American religious and political culture. In 1899, Pope Leo XIII, in the words of historian Scott Appleby, "warned Catholics against embracing American-style pluralism and voluntarism as norms for the universal church."[84] Vatican II effectively ushered in a new wave of Catholicism that emphasized individual faith while downplaying the hierarchy, and that was, for lack of a better term, "more American." For newly hyphenated, multi-identified Catholics, this shift could take them in any number of directions. For Paul Weyrich and other conservative Catholics, it took them down a path that would bring their religious faith and politics into ever closer congruence with that of conservative Fundamentalist and evangelical Protestants.

Even as Weyrich opposed the ecumenical reforms of Vatican II, they opened the door to his political activism on behalf of the NCR coalition. And while Weyrich rejected the limitations on political action imposed by *Gaudium et Spes*, the loosening of institutional authority and circumscription of the Catholic Church's political sphere opened the door for him to pioneer a new brand of religious political entrepreneurship premised on ecumenical coalition-building and on the adoption of a pro-family platform that was informed by Weyrich's traditionalist understandings of faith and morality, but constructed outside the formal institutional structures of the Church. Such a political coalition of conservative Protestants and Catholics was only imaginable in a post-conciliar and post-confessional state.

As we will see in the next chapter, over the course of the1970s Weyrich and other conservative activists worked with remarkable speed to remake the conservative institutional landscape and to advance a more radical, more purist understanding of conservatism—or as the journalist William J. Lanouette explained in 1978: "[The New Right] are 'right' on the nation's shifting and elusive political spectrum because of their avowed goal to make traditional American values—'freedom,' 'individualism,' 'family' and 'free enterprise'—the dominant features of the society and government." While the New Right has generally been treated as a secular movement, Weyrich's understanding of these values was deeply connected to his faith and, in turn, his social conservatism.

3

BUILDING THE NEW RIGHT AND THE NEW TRADITIONAL WOMAN

By the 1970s, the Right had been transformed into an institutionalized, disciplined, well-organized, and well-financed movement of loosely knit affiliates. Collecting millions of dollars in small contributions from blue-collar workers and housewives, the New Right feeds on discontent, anger, insecurity, and resentment, and flourishes on backlash politics. Through its interlocking network, it seeks to veto whatever it perceives to threaten its way of life—busing, women's liberation, gay rights, pornography, loss of the Panama Canal—and promotes a beefed-up defense budget, lower taxes, and reduced regulation of small business. Moreover, the New Right exploits social protest and encourages class hostility by trying to fuel the hostilities of lower-middle-class Americans against those above or below them on the economic ladder. Wholly bipartisan, though predominately Republican, the New Right network supports whoever shares its desire for radical political change and its resentments of the status quo. As such, the New Right is anything but conservative.

—Alan Crawford, *Thunder on the Right: The "New Right" and the Politics of Resentment*

Before a New Right Became *the* New Right

In 1968, in the midst of the Vietnam War, Richard Nixon was elected to the presidency, having pledged to restore "law and order" to a society that conservatives believed was coming undone. Facing a conservative challenge from the blatantly race-baiting third-party populist candidate George Wallace, Nixon campaigned as the true heir to the conservative rhetoric of individual freedom and fiscal responsibility promulgated by Barry Goldwater. But even before he was disgraced by the Watergate scandal, Nixon failed to deliver, expanding governmental regulation through the creation of the Environmental Protection Agency (EPA), establishing diplomatic relations with Communist China and negotiating a Strategic Arms Limitation Treaty (SALT) with the Soviet Union.[1] In response to Nixon's real and perceived failures to toe the conservative line, hardline conservative activists began floating the idea of challenging his reelection.

While not yet a cohesive movement in 1971, signs pointed to a rising wave of conservative activism. An article by the Republican strategist and writer Kevin Phillips, titled "The Conservative Revolt against Nixon," explained that there was an "insurgency" building against the president: "[Nixon's] problem is not a Reagan convention challenge. It is that many conservatives are beginning to ask, at least among themselves, whether they really care about the President's re-election."[2] Phillips coined the term "New Right" for the conservatives who sought to organize a pseudo-populist uprising, which aimed to reorient the American political system and forge more right-leaning conservative coalitions that could transcend party lines.

New Right political entrepreneurs were the intellectual successors to the fusionist conservative movement pumped by the *National Review*, but they were also strategically innovative and ideologically distinctive. Throughout the 1970s, the New Right worked with remarkable speed to create a new institutional topography for conservatives in American politics. In just four short years, between 1970 and 1975, New Right activists launched more than a dozen political organizations, including Analysis and Research Associates, the Heritage Foundation, the Center for the Public Interest, the American Conservative Union, Americans for Constitutional Action, Committee for Responsible Youth Politics, Committee for the Survival of a Free Congress, Free Congress Research and Education Foundation, National Conservative Political Action Committee, the Conservative

Caucus, and the Conservative Caucus Research, Analysis, and Education Foundation.

Paul Weyrich's political cunning lay in his early recognition that in order to redefine "conservativism" and create a political movement with the depth and breadth he envisioned, he would have to build it from the ground up. Initially, as is shown in this chapter, this meant creating a web of decentralized organizations and institutions, which ranged from think tanks to political action committees (PACs), congressional caucuses to grassroots organizations, direct mailers to newsletters, and magazines to broadcast television. The New Right not only embraced PACs and direct mail; it also abandoned ideological rigidity in favor of flexibility and pioneered a new coordinative discourse. Rather than attempt to coalesce around a singular conservative vision, the movement adopted a single-issue organizing strategy that enabled the movement to instrumentally jettison established conservative commitments to the free market and limited government. The shift from defining conservatism in relation to laissez-faire capitalism to defining it on the basis of right-wing Christian social values freed the New Right to promote a radical new vision of the purpose and function of government.

Over the course of the 1970s, a new right became the New Right. This chapter opens with an example of proto–New Right organizing, which suggests that from the very beginning, Catholic New Right (CNR) activists were focused on using federal social policy as a means of imposing conservative Christian social relations. This is followed by a discussion of how conservative Catholic political entrepreneurs manufactured a new conception of the traditional as a means of redefining conservatism. In short, the movement's aim of initiating "radical political change" is shown to be supported by a fundamental reconceptualization of conservatism. The chapter then turns to a nuts-and-bolts examination of the New Right's organizational strategy, which is to say, its development of a coordinative discourse. In the final analysis, the movement's embrace of single-issue politics is shown to facilitate the production of an ideology of victimhood among conservative White Christians. Taken together, the movement's redefinition of conservatism and adoption of new organizing strategies enabled it to begin to articulate a political vision that was concerned less with limiting the scope of government than with using the government to impose a new set of social relations predicated on a Catholic-inflected form of conservative Christianity.

In thinking about the role played by CNR political entrepreneurs in developing the New Right as a movement, this chapter is informed by Vivien Schmidt's methodological framework of discursive institutionalism. I find Schmidt's concept of "coordinative discourse"[3] helpful in conceptualizing the strategies and techniques employed by New Right activists to create the institutional and ideological foundations of the movement. I therefore understand the production of political institutions that inform policy, such as think tanks, the development of new movement-building strategies, such as direct mail, and the construction of coalition-building strategies, such as single-issue politics and co-belligerency, as all forming part of a New Right coordinative discourse.

Drawing from Schmidt's work, I conceive of coordinative discourse as operating on three temporal registers within the CNR: (1) In the short term and often with immediate effects, it functioned on the level of the production of policy and policy-related information as demonstrated by Connie Marshner's early intervention in the family policy arena and by the New Right's emphasis on the creation of think tanks; (2) In the medium-term, it consisted of programmatic ideas concerning electoral and coalition-building strategies; (3) In the long range, it helped shape the development of new modes of meaning-making and ways of political understanding,[4] as is demonstrated by the CNR's cultivation of an ideology of victimhood and its embrace of so-called culture war politics.

Focusing on the production of a coordinative discourse allows us to see how political entrepreneurs laid the foundations on which not only a new electoral coalition but also a new identity of Christian victimhood and a new political vision—premised on advancing White, male, and Christian supremacism—could be built. As much of the work of coordinative discourse production is undertaken by political elites,[5] this chapter focuses on the specific contributions of these actors. (The following chapter, which assesses parallel developments within the conservative Protestant community, focuses on the Reverend Jerry Falwell and theologian Francis Schaeffer on the conservative Protestant side of the aisle.)

While the New Right was a nonhierarchical, horizontally structured movement, it nonetheless was helmed by several conservative Catholics political entrepreneurs, including Paul Weyrich, Richard Viguerie, and Connaught Marshner. These CNR activists left a deep religious imprint on the ostensibly secular movement, directed its ideological and institutional development, and spearheaded the formation of a coalition with White conservative Protestants. In particular, I highlight the work of Marshner, a CNR political entrepreneur whose contribution to the New Right has not received the attention it deserves. Working alongside Weyrich, Marshner was a key architect of the new conservatism and helped to infuse the New Right and CNR with a distinctly Catholic worldview.

Women's (Right-Wing) Work

In 1971 a twenty-year-old White Catholic woman, Connaught (Connie) Coyne (later Marshner), began working in Washington, DC, upon graduating from the University of South Carolina with a bachelor's degree in secondary education. At the time, the Beltway was flush with both Republicans and conservatives, two groups that were not necessarily synonymous with one another.[6] The New Right would come to present itself as an outsider movement, but its core activists were consummate DC Beltway insiders, drawn from the ranks of conservative ideologues who worked within government during the Nixon administration. The young, not yet married Connie Coyne was both a Republican and a conservative, heavily involved in the Young America's Foundation (YAF) conservative youth group and a group of young congressional aides working to push a conservative agenda from the inside.

Details on Marshner's life are difficult to locate, but drawing from her curriculum vitae,[7] memos, and media clippings[8] archived at the American Heritage Center, the following can be gleaned: After graduation, she quickly landed at the Schuchman Foundation's Center for the Public Interest (CPI), which was headed by the conservative strategist and Capitol Hill aide Dan Joy.[9] Weyrich, then working as an aide to Senator Gordon Allott (R-CO), was also involved in the CPI in some capacity; however, it is not clear if he had a formal role at the institution. In the fall of 1971 Marshner was working closely with Joy and Weyrich on a host of conservative issues, but most centrally on opposition to "child development" legislation in Congress.

The Economic Opportunity Extension (EOE) Act, S. 2007, was passed by Congress in 1971. Included in the legislation was Title X, referred to as the "child development and child advocacy" programs, a provision for the creation of federally operated childcare centers, which would have resulted in the development of universal daycare. A 1976 report written by William Roth notes the act "was intended to establish a comprehensive system of child care."[10] The legislation was motivated, at least in part, by growing resentment toward the Aid to Families with Dependent Children (AFDC) welfare program. By providing access to childcare, Congress reasoned, single parents would be able to enter the workforce and become less dependent on government aid. As Roth explains, "Thus, if one extended the definition of the potential worker to include women involved with dependent children, one would increase markedly the number of people who potentially could be taken off welfare, and child care would thus be a tool allowing for the participation of mothers in the work force."[11] But conservative Catholic activists, like Marshner and Weyrich, did not want women to be freed from childcare obligations.

Despite the reality that 43 percent of women were already in the labor force in 1970[12] and that "households headed by a woman constituted only 14 percent of all persons but about 44 percent of poor persons,"[13] Marshner and her fellow activists argued that "child development" legislation would somehow harm women and children, and opposed the act on the grounds that it represented an unwarranted government intrusion into the family.[14] (Conservative activists also objected to the provision of federally funded legal services for the poor, which would eventually pass and come to be better known as Legal Aid, included in the 1971 EOE Act.) After the bill passed in Congress, conservative activists mobilized a multi-prong attack aimed at securing a presidential veto. A November 1971 memo from Dan Joy lays out the strategy: (1) circulate "Dear colleague" letters to change legislators' opinion on the bill; (2) promote a "congressional petition urging the veto and pledging their voting support to uphold it"; (3) generate negative press for the bill and positive press for the veto; and (4) form an "Emergency Committee for Children" to advocate for the veto and to represent religious, particularly Catholic, opposition to the bill.[15] These conservative political entrepreneurs also wrote speeches for elected officials to deliver during debate on the bill, and they claimed to have "constructed half of the total record on the subject."[16] While Marshner was actively engaged in all levels of the veto campaign, she was particularly influential in mobilizing a grassroots letter-writing campaign.

The historian Leo Ribuffo has credited Marshner with soliciting "hundreds of thousands of letters" in opposition to the bill from "local church women."[17] Memos from 1972–1974 shed light on Marshner's past and continuing role in securing letters through her work with Onalee McGraw, who headed up the National Coalition on the Crisis in Education

(NCOCE). Marshner described the NCOCE as "an information clearing-house for parents' groups, civic communities, and the like, all with a common interest in education in some aspect and all sharing a dismay at the 'new ethic.'" "They have an excellent cross-country communication network," she continued, explaining that "Mrs. June Larson, of Seattle, who is in charge of their mailing list, was very helpful to the Emergency Committee for Children (ECC) last fall, after first calling us when she saw a UPI article stating that branches of the ECC were springing up in different states."[18] In April 1972 Marshner recorded that "Onalee [McGraw] sent Paul's list of savable Senators to Mrs. June Larson in Seattle, who is in charge of the mailings to all the parents' groups. Mrs. Larson, thus, will get the word out across the country that these are the Senators to write to for maximum utilization of energy."[19] In yet another memo, Marshner remarked she had contacted Mrs. Larson, "with whom I have had regular communication since the Child Development battle in the Fall of 1971."[20] Marshner's memos indicate she was in regular and ongoing contact with a network of women mobilizing around parents' issues through the NCOCE's mailing lists. In this way, Marshner was able to "work with outside groups to generate pressure" and foster the appearance of widespread grassroots support for conservative issues. Tellingly, Marshner remarked, "While some of these groups produce numerous letters, they are rather unprofessional, to say the least. Nonetheless, that is not undesirable because they create the impression of widespread interest, which is the object."[21]

The multi-pronged strategy worked, and on December 9, 1971, Nixon vetoed the bill. Nixon justified his veto on the basis of support for small government, fiscal conservatism, states' rights, and, tellingly, parental rights. Echoing conservative activists' talking points, Nixon explained, "For the Federal Government to plunge headlong financially into supporting child development would commit the vast moral authority of the National Government to the side of communal approaches to child rearing over against the family-centered approach."[22] Marshner, Weyrich, Joy, and their conservative allies had succeeded in not only torpedoing universal childcare but also in framing the discourse of "child development" as an assault on the nuclear family and traditional gender roles. That a young professional woman played a pivotal role in ensuring other women would have a harder, rather than easier, time working outside of the home should not surprise us given the long history of right-wing women's activism.[23]

The veto of the child development provisions is instructive for several reasons. First, it demonstrates how, before there was the New Right, there was a new right-wing ethos operating in the District of Columbia. Second, it foreshadows the strategies and tactics the New Right adopted, as activists learned from scoring their first big win. Third, it illustrates the primacy of conservative Catholics in developing the New Right's agenda from its inception and the willingness of CNR activists to recruit Protestants. Finally, it highlights how, even as social conservatives asserted the primacy of the family and traditional gender roles, women occupied central leadership and organizing roles within the New Right. As the sociologist Rebecca Klatch noted in *Women of the New Right*, "what is unique about the New Right is the new activism of women."[24] What is less unique is how Marshner's ongoing role within the New Right and her influence on the development of the Christian Right has been largely neglected by scholars of both movements.[25] As this chapter shows, Marshner was there every step of the way.

Redefining "Conservatism"

In the beginning, the conservative activists who would come to form the New Right worked from within the government and were closely allied with conservative senators and representatives. As we saw in chapter 2, Weyrich got his start in DC working as an aide on Capitol Hill. Similarly, throughout the early to mid-1970s, Marshner worked at CPI and the Heritage Foundation as well as the Office of Economic Opportunity, a bureaucratic office created under the Johnson administration to implement War on Poverty programs.[26] While not wholly in sync with Nixon's agenda, the group's early aims were not out of step with those of other conservative Republicans working in government. These objectives were reflected in a memo recording the events of a July 1972 meeting, attended by Walt Mote, Paul Weyrich, Jerry James, Dan Joy, Connie Coyne, Phil Truluck, and Mary Claire Davies. Weyrich recorded the following immediate goals for the group: oppose any welfare reform; keep the Legal Services Corporation from being created; "prevent passage" of a new child development bill; ensure the passage of a one-year funding bill for public broadcasting "in order to make sure that the goal of preventing a federalized TV network and preventing radical programming on the air is achieved"; ensure the passage of the Curtis amendment to the Occupational Safety and Health Act (which would have prohibited "the use of funds in the bill for inspection of firms employing 25 or fewer persons"[27]); promote passage of defense programs related to SALT; and "engage in an operation under the umbrella of the Vice President's office, which will take us through the elections, the purpose of which is to aid selected non-incumbent candidates for Congress, especially the Senate." Many of these issues served as foundation of the New Right's political program as it developed in the mid-1970s.

But, in looking to long-range goals, Weyrich reported, "We want to go on the offensive to develop an 'activist' program."[28] It was this desire to play offense that prompted the creation of the New Right as an insurgent movement and distinguished it from mainstream conservatism. To transform the Republican Party from the outside in, the New Right believed it had to disrupt the usual workings of the establishment, Republican and Democrat, in the name of a truer "conservatism."

But what exactly did Weyrich and others mean when they called for a conservative revolution in the mid-1970s? To understand how the New Right determined the issues it embraced and built its platform, and how the CNR came to inform the broader New Christian Right (NCR), we must first understand how CNR activists reconciled their radical agenda with the commitment to inhibit change and "conserve" the past—that is, the basic tenet of conservatism. To justify a transformative and proactive agenda, conservative Catholic activists reinvented the "traditional" and, in the process, redefined conservatism.

We can see the beginnings of this religious conservativism at work in remarks Weyrich make to the Republican Platform Committee. In a "Statement before the Republican Platform Committee" in August 1976, Weyrich put forward a definition of conservatism as he understood it:

> It means, first, that the Federal government should be strong in those arenas where it has a legitimate function, and second, that it should remain out of many areas of the national life where it has no business being. Since the Federal government has the sole responsibility for defending the Nation and conducting foreign affairs, it should be much stronger and more resolute in these areas than it now is, even under a Republican administration. It is also responsible for the maintenance of public order through the courts.[29]

This is a seemingly straightforward expression of post–World War II conservatism; however, later portions of the statement present a more complicated critique of government overreach in relation to the expansion of abortion, women's rights, and civil rights. The extension of individual liberties to marginalized members of society was presumed to have a deleterious impact on the rights of others, leading Weyrich to frame conservatism's greater aim as the protection of the (White) family and society:

> The Republican Party should draw the lines very clearly here, in its defense of the family and family values. That means that it should defend the right to life, oppose the Equal Rights Amendment, expel the Federal government from its role in the design of elementary and secondary school curricula intended to undermine the family and the Judaeo-Christian ethic on which our society is based, stop forced busing, eradicate child development legislation, and so forth. The Republican Party must defend the family structure, and the right of the individual to live his own life.[30]

Together, Weyrich's two statements represent the nexus of single issues taken up by the New Right, and the movement's emphasis on social policy.

In *Women of the New Right*, Klatch recognized a "schism" within the New Right, identifying the existence of two right-wing camps within the movement in the1970s: those who held a laissez-faire economic worldview and those who were religiously and socially conservative.[31] While Nixon, for example, fell into the former camp, Weyrich and Marshner were representative of the latter. As CNR activists, they were ideologically committed neither to fiscal conservatism nor limited government as structuring principles. Instead, they were committed to using the government to coerce society to take on the shape and form of an idealized Christian polity. To maintain that to do so was to "conserve" the past, the New Right engaged in a double move: it reconstructed the "traditional" and claimed it was under attack. In the process, the movement obscured its proactive and illiberal agenda behind a veneer of defending innocent Christian victims.

The work of redefining conservatism and the traditional is perhaps most clearly embodied by the New Right's women activists. "The social conservative world," Klatch writes, "is rooted in a firm conception of the proper roles of men and women, which divinely ordained are essential to the survival of the family and to the maintenance of a moral, ordered, and stable society. Men and women have clearly defined, separate functions. Because gender is delineated in such unambiguous terms, any blurring of these roles is viewed as a threat."[32] In the hands of conservative female activists, including Marshner and Phyllis Schlafly, social conservative politics and policies became premised on the need to protect women from victimization at the hands of progressives and "secular humanists"—an all-encompassing and expansive term that incorporated liberals, progressives, feminists, homosexuals, and communists in equal measure. Of particular note is Klatch's identification of how the social conservative worldview of New Right women was articulated in stark opposition to what they termed the "macho feminism" of progressive female activists. She explains that these activists justified their own political activism on the grounds of "moral conviction" and made sense of their political work, which necessarily took them outside of the home, as a sacrifice required for the greater good of society.[33]

New Right women were at the forefront of redefining the traditional even as their very role as activists highlighted the inconsistency of their ideological positions. Marshner was particularly emblematic of this contradiction. In the mid-1970s she followed Weyrich to his newly founded organization, the Committee for the Survival of a Free Congress (CSFC), first as a field director and later as the director of the Family Policy division. By 1975 Marshner had become a legislative director for the CSFC, was preparing memos for the Republican Study Committee and the Senate Steering Committee (both conservative committees), and outlining talking points for why elected officials should object to child development legislation. Marshner was, in short, a modern career woman. A 1984 profile in the *Dallas Herald* noted the seeming contradiction between Marshner's expressed values and behavior:

> The conservative pro-family movement is dedicated to preserving what Mrs. Marshner calls traditional Christian values: the husband as head of the family; parents staying together for their children's sakes instead of divorcing; God's commandments, not man's, as the center of family and social order. Connie Marshner regards herself as doing God's bidding, and her mission is to fight government policies that she says interfere with family life. . . . Dedicated as she is to promoting black-and-white standards of the pro-family line, Mrs. Marshner admits the way she leads her life falls into a more uncertain gray area. She personifies, in effect, some of the contradictions between the traditional Christian values she supports and the realities of life in the 1980s.[34]

The reporter, Anita Creamer, allowed Marshner to maintain control of the narrative, quoting her as saying, "It is a contradiction for me to work. . . . I agonize over it constantly. . . . If I were just working in a factory or in an office, I'd take a different approach. This is more like a calling than a job."[35] Marshner was far from the only woman to have such a "calling" and make a career out of advocating for essentialized gender roles that consigned women to the home.

In addition to Marshner, Phyllis Schlafly was central to the development of a new social conservatism and was closely allied with the New Right and the NCR even as she maintained her autonomy from both groups. While much has been written by and about Schlafly,[36] it is worth revisiting her activism here to focus on her role in crafting and mobilizing the narrative of victimization that would become central to the movement's communicative discourse. In brief: like Marshner, Schlafly was a conservative Catholic and was married with children. She first rose to national prominence in 1964 with the publication of a book written in support of Goldwater's candidacy titled *A Choice, Not an Echo*. One of the most innovative strategists of the conservative movement in the 1970s, she led the fight to stop the ratification of the Equal Rights Amendment (ERA).

Schlafly mastered the art of the retorsion argument to reframe debates around the ERA and marshaled a grassroots army of aggrieved housewives, who rallied around her and racked up wins as they pushed for state after state to either vote against or rescind ratification of the bill. Beginning in the early 1970s, Schlafly asserted that the ERA would deprive women of the "protected status" they had secured on the basis of Christian tradition. Writing in the February 1972 edition of "The Phyllis Schlafly Report," she argued:

> We are fortunate to have the great legacy of Moses, the Ten Commandments, especially this one: "Honor thy father and thy mother that thy days may be long upon the land." Children are a woman's best social security— her best guarantee of social benefits such as old age pension, unemployment compensation, workman's compensation, and sick leave. The family gives a woman the physical, financial and emotional security of the home—for all her life.
>
> The second reason why American women are a privileged group is that we are the beneficiaries of a tradition of special respect for women which dates from the Christian Age of Chivalry. The honor and respect paid to Mary, the Mother of Christ, resulted in all women, in effect, being put on a pedestal.[37]

Schlafly deftly cast women as victims of change by asserting they would lose their "unique status" in American society and law. But her argument was fundamentally disingenuous: women in the 1970s objectively did not occupy a special or protected place in the law or broader culture[38]—and they never had. Rather, Schlafly's argument mirrors the temporal politics of backlash discourse: it manufactures a fictionalized narrative about the past in order to construct a before and an after, which, in turn, serves as the justification for advancing a new political vision and corresponding set of social relations. In other words, Schlafly's writing shrouds an essentially prefigurative politics—premised on a new integration of Christian values and morality into American law and politics that would demand social relations conform to a conservative Christian worldview—in the language of victimization and self-defense. In this way, the development of a proactive agenda aimed at instituting new forms of social relations could be presented as reactionary and backlash driven.

Like Schlafly, Marshner's work reflected a prefigurative politics as she sought to advance family policies that would harness the state's coercive capacities to enforce a particular set of familial social relations. In a later writing, titled "Who Is the New Traditional Woman?," Marshner reimagines a new traditional identity for women. Marshner begins by acknowledging the nation's historical ambivalence toward Christian values, writing, "In the Founding days, most people adhered to the Judeo-Christian ethic even if they lacked faith in it, because it was the only real option."[39] She further deconstructs the idea that there is a static and objective "traditional woman," asserting that women became "enchanted with the images and phoniness of Hollywood's depiction of [domestic] 'reality'" in the 1950s. And yet, she preemptively concludes, "To summarize the points developed so far: (1) the key to the New Traditional Woman is not the conventions of yesteryear but the abiding values. (2) I hope I have sharpened up the distinction between conventions and values." Thus, the "new traditional woman" is neither Norman Rockwell's well-heeled housewife nor a pre-modern domestic submissive. Marshner effectively constructs a universal and static set of Christian gender-based values while simultaneously acknowledging that these values have failed to ever be fully implemented in American social or political conventions. And yet, the "new traditional woman" "rejects the inevitability of social decay," instead projecting herself into a future where New Right social policies have successfully fused Christian values with a new set of conventions.

Taken together, Schlafly and Marshner's work helped to redefine conservatism and coopt the debate over the expansion of rights for minoritized and marginalized groups. By positing that the ascription of rights to these groups would pose an imminent and existential threat to the "traditional" rights of women and families, they appropriated the liberal discourse of rights even as they advocated for the passage of illiberal policies.[40] Conservatives adopted the discourse of rights, as Andrew R. Lewis has shown in *The Rights Turn in Conservative Christian Politics*.[41] But, I argue, they did not do so from within a liberal framework that gives primacy to the rights of all individuals equally. Rather, as we see in the epilogue, they operationalized the rights framework from a distinctly illiberal perspective that centers on the protection and supremacy of the White, cisgender, heterosexual, and heteronormative family.

The New Right

To understand how the New Right manifested and operationalized this new conservatism, we need to look at how the movement functioned. To do so is to avoid falling into the trap of "fail[ing] to see the mutually supportive roles of the conservative political action groups, think tanks, and other sectors like the corporate community,"[42] which made the New Right an effective movement. The following sections, therefore, assess the movement's development of single-issue politics in relation to its organizational strategy. The issues, strategies, and tactics adopted by the New Right— that is, its coordinative discourse—worked hand-in-hand with the movement's development of a politics of victimhood, which was used, on the one hand, to bring conservative Christians together and, on the other hand, to obscure the radicality of the conservative Christian political platform.

Organization

Between 1971 and 1977, Weyrich and other New Right political entrepreneurs, including Ricard Viguerie, John Terry Dolan, Howard Phillips, and Marshner, used their DC political insider status to build the organizations that would anchor an ostensibly outsider movement. The first incarnation of New Right institutions, for example, Analysis and Research Associates (ARA) and Heritage Foundation, focused on producing policies and setting legislative agendas, but changes in the political climate coupled with campaign finance reform created an opening in the political opportunity structure that New Right activists rushed to fill via the creation of conservative fundraising institutions.

Two unexpected gifts contributed to the political mobilization and institutional growth of the New Right: the first came from the Republican Party, as President Nixon's perceived failure to act like a true conservative fueled right-wing activism.[43] After Nixon's impeachment and resignation, conservative disenchantment with the establishment Republican Party increased dramatically. It rose to a fever pitch when Gerald Ford selected the moderate Nelson Rockefeller as his vice president in 1974, a move New Right activists viewed akin to high treason. The second offering came from the Democrats and arrived in the form of poorly conceived reforms to campaign finance law. That same year, the Federal Election Campaign Act of 1972 was amended to place limits on campaign donations. But rather than curtail the role of outside money in congressional races, it had the unintended consequence of benefitting nonestablishment and insurgent New Right candidates because it "forced candidates to find ways to finance elections outside the normal two-party structure."[44]

By 1974, fearful that conservative Republicans would be voted out of Congress on a national wave of disgust with the Nixon-scarred GOP, New Right activists shifted their focus to reelecting incumbents.[45] Relying heavily on direct-mailing lists cultivated by the CNR entrepreneur and publisher Richard Viguerie and his direct mailing company, the Richard A. Viguerie Company (RAVCO), a host of PACs formed (including Weyrich's Committee for the Survival of a Free Congress). These organizations "are smaller than their liberal counterparts, raise less money, give to fewer candidates and are much more intensely motivated ideologically," *Congressional Quarterly* reported. "They want to elect not just conservatives but committed, ideological conservatives who will score high on the Americans for Constitutional Action and American Conservative Union vote ratings."[46] According to Viguerie, the movement was intentionally nonhierarchical and relied on forming loose issue-driven coalitions within the two-party system "to create conservative majorities [or elect conservative candidates] in both parties."[47] Subsequently, the New Right prided itself on supporting conservative candidates within both parties as a means of disrupting the status quo and on utilizing an "informal way of operating."

The New Right's coordinative discourse was premised on a reconceptualization of how a political movement should strategically function. The 1976 strategy was, in Weyrich's words, "organization." "We preach and teach nothing but organization," Weyrich told *Congressional Quarterly*. "Conservatives are notorious for feeling that if they are right on the issues, they will win the election. This is nonsense," he continued, stressing instead the need for sustained and protracted fundraising and political action.[48]

In the mid-1970s, organization took the form of institutional prolif-eration as a veritable alphabet soup of organizations was cooked up by the New Right. The central institutions of the New Right that developed between 1973 and 1976 included the Committee for Survival of Free Con-gress, National Conservative Political Action Committee (NCPAC), Con-servative Caucus (CC), Conservative Victory Fund (CVF), Committee for the Republic (CFTR), Republican Study Committee (RSC), Senate Steering Committee (SSC), Committee for the Right to Keep and Bear Arms (CRKBA).[49] Weyrich was eager to credit the movement's success to these organizations, highlighting the relative strengths and contributions of each:

> The advent of the Heritage Foundation, which gave tough minded conser-vatives in Congress a data base for their efforts; the Conservative Caucus [led by Howard Phillips], which sought out leadership to form coalitions at the local level to mobilize grassroots sentiment; the Committee for the Survival of a Free Congress and the National Conservative Political Action Committee [led by John (Terry) Dolan], which brought the technical ex-pertise and training which the Left had used for years to win elections to right-of-center candidates in both parties, helped to articulate a new brand of practical yet principled conservatism to Congress, to the candidate and to the public.[50]

In 1976 *Congressional Quarterly* reported on the New Right's explosive in-stitutional growth, crediting much of its success to Viguerie's direct mailing lists, noting the lists were "built up over the past decade of work for private as well as political clients, [and] have been the basis for fund-raising this year by three important new groups—the National Conservative Political Action Committee, the Committee for the Survival of a New Congress, and the Gun Owners of America."[51] However, the proliferation of organi-zations and their shared reliance on Viguerie posed a significant problem for the New Right: the same potential donors were endlessly spammed with fundraising requests, and conservatives and liberals alike suffered from "the incestuousness of their mailing lists."[52]

As the primary supplier of conservative donor lists and mailers to New Right fundraising operations, Viguerie got rich, and the recipients of his letters got fed up. For example, mailings from the CSFC during this period included apologies from Weyrich for subscribers having been spammed by unsolicited fundraising mailers from RAVCO, but Viguerie himself was unapologetic. Instead, he dedicated one of his monthly "From the Publisher" pieces to "The Importance of Direct Mail," using the occasion to explain to *Conservative Digest* readers that "without the mails, most conservative activity would wither and die. . . . There *is* one method of mass communication that the liberals do not control—*direct mail*. In fact, conservatives excel in direct mail."[53] While Viguerie was telling his audience that direct mail was responsible for building the movement, it was also making him a very rich man. As previously noted, campaign finance reform had opened the door to the creation of PACs, which in turn encouraged the proliferation of small, individual contributions. But the 1974 campaign finance amendments did nothing to ensure that the money given in support of candidates actually went to them—and, in fact, very little of it did.[54] Nonetheless, even if direct mail was not exactly padding campaign war chests, it was bringing a new conservative political program, premised on single-issue politics, into the homes of millions of Americans every day.

Single-Issue Politics

During this same period, throughout the mid-1970s, the New Right endorsed not only a plurality of conservative groups but also a broad set of political issues that were prone to shifting and did not neatly comprise a coherent political ideology. The movement adopted, cast off, and elaborated on a number of single-issue positions. While the New Left mobilized around civil rights, women's rights, and ending the Vietnam War as single-issue agendas that were framed in relation to a rights-based moralism, the New Right adopted a broader array of issues that included social conservatism, fiscal conservatism, and anticommunism. Largely framed in relation to a defensive posture, these issues included opposition to abortion, pornography, SALT II, ratification of the Panama Canal Treaty, and the Equal Rights Amendment. On the affirmative side, they included the embrace of gun rights and parental rights, but even these issues were cast as being in response to left-wing threats reflected in the backlash reference in the opening epigraph.

Single-issue agendas tend to be comprised of positions that are framed as being moralistic and nonnegotiable, two characteristics the New Right exploited to their advantage. For example, early on, in 1974, Marshner recognized the untapped potential for mobilizing voters around abortion as a single issue. Reflecting on the 1974 midterm elections in a memo, she wrote:

> Right to lifers are not generally highly sophisticated politicoes. But their motivation is high. End-the-war freaks and eco-nuts were not politicoes when they start out, either (though the pro-abortionists of the '60's by and large were politically sophisticated). All indications are that abortion will be an issue in the November elections, more than a heck of a lot of candidates would like it to be. If one feels any loyalty to James Madison's belief in countervailing "factions," however, one must welcome the appearance on the scene of active right to life political organizations. Elections are going to be close in November, 1974. . . . The injection of a very solid, very clear-cut issue into the races can help separate sheep from goats. It will at least be a real grounds for decision by some voters.[55]

Marshner was prescient about the power of mobilizing single-issue anti-abortion voters, but it took six years for the issue to acquire the influence she anticipated. In the intervening years, single-issue organizing served an important purpose: it helped to solidify and radicalize the conservative positions held by members within these groups.

As Cass Sunstein has suggested, rather than groups or coalitions having a moderating impact on members' positions, there appears to be a "group polarization" effect, whereby members strengthen one another's preexisting positions. Sunstein proposes, for example, that "religious organizations tend, for example, to strengthen group members' religious convictions, simply by virtue of the fact that like-minded people are talking to one another."[56] And so, by refusing to bring the plurality of conservative issues under a single partisan umbrella or create ideological synthesis, the movement was also able to resist the effects of the "moderation thesis," which holds that the process of coalition-building tempers radical platforms as movements seek legitimacy and electability.[57] Thus, as single-issue groups grew in size and institutional sophistication, absorbing more grassroots members and finding allies in elected officials the New Right helped put into office, they not only maintained their original conservative positions but also adopted increasingly hardline, nonnegotiable stances on issues like abortion, pornography, parental rights, and communism.

Taken on its face, the New Right's embrace of single-issue politics can be seen to have laid the foundation for the explosion of what came to be referred to as the "culture war" politics of the 1980s. The sociologist James Davison Hunter explains, "The culture war emerges over fundamentally different conceptions of moral authority, over different ideas and beliefs about truth, the good, obligation to one another, the nature of community, and so on. It is, therefore, cultural conflict at its deepest level."[58] This understanding of single-issue politics is the one CNR activists sought to cultivate as the coordinative discourse surrounding single-issue politics was communicated to the grassroots using the language of truth and morality, and through the cultivation of an existential fear of the dangers wrought by "progressive" change.

Single issues, such as opposition to school busing as a means of desegregating public schools, constructed political issues in terms of the innocent victim and the evil perpetrator, the persecuted White Christian child and parent and the persecuting civil rights crusader. In this way, single issues not only served to galvanize the grassroots around moral issues but also helped construct a Manichean worldview and a political identity premised on an ideology of victimhood. By casting single issues in this light, the CNR was able to deflect attention from the radicality of its political positions, even as it proclaimed itself to be composed of "radicals" and to assert its actions were defensive—and even as it actively sought to use issues like "child development" to assert the supremacy of the straight, White, Christian man and the racialized, heteronormative family (via the rejection of school integration schemes, the embrace of a patriarchal traditionalist conception of the family, and essentialized gender roles).

In practice, the New Right's focus on single-issue politics also afforded the movement the flexibility to test out the adoption of positions that contradicted those held by fiscal conservatives without formally disavowing the free market. This strategy was aimed at courting voters who were cut out off from the Republican Party, especially blue-collar union workers. Viguerie especially was a proponent of "lunch bucket" politics, emphasizing "issues that appeal to rank-and-file workers beset by high prices, factory closings and stiff foreign competition."[59] For the New Right, single-interest issues and coalition politics were both a means and an end to breaking with the fiscal conservatism that was a hallmark of conservative ideology and of the Republican Party establishment. Contrary to Alf Tomas Tønnessen's claim that the New Right was comprised of "ideologically conservative, so-called three-legged-stool conservatives (economic, social, and defense),"[60] the movement was in more than name symptomatic of a *new* right that was willing to jettison economic conservatism in order to both pander to voters and pursue a conservative Christian social agenda.

Abandoning the GOP's embrace of Big Business and its commitment to limited government spending on social welfare programs that benefited the working class signaled not only a disavowal of the Republican Party but also a shrewdly pragmatic shift on the part of the New Right. Increasingly, the New Right sought out unorthodox coalition partners, looking to ally with "groups like labor, the environmental movement, Common Cause, and even Democrats." In doing so, Clay F. Richards reported in the *Boston Herald American*, the movement was embracing "pragmatism" and "forsaking the ideological orthodoxy that was the hallmark of the Barry Goldwater generation of conservatives."[61] It should come as no surprise that this move alienated more orthodox conservatives. The self-identified conservative journalist Alan Crawford observed:

> Pointing to the ease with which Viguerie and his cohorts have, at least publicly, agreed to surrender as essential a part of American conservatism as "the free market," some conservatives dismiss their views as mere electioneering. Others, however, believe they detect something far more serious—a general indifference to ideology, which is apparently of so little concern to "New Right" publicists that they quite willingly broadcast a set of opinions merely to drum up support.[62]

In particular, those who saw themselves as "traditional" fiscal conservatives were concerned about the New Right's incoherent economic positions. Kevin Phillips, an early supporter of the movement, hinted at discontent with the movement's abandonment of fiscal conservatism when he described it in the following terms: "What they [the New Right] really are, generally speaking, is a group of anti-Establishment, middle-class political rebels more interested in issues like abortion, gun control, busing, ERA, quotas, bureaucracy, and the grassroots tax revolt than in capital gains taxation or natural gas deregulation."[63] In other words, the New Right was viewed as dilettantish, neither truly committed to fiscal conservatism nor truly reflective of a populist working-class movement.

In short, the movement's shifting identification of issues around which to mobilize suggested an instrumentalist approach to politics and a lack of "pure" ideological commitment. Writing for *The Nation* in 1977, Crawford remarked on both the fragmented nature of the New Right and its use of single-issue politics to mobilize voters:

The lack of a defined program—and lack of interest in defining one—manifests itself, they say, in an emphasis in "Red Flag" issues, for example, busing and gun control, to the exclusion of more substantive—and complex—ones. . . .

Howard Phillips of Conservative Caucus defends the emphasis on emotionally charged "social issues" (in tune with Viguerie's own belief that it is impossible to raise money unless you conjure up an enemy), contending that voters are not ideological but motivated by strong leadership—a statement that impresses some traditionalists as a call for demagoguery.[64]

Rather than see the charge of demagoguery as a shortcoming, CNR activists persisted in viewing their instrumentalism as an asset. "Conservatives have been led by an intellectual movement but not a practical movement up to now," Weyrich was quoted as saying in an article in *National Affairs*. "We talk about issues that people care about, like gun control, abortion, taxes and crimes. Yes, they're emotional issues, but . . . it's better than talking about capital formation."[65] In the hands of the CNR, single-issue politics were used to emphasize the cultural and emotional dimension of politics, frame political conflict in oppositional terms, and construct conservatives as victims of a progressive assault. But the New Right was not purely, or even primarily, driven by pragmatic considerations. While some issues were seemingly adopted instrumentally, many of the signature social conservative single issues adopted by the movement reflected both the personal religious commitments and political positions of CNR activists as well as trends they saw happening on the ground.

The lack of a cohesive political program that Crawford quite rightly pointed to should not, however, be confused for the lack of a cohesive worldview or a failure to devise comprehensive programs around specific single issues. For example, opposition to "child development," a signature single issue for the New Right early on, extended far beyond just advocating for a veto of the EOE. While framed by activists and observers alike as a backlash campaign, the New Right "child development" agenda quickly developed into a proactive program. This is evidenced by a 1974 memo by Marshner on "Brainstorming for a 'Family Consolidation Act,'" in which she spitballed ideas for advancing a comprehensive right-wing vision of the relationship between the state and the family. Included in Marshner's list were the following proposals:

1. *Dismantling of public secular education,* which would include an end to compulsory schooling, the creation of a voucher system to be used for public and private schools, the elimination of school busing programs, and recognition that "Parents should have some significant say in planning curriculum at all levels, not just through PTA nonsense, but in some more effectve [*sic*] manner";

2. *Adoption of a doctrine of parental rights,* which would require a statement affirming that the government recognizes "The parent(s) are presumed to have the good of the child at heart in all matters, and this presumption shall carry over into courts in all phases of judicial action and interest," and a "Statement of parental sovereignty over all aspects of their children's growth and development and education";

3. *The creation of a nuclear family centered economics,* which would necessitate changes to the IRS tax code to allow deduction of childcare expenses paid to relatives, a progressive tax exemption for children, and a scheme to encourage women to take maternity leave from paid work. Marshner proposed that the government "Guarantee a woman's job for a year, or whatever, so that if she has to work, she can nonetheless spend the all-important first year with her baby, and be assured of a job awaiting her." She also proposed the creation of a "system of child allowances" for families that relied on two incomes, proposing that "the government shall financially assist such parents so that the equivalent of the after-tax income of the previously-working spouse, at an average of the last three-years' employment, shall be provided. One-half of such amount is to be taken as a direct tax credit from the tax bill; the other half by direct grant from XXX."[66]

Marshner's notes for developing a "Family Consolidation Act" reflected not only her conservative Catholic beliefs about gender and the family but also a new approach to government, which sought to limit its scope in some areas (education) while simultaneously strengthening and expanding its capacity in others (mandating government payments to encourage stay-at-home parenting). It is easy to see, based on these proposals, how the New Right could be attacked for not promoting a standard, limited government, fiscally conservative ideological line. Moreover, it is easy to see why Crawford would charge the movement with seeking "radical political change" and being "anything but conservative."

Within a decade, Marshner's sweeping vision would, in many ways, come to serve as the basis for conservative Catholic and Protestant coalition-building and define the NCR. But, in the mid-1970s, single-issue organizing was the name of the New Right's game, and it resulted in the proliferation of narrowly targeted groups dedicated to advancing their specific cause. Writing in 1983, the sociologist Jerome L. Himmelstein observed that throughout the 1970s, the New Right's single-issue organizing strategy led the movement to attempt to "tie together" a staggering number of single-issue groups:

> antiabortion groups as the National Right to Life Committee, the National Pro-Life Political Action Committee, the Life Amendment Political Action Committee, and the American Life Lobby; such antigun control groups as the Citizen's Committee for the Right to Keep and Bear Arms and Gun Owners of America, such antifeminist groups as Stop ERA and the Eagle Forum; such anti-pornography groups as the National Federation for Decency and the Coalition for Better Television; and the antiunion National Right to Work Committee.[67]

On the one hand, the sheer number of single-issue organizations—as well as the additional working groups and coalitions, such as the Kingston Group (dedicated to economic issues) and the Stanton Group (focused on foreign policy issues), that Marshner and Weyrich were connected to—was, in and of itself, part of the New Right's coordinative strategy. Casting a wide net enabled the New Right to attract and mobilize a broader swath of the conservative electorate than could mainstream Republicans. On the other hand, single-issue politics posed a significant challenge for the New Right: each set of single-issue groups focused almost exclusively on its siloed agenda, and affiliations bridging single-issue groups tended to be loose and unstructured.

While embraced for its ability to mobilize the grassroots and encourage the formation of ad hoc and horizontal coalitions, the fragmented and instrumental nature of single-issue politics inhibited the cultivation of a broad and widely shared "conservative" identity, even as CNR activists sought to redefine what "conservative" meant. And so, while New Right political entrepreneurs thrilled to see their coalition partners adopt "true" conservative positions, they struggled to build alliances across single-issue groups and could not guarantee that, for example, pro-gun conservatives would turn out en masse to vote for a conservative candidate whose primary campaign issue was pornography or school busing.

Concluding Thoughts

Throughout the 1970s, CNR activists sought to redefine conservatism while also framing their movement in terms of a backlash to the left. By casting single issues in terms of backlash, the movement mobilized a narrative of victimization that, in turn, helped rationalize the movement's aims as reactionary and defensive. Single-issue campaigns were critical to the early development of a coordinative discourse within the New Right as they helped polarize conservatives and fostered short-term alliances, but their resultant coalitions could not be sustained or expanded beyond the issue at hand. The movement seemingly lacked an ideologically coherent and consistent base of support. While single-issue politics facilitated the creation of multiple new coalitions and encouraged the adoption of an ideology of victimhood, they are also shown to have inhibited the creation of a singular broad-based coalition.

In order for the New Right to manifest its political ambitions, it needed to identify and secure access to a large, cohesive, and reliable grassroots that could be mobilized nationally. That is, the movement needed to bring White conservative Protestants into the coalition. Early in 1976, CNR activists recognized the potential of tapping into the conservative Christian grassroots and put together a plan titled "Project Survival." Conceived of as "an audacious plan to register 12 million new voters" before the presidential election, Project Survival would be "an extraordinarily low cost quiet 'blitz-krieg' to activate these conservative Christians in the next 10 months by showing them precisely the why, where and how of registering and voting." While Project Survival included a fundraising pitch and a proposal for the use of direct mail, it does not seem to have gone far beyond the conceptualization of the project—at least in 1976.[68]

Two years later, in the leadup to the 1978 midterm elections, the New Right remained committed to the instrumentalization of "emotional" issues, but it was increasingly aware of the power of consolidating these issues and the growing influence of the CP grassroots movement. For this reason, the New Right encouraged its base to identify with the broader "conservative" label and to embrace coalition politics.[69] Weyrich and Viguerie, in particular, became vociferous proponents of "coalition politics," maintaining they had learned the pragmatic strategy from the left.[70] The New Right leaned heavily on the concept of coalition, at least in part to address one of the limitations of ad hoc single-issue organizing, which discourages the development of broad-based movements. Arguably useful as a mathematical strategy for garnering support, the logic of coalition suggested that single-issue voters could be counted on to vote en masse for a candidate that represented associative issues. That November, the New Right claimed electoral success for having unseated eight senators who had voted for the Panama Canal treaties were unseated, and it attributed the movement's success to an enthusiastic embrace of single issues, stating, "The nation owes a debt of gratitude to single purpose groups in the areas of right-to-work, right to life, tax limitation, defense and pro-gun activity."[71] And yet, despite the seeming excitement expressed in *The New Right Report*, "the GOP gains weren't impressive," as the New Right had primarily turned moderate Republican seats into conservative Republican seats, which was not precisely a model for enacting large-scale change.

It turned out that while single issues had been effective at mobilizing deeply invested and committed voters, the New Right had faced difficulty attracting members to multi-issue conservative groups, such as Howard Phillip's Conservative Caucus, and it faltered when it tried to corral voters under a too loosely constructed "conservative" umbrella.[72] And so, while the plurality of issues and ad hoc coalition strategy initially adopted by the New Right helped it to grow, these strategies and tactics also posed significant challenges that, by the end of the decade, led the movement in need of both a more cohesive conservative platform and new coalition partners. Only by the end of the decade were CPs poised to join forces with their CNR counterparts.

Conservative Catholics were not the only Christians to have undergone an institutional and ideological transformation in the 1960s and 1970s. Just as religious and social transformation within the Catholic Church set Weyrich on the path to conservative political organizing, Bible-believing Protestants experienced their own revolution during this period. Internal transformations within evangelical and Fundamentalist Protestantism, alongside broader social changes, politically galvanized CP elites and the grassroots, as we will see in the following chapter.

4

JERRY FALWELL

A Fundamentalist Phenomenon Rises Up to Meet the Grassroots

There was, in fact, a moral majority of sorts who were in power in this country for many years, into the early part of the century. But the Scopes trial and the revolt against Prohibition swept those fundamentalists, if you will, out of power, and they have been on the defensive ever since, until recent times.

—Paul Weyrich

All over the country there were little clusters of mainly mothers, evangelical, fundamentalist Moms' groups, who were in very—they were unstructured, they didn't have an organization, they were just in touch with each other, and they were beginning to be aware that there really was a problem here. They didn't know what it was, they didn't know how to define it, but when they read this and they realized that government was—that liberals in Congress were trying to design things so that government would prevent parents from raising their children, they—they knew was something wrong, and they responded to that. . . . But, ultimately, I think, those people, those real, true grass roots, real Americans, are the ones who provided, then, the—the blood . . . and the bones for what became an organized movement. . . . These people, by and large, were disenfranchised, they went to church faithfully but they didn't vote faithfully, in many cases they weren't registered, they did not participate

in the political process, uh, but they were the real Americans who had
been sleeping through the '60s.

—Connie Marshner, discussing the Economic Opportunity Child Development veto letter campaign

Never one to shy away from self-aggrandizement, Paul Weyrich claimed
to be responsible for bringing White conservative Protestants (CPs) into
the right-wing political fold. As recounted in chapter 1, prior to the late
1970s, Weyrich said he had tried to interest Protestants in politics for
years, shopping them a number of issues, including abortion, but nothing
captured the interest of Protestant elites until the segregation academy issue caught fire. While the backlash discourse of this narrative has already
been problematized, there is another side of the story that deserves our
attention: Weyrich's claims suggest that conservative evangelicals and fundamentalists were essentially apolitical, passively waiting to be awakened
by the knock of the federal government when it forced politics into their
homes and schools by seeking to impose racial integration through the
threat of levying additional taxes. But this story is apocryphal. Neither the
IRS nor Paul Weyrich deserves the credit for politicizing CPs in the 1970s;
they were already politicized.

Throughout the decade, CPs rose up to meet the counterculture revolution with a cultural and religious revolution of their own. However, they
were not effectively mobilized in support of a comprehensive conservative
political platform or on behalf of the Republican Party. And so, it would be
more accurate to say that Weyrich was a savvy political entrepreneur who
saw an opening in the political opportunity structure emerge in response to
the segregation academy controversy. Stepping in to fill CPs' institutional
needs, Weyrich and the New Right capitalized on the internal political
and theological transformation of fundamentalists to satisfy the political
needs of his own New Right movement. But the conditions of possibility existed independently of Weyrich and were the result of theological
developments and institutional changes taking place within religiously
conservative Protestant communities. Just as changes within Catholicism
created space for Weyrich to develop a conservative Catholic identity, so-
ciohistorical changes within American Protestantism created space for the
development of a politically conservative Protestant identity.

This chapter explores the theological, organizational, and political conditions that made possible the New Christian Right (NCR) coalition. It begins with a brief overview of the development of American Protestantism in the early and mid-twentieth century to contextualize the political identity formation of CPs. To effectively shape American secular society and transform the nation's politics, fundamentalists in the mid-twentieth century became less apart and more in line with a mainstream they had sought to keep at bay. As traditionally independent and particularized congregants tuned in to watch mega pastors deliver targeted sermons, the conservative Protestant base became ever more coherent at the same time as it grew increasingly politicized as a result of grassroots activism. For CPs, specifically fundamentalists, separatism gave way to increased engagement with the outside world, which entered their homes and consciousness through television screens, direct mailers sent to hundreds of thousands of mailboxes at a time, and grassroots mobilizations at the local level. Driven by a desire to exert more political control and guided by religious leaders who acted as power brokers, we see how fundamentalists learned to embrace modern technologies, overcome their antipathy to other Christians, and found coalitions with partners who could provide them with strong institutions and establish intellectual frameworks to support a faith-based politics.

Given the absence of a universal hierarchical structure, such as the Roman Catholic Church, the process of conservative Protestant transformation was diffuse and driven by what I term "religious political entrepreneurs," with the Reverend Jerry Falwell at the helm. While Falwell was by no means the only—or perhaps even most effective—religious political entrepreneur, he was the most visible face of fundamentalism in the 1970s and became the spokesperson of the largest Christian Right organization, the Moral Majority, at its founding in 1979. In keeping with the emphasis on political elites and examination of the development of NCR and CNR coordinative discourses, the bulk of this chapter focuses on Falwell's religious-political development.

Responding to outside changes, capitalizing on an existent political ideology of anticommunism, and drawing on the energy of politicized grassroots activists, Falwell brokered new institutional alliances outside the faith and helped fundamentalists become active participants in the mainstream of American politics. Throughout the 1970s, we see how Falwell helped convince CPs to overcome the tendency toward political withdrawal and theological separatism, and instead to enter into dialogue and coalition with other conservative religious groups—even Catholics. Alongside other religious political entrepreneurs embedded in the fundamentalist faith, particularly the theologian Francis Schaeffer, Falwell is shown to have begun the process of building a conservative Protestant political movement from the inside out well before Weyrich stepped into the fray.

During the early- and mid-1970s, the coordinative discourse of conservative evangelical/fundamentalist Protestants developed independently from that of the New Right. However, the parallel structure of developments within both movements occurred in such a way as to make the confluence of these groups and the formation of the NCR not only possible but necessary. In short, this chapter brings us to the threshold of conservative Catholic and Protestant political convergence. Recognizing the respective limitations of CP and CNR strategies helps explain why the CNR pivoted from a single-issue coalition strategy to the promulgation of an ideologically cohesive, multi-issue "pro-family" platform. It also helps explain the coordinative work and strategic mobilization that was behind the seemingly explosive emergence and subsequent growth of the NCR.

The Fundamentals

For CPs to forge an ecumenical Christian Right, they had to overcome not only centuries of antipathy toward Catholics but also deep-seated internal conflicts. Fundamentalists, in particular, had to transform how they viewed themselves in relation to other Christian denominations, secular society, and the state. The following discussion provides a brief overview of the development of American Protestant fundamentalism and demonstrates how 1970s fundamentalists underwent significant changes on their road to forging the NCR. However, they are shown to have retained two key features of fundamentalist culture, which informed the political shape of the NCR: a deep-seated animosity toward liberalism and the cultural identification as victims of modernism.

American fundamentalist Protestantism began with the publication of a series of tracts, *The Fundamentals*, written by theologians affiliated with the Bible Institute of Los Angeles in 1909 and 1910. The texts' "prime purpose was the defense and exaltation of traditional views of the Bible."[1] While *The Fundamentals* would birth a diverse movement encompassing a number of congregationalist and Baptist churches, the faith system can be summarized as "a form of conservative evangelical Protestantism, [that] may be distinguished from other types of evangelical churches by its intense opposition to modern scientific theories and many aspects of popular culture."[2] This means fundamentalists embrace the basic tenets of conservative evangelical Protestantism, which include the belief in the need to be "born again," the primacy of the Bible, the centrality of the sacrifice of Jesus on the cross (crucicentrism), and the need to share God's word or evangelize.[3] *The Fundamentals* included five additional elements: "the inerrancy and full authority of the Bible, the virgin birth of Christ, a belief that Christ died for man's sins (substitutionary atonement), the bodily resurrection of Jesus, [and] the authenticity of miracles."[4] An essential opposition to the social and economic changes wrought by industrialization, broadly termed "modernism," developed alongside these doctrinal tenets. Subsequently, antimodernist sentiments manifested in fundamentalist theology, culture, education, and politics.

The work of the historian George M. Marsden frames the development of fundamentalist Protestantism as being directly in conversation with, and responsive to, broader changes in American political development. Fundamentalists have been caught in what Marsden terms an "establishment-or-outsider paradox." Arising from the contradiction between viewing themselves as heirs to mainstream American culture, which they saw as synonymous with evangelicalism, and perceiving themselves "as a beleaguered minority with strong sectarian or separatist tendencies," the establishment-or-outsider paradox infused the religious development of fundamentalists and their relationship to American political culture.[5] Torn between the desire to lay claim to the nation's cultural and political institutions or protect themselves from an ever more hostile and sinful world, fundamentalists have oscillated between being engaged political actors and passive observers of a nation in decline. Marsden identifies four distinct periods in the development of fundamentalism, reproduced in abbreviated form in table 4.1, and to which I have added a column addressing their relationship to the broader political culture.[6]

Anticipating the End Times

As the table demonstrates, in the nineteenth century evangelicals viewed themselves as part of the social and political establishment, or rather, they understood themselves to be representative of the dominant (White) culture. In the late nineteenth and early twentieth centuries, some faith

Table 4.1. Evangelical and Fundamentalist Development Chart

Era	Religious Identity	Description	Relationship to Political Culture
Nineteenth century	Evangelicalism	"Includes most major Protestant denominations and also newer revivalist groups including holiness and premillennialists."	Establishment/Insider: the political system is viewed as a product of/ responsive to the evangelical worldview.
1920s	Fundamentalism	Encompasses "a broad coalition of conservatives from major denominations and revivalists (prominently including premillennial dispensationalists).	Other/Outsider: the political system is viewed as separate from/ antithetical to the fundamentalist worldview.
1950s– mid-1970s	New Evangelicalism and Fundamentalism	"New Evangelicals (eventually just 'evangelicals'), most of whom have a fundamentalist heritage form the core of a broad coalition that draws in related theological conservatives ... who emphasize positive evangelism, best exemplified by Billy Graham. Fundamentalism is used as a self-designation almost only by ecclesiastical separatists with Graham. Almost all are dispensational premillennialists, as	Establishment/Insider vs. Other/Outsider: in the context of the Cold War, the political system is viewed as a product of/ responsive to the evangelical worldview. Fundamentalists remain critical of and apart from the political system, but simultaneously perceive US government as sinful/ corrupted and as a bulwark against Godless communism.

		are some separating evangelicals."	
Late 1970s to early twenty-first century	Fundamentalistic Evangelicalism	"The Religious Right... includes 'fundamentalistic' militants from not only separatist fundamentalist groups, but also from almost the whole spectrum of evangelicals."	Advancing the Creation of a New Establishment/ New Insiders: the political system is viewed as the proper domain for Bible-believing Protestants to advance their worldview, and they view themselves as ordained by God to save America from the scourge of Godless liberalism.

Source: Adapted from George M. Marsden, *Fundamentalism and American Culture*, 2nd ed. (Oxford: Oxford University Press, 2006), 234–235.

leaders, such as the pastor Isaac M. Haldeman, believed that premillennial-ism called for an absolute retreat from social engagement with the outside world, as any attempts to improve upon it were not only futile but part of the devil's plan to patch up a broken world in order to blind the faithful to the crises enveloping it. On the other end of the spectrum, during the same period, premillennial thought also produced social service ministries aimed at helping the poor and spearheaded social reform movements, such as Prohibition.[7] These dueling viewpoints can be explained, at least in part, by the existence of two distinct eschatological interpretations.

Both pre- and postmillennialism are dispensationalist doctrines that seek to produce an account of how God's plan for man's final salvation will unfold. Postmillennialists believe that they must create the conditions for the thousand years of peace, or the establishment of God's Kingdom, on earth as it were.[8] In the nineteenth century, postmillennialism encouraged social reform, as "it was incumbent on the faithful to reform society and pave the way for the 'second coming' of Jesus."[9] While some postmillen-nialists interpret the doctrine as a call to provide social welfare services and do good works, others, like R. J. Rushdoony, take it as their marching orders for constructing a Christian theocracy.[10] Premillennialism, in com-parison, teaches that the Second Coming of Christ will occur after the trials and tribulations, but before a thousand-year reign of peace on earth is established. Worldly affairs are understood to have no bearing on the Sec-ond Coming, leading many premillennialists to focus on saving individual souls in advance of the Second Coming. While it is not a requirement for fundamentalist Baptists, like Jerry Falwell, to ascribe to a premillennialist eschatology—that is, the belief that the end times will occur prior to the establishment of God's kingdom on earth—the vast majority do.

Marsden has a tendency to describe fundamentalist thought in terms of Manicheanism, or the dividing up of the world into distinct spheres of "ab-solute good and evil," with both God and the devil taking an active and ma-terial role in daily affairs. Doing so helps makes sense of the development of "super-patriotic premillennialism," or the 1950s premillennialist poli-tics that led CPs to view the Cold War as a cosmic war between God and the devil. The tendency within premillennialist thought to view all things in terms of God and Satan extends beyond anticommunism though, as fundamentalists are "disposed to divide *all* reality into neat antitheses: the saved and the lost, the holy and the unsanctified, the true and the false."[11] When transposed onto the political arena, premillennialist theology can produce an impassioned but conflictual approach to politics, characterized by the "establishment-or-other" paradox. Its adherents stand firm in their convictions and believe they are called to save their fellow man's soul, but they often wrestle with what—if anything—is to be done.

By the 1920s, fundamentalist teachings cultivated hostility toward modernism, intellectualism, and those outside of the faith; fostered distrust of political institutions; and promoted a deep embrace of hyper-individualism among its adherents. But, believing themselves to be keepers and speakers of the truth, throughout the twentieth century fundamentalists struggled to determine if they should fight to occupy a position of power in society in order to save souls or retreat to the fringes to keep from being corrupted by secular influences. And so, as fundamentalists tried to determine whether the road to salvation could be found only within the four walls of their churches or if it ran throughout society, they also strove to determine whether they should remain "other" and keep themselves separate from the rest of society, or if they should play an active role in shaping society with the intent of influencing the "establishment."

From Establishment to Outsider: Becoming Victims

As reflected by Paul Weyrich's statement quoted in the opening epigraph, one popular and enduring narrative concerning fundamentalists begins with the Scopes "Monkey" trial in 1925, which saw fundamentalists challenge the teaching of evolution in American schools. Although the plaintiffs technically won the case, they were lambasted in the court of public opinion, with major newspapers representing Tennessee Christians as antimodern and backward-looking. Williams Jennings Bryan, the charismatic politician who testified on behalf of the fundamentalist opposition to evolution during the trial, was thoroughly ridiculed during cross-examination and widely mocked by the press. He died less than a week after the trial concluded, ending an otherwise illustrious career in public service on a rather inglorious note. Historian Barry Hankins summarizes popular media perceptions of the trial as having "marked the decline of fundamentalism. The old religion met the new science, and the old religion lost."[12] Struck by the caustic example that was made of Bryan for having dared to defend the Bible and wounded by their public humiliation, American fundamentalists are often thought to have retreated from American politics to lick their wounds in private for the next fifty years.

The reality was quite different, and while fundamentalists were relatively quiet during the Great Depression, they were political actors both
before and after the Scopes trial. Fundamentalists led social reform movements before 1925, taking an active role in Prohibition, waging war on
the national broadcasting network throughout the 1930s, and enthusiasti-
cally diving into the anticommunist movement post-WWII.[13] The Scopes
trial narrative of fundamentalist retreat worked to eclipse fundamentalists'
ongoing political efforts—and to encourage the identification of fundamentalists as victims, pushed out of society by a Godless embrace of modernism and liberalism.

During this period, liberalism came to be associated with modernism,
as the liberal emphasis on the secular rights of man and the inevitability of
progress was seen to supplant a more fundamental understanding of natural rights originating from God and the depraved nature of man absent
God's grace. Writing about the (nonfundamentalist) Protestant theologian
Karl Barth's turn away from liberalism in 1919, historian Mark Taylor Dalhouse explains, "The war and its immense toll shattered, for Barth, the liberal view that man by his own efforts could bring the Kingdom of God to
this earth. Barth now understood that liberal theology, in remaking Jesus
into a simple teacher of ethics and a good example for people to follow,
had in fact destroyed what humans needed most: a savior to rescue them
from their fallen, sinful natures."[14] Concerns about the danger posed by the
primacy of man in liberal thought motivated much of the fundamentalist/
modernist conflict, which centered around whether primacy should be accorded to faith in the Bible—God's word—or to man's word, conceived of
as the individual's intellectualized interpretation of religion as a system of
ethics.[15]

In *The Fundamentalist Phenomenon*, a political how-to manual for fundamentalist organizing that was first published in 1981, Jerry Falwell and
his coauthors, Ed Dobson and Ed Hindson, embrace Marsden's work,
homing in on the confrontational elements of the religious movement
and defining fundamentalism as the "militant opposition of Liberalism."[16]
Reframing the fundamentalist/modernist debate in starkly martial terms,
they write, "It was the threat of a common enemy [modernists] that caused
Bible-believing Christians from every conceivable kind of denominational
background to form a mutual alliance of self-defense."[17] Here, we can identify both backlash and victimhood discourses at play, as the authors cast
modernist Christians as perpetrators and Bible-believing Christians as

innocent victims, forced to take action in response to an unprovoked liberal assault. The centrality of an identity of victimhood to the fundamentalist origin story likely helped make Bible-believing Christians more, rather than less, receptive to the New Right's emotionally charged framing of single-issue politics discussed in the previous chapter. Also of note is how Falwell understood fundamentalism as the antithesis to liberalism. This should give us pause when considering how Bible-believing Christians approach the discourse of rights and suggests we should not read CNR and CP actors' embrace of the rhetoric of "parental rights" and the "rights of the unborn" as signaling an acceptance of liberalism.

Establishment/Outsider Oscillation

While the pre-war dispute between modernists and fundamentalists certainly created a divide within the Protestant community, the definitive split between what we might think of as hardline or separatist fundamentalists and the new evangelicals occurred somewhat later, spearheaded by fundamentalist firebrands like the Reverend Bob Jones Jr. during the 1950s. It is this deeper rift that Falwell was both shaped by and had to overcome.

In the late 1940s and 1950s, CPs of all stripes were actively developing a political ethos founded on anticommunism and hyper-nationalist sentiment.[18] Angela Lahr's history of the relationship between the Cold War and conservative Protestant politics details the extent to which CPs were politically active in the post-war period and to which they influenced mainstream American culture. It also demonstrates the difficulty of maintaining a stark taxonomy of Protestant beliefs and identities as considerable ideological blurring took place between new evangelicals, fundamentalists, and members of secular society who collectively fused apocalyptic beliefs with Cold War fears of a communist takeover and American patriotism.

Soon after the close of World War II, anticommunism provided a conduit for many new evangelicals to join in the hyper-nationalist rhetoric of a scared and bellicose post-war America. New evangelical faith leaders, like the Reverend Billy Graham, whose first massive religious crusade was in 1949,[19] began mixing fears of nuclear annihilation with Biblical end-time beliefs.[20] Anticommunism did not just provide a framework for injecting God into the public sphere; it also facilitated opposition to growing calls for racial equality. As the theologian Anthea Butler explains, "The linkage of communism with civil rights work—combined with evangelicals' fear of the end times and the Antichrist—instilled fear and determination in evangelists and evangelical listeners alike."[21] By calling those who advocated for Black civil rights "communists," and equating communism with God-lessness, new evangelicals succeeded in defining anticommunism in relation to White Christian supremacism.

By the early 1950s, new evangelicals shed the movement's fundamentalist image to move closer to an "establishment" model, both theologically and politically. Adopting a softer and more accessible image, new evangelicals claimed to speak on behalf of a White Christian nation at war and took up the mantle of their nineteenth-century predecessors who had viewed themselves as the righteous and rightful representatives of American society. For some, like the activist Fred Schwarz, who started the School of Anti-Communism and the Christian Anti-Communist Crusade, fundamentalist separationism gave way to new evangelicalism in the name of fighting communism. For others, such as the pastor Billy James Hargis, who founded the Christian Crusade, joint membership in groups like the John Birch Society opened a door to secular conservatism.[22] Across the board, ready to do battle against atheistic communism, both new evangelicals and fundamentalists became God's chosen White patriots.[23] Moreover, Christian anticommunist crusades temporarily enabled CPs and Catholics to work together;[24] their shared hatred of communism temporarily overcame their antipathy toward one another—at least until John F. Kennedy's presidential campaign revived tensions in 1960.

Nonetheless, it should be noted that many fundamentalists of this era embraced a doctrine of strict theological separationism, which held they must keep themselves apart from the outside world and operate in relative institutional isolation from other conservative political movements (i.e., the outsider model). Fundamentalist separatism demanded separation not only from anything that could be deemed modernist, both in theological, political, and cultural terms, but also from anyone who fellowshipped with modernists or liberals. (Hence the public split from the wildly popular, big-tent, new evangelical Reverend Billy Graham, noted in table 4.1.) It would, however, be a mistake to think the radically "other" theological position adopted by fundamentalist preachers, like Bob Jones Jr. and Carl McIntire, cleaved a neat line of ideological separation between their world and that of either the new evangelicals or secular America.

Surveying the devastation of World War II and facing what they perceived to be an existential threat from communism and "the menace of atheistic secularism promoted by big government at home,"[25] fundamentalists doubled down on their opposition to liberalism and commitment to theological separationism. Anticommunism facilitated the crossover of Christian apocalyptic thought into secular politics and encouraged conservative Protestant political activism and engagement. At the same time, however, hostility to liberalism and distrust of big government reinforced fundamentalists' antiestablishment impulses and antipathy toward large-scale institutions. Thus, the post-war era was a period of oscillation between establishment and outsider positions, both between new evangelicals and fundamentalists and within fundamentalism.

On one hand, new evangelicals increasingly positioned themselves as the establishment and fundamentalist separatists claimed the outsider mantle. On the other hand, separatist fundamentalists simultaneously advocated for institutional isolation and threw themselves into anticommunist political organizing, oscillating between sociopolitical engagement and disengagement. And while premillennialism encouraged saving individual souls over social reform, it left open the question of how to save the most souls. There is a mistaken tendency to view postmillennialism as having an exclusive purvey to encourage aggressive political engagement when, in practice, theological and political distinctions are not so clearly drawn. Rather, premillennial dispensationalism has produced conflicting attitudes toward social and political engagement, as is clearly evidenced in the following section detailing Falwell's progression from preaching the righteousness of political disengagement to spearheading the Christian Right.

By the 1970s, as a new fundamentalist culture emerged, Falwell sought to resolve the "establishment-or-other" paradox in favor of manifesting a new establishment and creating a new political order in his fundamentalist image. In many ways, oppositional fundamentalist outsider attitudes—most notably the hostility to liberalism and secularism—were incorporated into the ideological foundation of the Christian Right. But, in order for the movement to be formed, the basic tenet of fundamentalist separatism first had to be tempered.

A Man of His Time

Born in 1933, Jerry Falwell grew up in Lynchburg, Virginia, a privileged son (along with a twin brother, Gene) of a self-made entrepreneur. World War II took a toll on Lynchburg, and Falwell's father's "business empire began to collapse during those painful years."[26] An alcoholic, Falwell's father was emotionally unavailable to his boys. Yet after the war, the economy picked back up, and the Falwell boys came of age in a relatively prosperous community. As a result, according to the historian Daniel K. Williams, "he developed a strong faith in the private sector and became an enthusiastic advocate of a strong defense policy."[27] These traits closely mirror those of Falwell's right-wing contemporaries—both secular and religious—whose conservatism was predicated on a deep and abiding love for American capitalism and small government, and a simultaneous dependence on government defense spending.

At age nineteen, Falwell underwent a conversion experience and joined an evangelical Baptist church in Lynchburg. On the recommendation of his pastor, Falwell chose to attend Baptist Bible College in Springfield, Missouri, which specialized in training ministers. He embarked on his training for the ministry with an experiential knowledge of his faith and with the knowledge "that the principal task of the Christian is to evangelize."[28] At Baptist Bible College, Falwell was steeped in the history and theology underpinning fundamentalist Protestantism. In 1956, having completed his education, he returned to Virginia to found an independent fundamentalist church, the Thomas Road Baptist Church (TRBC) in Lynchburg. The same year, he began to broadcast an "Old Time Gospel Hour" on radio, a program that eventually turned into a nationwide television broadcast and attracted millions of viewers. As we will see, Falwell's theological antimodernism did not extend to new technology, especially not when used in the service of bringing souls to Jesus.

Long before he officially entered the political arena, Falwell grew his congregation quickly and drew a committed following that was drawn to his fire-and-brimstone sermons. As one of Falwell's most comprehensive biographers, Michael Sean Winters, explains,

> The televised services of the 1970s may have been dressed up—broadcast from a larger, sleeker sanctuary and featuring bigger and better choirs—but the content of his sermons was mostly what it had been when Falwell first preached to the thirty-five dissidents in the old Donald Duck building. The wages of sin is death. Christ dies to take away our sins. The Christian has only to be born again to receive eternal redemption. Once saved, Christians should live godly lives lest the Enemy tempt them to unbelief. Week in and week out, these were Falwell's most common themes, running even through

those sermons that began to tiptoe into the political realm, such as his de-nunciations of communism.[29]

While Falwell slowly began to include pointed political asides in his ser-mons, he maintained a separatist stance and explicitly opposed mixing reli-gion and politics throughout the 1960s—at least when it came to ministers playing an active role in the civil rights movement.

In a widely distributed 1964 sermon condemning Martin Luther King Jr.'s role in leading the march on Selma, Alabama, Falwell famously pro-claimed, "Preachers are not called to be politicians, but soul winners." Rather than being called to advocate for racial justice, Falwell believed preachers should redouble their efforts to save souls, alleging, "If as much effort could be put into winning people to Jesus Christ across the land as is being exerted in the present civil rights movement, America would be turned upside down for God." For Falwell, the godly thing to do was not call for racial equality, but for conversion, leading him to "feel that we need to get off the streets and back into the pulpits and into the prayer rooms."[30] Falwell's sermon reflected a premillennialist and separatist religious mindset that prioritizes individ-ual salvation and demands the rejection of secular politics.

For many, including Falwell, premillennialism absolves individuals of their obligation to act in defense of the oppressed and subjugated. But by disavowing action in the face of injustice, this version of premillennialism lends its support to the maintenance of supremacist systems. While sep-aratism can, in some contexts, be an act of resisting supremacy, to choose separatism requires that one is, first and foremost, free to choose and, sec-ond, that one can largely live independently of existing institutions. In the context of Jim Crow America, then, racial privilege served as a prerequisite to fundamentalist separatism. For Falwell, premillennialism worked in the service of segregation, as he interpreted it as a justification for inaction. Thus, his sermon reflected a White supremacist mindset, requiring not only a fundamentalist separation from politics but the ongoing separation of White from Black people. The two mindsets—sociopolitical and ra-cial separatism—were inseparable for Falwell and many White American fundamentalist Christians in the 1960s. In the 1970s the trick for Falwell would be to figure out how to finesse the reactionary doctrine of premi-llennial separatism into a future-oriented and proactive doctrine that could be used not just to maintain but to advance a politics of White, Christian, male supremacism.

The Grassroots: With or without Falwell, a New Fundamentalism Grows from the Ground Up

Whether or not Falwell was ready to take on the forces of secular politics in the late-1960s, the conservative Protestant grassroots certainly was.
Anticommunism not only opened the door for the mainstreaming of new
evangelical premillennial thought but also introduced CPs to conservative
activists from whom they could learn hyper-local organizing strategies. As
Lisa McGirr's work has shown, over the course of the 1960s and early
1970s, suburban Orange County, California, conservatives, much like their
East Coast New Right counterparts, transitioned from anticommunism to
single-issue campaigns, focusing on local sex education initiatives, school
busing, gay rights, pornography, and abortion.[31]

Contrary to Connie Marshner's claim, quoted in the epigraph to this
chapter, that mothers were unorganized, unaware, and politically disen-
gaged prior to the Child Development veto campaign in 1971, parents'
groups, largely comprised of evangelical and fundamentalist Protestants,
were raring to go by 1969. One such campaign, in Anaheim, California,
was launched in 1968–1969 to oppose the introduction of the Family
Life and Sex Education (FLSE) program and was premised on concerns
that the introduction of a sex-ed curriculum would not only expose children to inappropriate material but also undermine the authority of parents to determine how best to educate their children.[32] A "Parents' Action
Guide" from this period warned that "[children's] individual rights and
freedoms are eroding quickly. Discrimination against Christian parents
and children is becoming widespread."[33] Illustrated with drawings of con-
ventionally attractive parents and with ample use of checklists and bullet
points, the accessible, easy to follow, and engaging guide laid out a comprehensive plan of action for conservative parents to follow in order to
have their voices heard. Intended to "help you to become a 'voice of reason' in the spiritual battles facing the Church today," the Action Guide
proposed parents recruit like-minded parents to form a "Public School
Awareness committee." Mirroring the coffee klatch strategy employed by
the John Birch Society, the guide encouraged serving refreshments and
recruiting members through personal social and church networks. The
end goal was to craft a unified agenda centered on concrete actions that
parents could easily undertake, including launching a petition, organizing
a letter-writing campaign, running a phone call campaign targeting local

elected officials, engaging talk radio hosts, swamping school board meetings, and running for office.

Anti–sex education campaigns such as this one drew support from right-wing anticommunist organizations, including Billy Hargis's Christian Crusade and the John Birch Society's Movement to Restore Decency (MOTOREDE). Campaigns and organizations cropped up across the country, from California to Michigan to Oklahoma, as did right-wing organizations expressly formed to target FLSE.[34] A 1973 study written by Lawrence J. Haims identified an extensive list of groups that were working to combat sex education curricula. Alongside MOTOREDE, Christian Crusade, and "two other far-right organizations . . . Let Freedom Ring and the American Education Lobby," these included Sanity on Sex (SOS), Mothers Organized for Moral Stability (MOMS), Citizens for Parents Rights (CPR), People Against Unconstitutional Sex Education (PAUSE), the Citizens Committee of California Incorporated (CCCI), Mothers for Decency in Action (MDA), Friends of the (name of state) Schools, Concerned Citizens Information Council (CCIC), Parents Opposed to Sex Education (POSE), Citizens for Moral Education of Central Florida (CMECF), Concerned Citizens of Hawaii (CCH), Parents Opposed to Sex and Sensitivity Education (POSSE), Illinois Council for Essential Education (ICEE), Committee to Halt Indoctrination and Demoralization in Education (CHIDE), and Associate Citizens for Responsible Education (ACRE).[35] The study further identified:

> tactics [that] have been employed in virtually every local anti-sex education campaign: 1) Committees spring up . . . ; 2) Speakers arrive on the scene . . . ; 3) Some churches give support . . . ; 4) Meetings are disrupted . . . ; 5) Half-truths and dubious documentation start making the rounds . . . ; 6) Emotional appeals are made . . . ; 7) Teachers and other school people become suspect . . . ; 8) Publications are passed around . . . ; 9) Letter writing starts . . . ; 10) Radio and TV get into the act; 11) Pressure is put on public officials . . . ; 12) Dark hints of future evil are issued . . . ; 13) Threats and intimidation become commonplace.[36]

Archival documents such as these amply demonstrate that by the late 1960s and early 1970s, conservative Christians had access to a blueprint for organizing in opposition to sex education and a host of ad hoc groups providing organizational support. The Kanawha School Board controversy in West Virginia during this time illustrates both how closely the above tactics were followed and the growing political engagement and activism of CP parents. It also demonstrates how CNR activists began to provide institutional support for the CP grassroots in the mid-1970s.

Beginning in 1969, the county of Kanawha became embroiled in a long-running battle over public education curricula, when a local woman, Alice Moore, or "Sweet Alice" as she came to be called,[37] won election to the local school board on a platform of fighting mandatory sex education. A fundamentalist originally from Mississippi, Moore drew on a national right-wing discourse that connected sex education to communism, and "within months of taking office in early 1970, [she] had managed to overcome opposition to her view that the sex-ed curriculum was anti-Christian, anti-American, and indoctrinated students with an 'atheistic and relativistic view of morality' that ran counter to her own firm conviction that God's law is absolute."[38] While Moore won and the skirmish over sex education was relatively quiet and quick, the next controversy resulted in a protracted and bloody battle.

In March 1974 Moore turned her attention to textbook selection and launched a campaign to block the inclusion of books that advanced multiculturalism, secular humanism, or any values that did not comport with those held by fundamentalists. John Egerton, writing for *The Progressive* in 1974, reported, "Mrs. Moore's assertion was that most of the books on the language arts list contained material that was disrespectful of authority and religion, destructive of social and cultural values, obscene, pornographic, unpatriotic, or in violation of individual and familial rights of privacy."[39] According to a chronology of the events in Kanawha from the William Martin archive, early in the controversy, in April 1974, Moore reached out to Mel and Norma Gabler, a fundamentalist Texas couple who spearheaded the textbook challenge movement. Over the next several months, the playbook identified by Haims's study was operationalized as committees were formed, churches became involved on both sides of the debate, Moore went to the media, petitions were launched, and school board meetings were flooded with concerned parents. In June, "a Concerned Citizen Group formed," and "over the summer the Christian-American Parents Association embarked on [a] letter-writing campaign [and] held [a] rally at Municipal Auditorium." Dubious documentation took the form of protest fliers that included excerpts from books "that were never a part of the lang arts program." By the fall, the Kanawha County controversy expanded to include a school boycott, picketing at "mines, schools, school bus garages, industry, [and] trucking companies," devolved into violence (including fire bombings and a shooting), and began to attract national media attention and draw in outside actors.[40]

On one side were fundamentalist parents, faith leaders from the surrounding areas, and national conservative activists, including representatives of the Heritage Foundation and the John Birch Society. On the other side were liberal parents, the majority of Black churches, the school superintendent, and representatives of the West Virginia Human Rights Commission, National Association for the Advancement of Colored People (NAACP), and the Young Women's Christian Association (YWCA).[41] Of note, Connie Marshner personally went to Kanawha County to provide Moore's camp with assistance and to lead a training in January 1975.[42] On one hand, the need for outside support and intervention from groups like the Heritage Foundation and MOTOREDE points to a recognition of the power of the fundamentalist grassroots on the part of these organizations. On the other hand, fundamentalists' willingness to accept support demonstrates a surprising openness to work with those from the outside and suggests a transformation in separatist attitudes was underway.

In her study of the Kanawha controversy, Carol Mason, a gender and women's studies scholar who studies the right, draws attention to the gendered and racialized dimensions of the conflict while cautioning against any oversimplification that reduces the matter to racist backlash. Mason argues that adopting a backlash frame can obscure the "very legitimate claim that the protest, and other curriculum disputes, made: that new schooling *can* yield an altered sense of community with new social identities and different social relations."[43] Read in this way, anti–sex education campaigns and conflicts over school curricula should be understood as political struggles to impose one particular set of social relations over and above all others through ideological production and policymaking. Rather than recognize the radicality of what they were trying to do, conservative Christians used the discourse of backlash to claim their actions were defensive. To illustrate how this process played out, it is worth quoting at length from Clayton L. McNearney's depiction of the controversy:

> So, what seems to be the case in Kanawha County is that the protesting parents have simply turned the [Health, Education, and Welfare curricular] guidelines to their own advantage. In doing this, the protesters have had to restructure their own thinking and begin to see themselves as a

minority. This, of course, has been a more difficult thing for them to do. The opponents of the texts began, as we said, with the largely unquestioned assumption that they represented the majority. They have found that their effectiveness locally, i.e., in Kanawha County, has been dependent upon their ability to demonstrate that they are, in fact, the majority. Or, at least, it is dependent upon their ability to cause the politicians and other powers that be to re-examine the question and, therefore, not automatically deal with them as simply an insignificant disgruntled minority. At the same time, the arguments they have found to receive the most sympathetic hearing nationally and which would seem to be most effective in preserving their way of life have been those which are derivative from the recent Court cases and the HEW guidelines, i.e., arguments of a minority.[44]

Thus, while CPs framed their campaigns in relation to a defense of the majority's "traditions," they also actively reconfigured what was meant by the "traditional" and cast themselves in the role of a victimized minority. The discourse of "secular humanism" further contributed to the sense that CPs were victims.

Mason argues that Moore played a pivotal role in bridging the anticommunist rhetoric of the 1960s with the antisecular humanist language of the 1980s, a move that Mason correctly asserts is often elided by scholars of the NCR.[45] Coded in terms of "humanistic philosophy" by Moore, the fears conjured by secular humanism functioned as an empty signifier for right-wing Christians. Instrumentalized by Moore and taken up by the media, "the specific term 'secular humanism' gained widespread popularity and currency as *the* name of the dreaded conspiracy against 'our children.'"[46] As we will see in chapter 5, the boogeyman of "secular humanism" helped unify a host of perceived threats to the family and facilitated the convergence of a plurality of single issues under the umbrella of "pro-family" politics. In speaking to conservative Catholics' rejection of secularism and to fundamentalists' rejection of modernism and liberalism, it also helped to fuse both groups' shared sense of victimhood as they believed they were faced with a common enemy.

The Kanawha County textbook controversy is just one example of many that demonstrate how, by the early 1970s, the fundamentalist grassroots were reconsidering their place relative to the political culture. While anticommunism had politicized fundamentalists, pulling them toward engagement with secular society and facilitating the development of a religiously informed political worldview, strict separationism had demanded they adopt an isolated and removed posture. Generations of the fundamentalist faithful had been raised straddling the "establishment-or-outsider" paradox, taught to embrace an experiential faith that eschewed rationalist thought and modernism, and encouraged to embrace the mandate to save souls, but not clear if that required standing apart from or intervening in secular society. But, as the 1960s gave way to the 1970s, local activism and grassroots organizing suggested that strict separationism might not be as important as some had thought.

Falwell Finds Politics

The fundamentalist grassroots appeared ready to publicly claim a stake in the political future of the country. But in the early 1970s, it was less clear where fundamentalist elites stood. Just one year before conservative Christians in Anaheim, California, launched their anti–sex education campaign, Falwell had, after all, called on Christians to stay out of politics. And so, before Falwell could become a religious political entrepreneur, he had to undergo a transformation that would resolve his own establishment-or-outsider paradox in such a way as to justify a newfound embrace of political activism.

Much like Paul Weyrich, Falwell was prone to self-mythologization and frequently claimed that abortion motivated him to become a political actor. But the timeline for Falwell's political awakening in the mid-1970s does not neatly align with the 1973 Roe decision, and there is little evidence that abortion was a significant motivator for him early on. What then drove Falwell to reject his earlier claim that preachers should be "soul winners" and instead embrace preachers being "called to be politicians"? In all likelihood, Falwell was motivated in response to federal government action—just not on abortion.

In 1973 Falwell was more focused on the Securities and Exchange Commission (SEC) than the Supreme Court. In the span of fewer than fifteen years, Falwell had built his Thomas Road Baptist Church in Lynchburg from the ground up, created one of the nation's most enduring megachurches, and began broadcasting his "Old Time Gospel Hour" sermons over the radio and on local television. He then turned his sights to the creation of a mega-televangelist ministry and what would become a world-renowned fundamentalist Baptist university. But to expand his televangelist reach to national television and build a university, Falwell needed to raise a large amount of capital in a short amount of time. To raise funds, he launched a campaign that relied on what Susan Friend Harding has termed "sacrificial giving." As Harding explains, "the whole point of giving to a God-led ministry is to vacate the commercial economy and to enter another real, a Christ-centered gospel, or sacrificial, economy in which material expectations are transformed."[47] In need of cash to expand his operation, Falwell turned to his flock. Persuading his followers to glorify God by digging deep into their bank accounts, he sold bonds with an 8 percent return. Within a short time, he had raised almost $6 million. By 1972, Liberty University was under construction, the "Old Time Gospel Hour" was being televised nationally—and Jerry Falwell was under investigation for financial fraud.[48]

In Falwell's telling, the SEC "inquiry was to determine if any literature had been supplied to potential buyers of the bonds that was false or misleading," but the federal complaint alleged the church engaged in financial "fraud and deceit."[49] Regulators suspected that the Thomas Road Baptist Church had insufficient collateral assets to support the bond sale. Although Falwell was eventually cleared of "intentional wrongdoing," he was ordered to call in the bonds and TRBC's finances were put into receivership.[50] Falwell's recollection of being informed he was under investigation is telling: he writes, "My nerve endings begin to tingle at the very first sign of government interference in the work of the church."[51] For Falwell, the SEC investigation was not the result of his own financial mismanagement of TRBC but rather was evidence of federal persecution. Much like the IRS taking action to enforce the desegregation of Christian schools, the SEC investigation was a targeted financial attack that was read through the lens of "religious freedom." It is, therefore, likely that Falwell viewed the SEC's actions as a personal threat to both his religious and economic freedom.

And yet, we might contest this understanding of the SEC investigation: the government did not come knocking on Falwell's door without first receiving an invitation. As Falwell built his televangelist empire, he embraced modern technology and began to take on an increasingly prominent public persona. While still theologically committed to separatism, Falwell began shedding his "otherness" and rushed out to greet the rest of the world. The tension between being an insider/outsider and adopting an inward-looking/outward-facing worldview (i.e., the fundamentalist paradox) was never far from the surface of the institutions Falwell built during the 1970s. This tension was particularly acute in Falwell's approach to media and technology.

Much like his New Right counterpart Richard Viguerie, Falwell was a pioneer in the use of computerized direct mailings. Beginning in 1976, Falwell became the first televangelist to start using Epsilon Data Management to solicit donations. Reporter Dirk Smillie writes, "Falwell crafted his letters with theological abandon, hitting his mortal enemies with blunt force. With Epsilon's help Falwell added urgency to his appeals, pushing donors to act fast. Epsilon led Falwell to discover that the secret to steady income is consistency; getting lots of donors to give a little, but regularly."[52] A typical Thomas Road Baptist Church solicitation letter would be personally addressed and might warn of the impending financial collapse of the ministry if the addressee did not pledge to give ten dollars every month to keep the broadcasts up and running.

While Falwell's political awakening likely began in response to both CP grassroots organizing and the SEC investigation, it crystallized with a series of "I Love America" rallies, which were held in state capitals and other cities across the nation beginning in 1976.[53] That year, Falwell and a collection of singing students "visited 141 cities in America, performing, preaching, and praying in huge churches, public auditoriums, and great coliseums to standing-room-only crowds of enthusiastic, grateful pastors and their people."[54] The rallies were intended as a "call to political action," meant to exhort religious folks to take back their country from immoral and sinful actors.[55] And while the rallies were in many ways an expression of Falwell's morality politics, focusing on the evils of pornography, homosexuality, and abortion, they were also a continuation of an older anticommunist politics. Falwell elaborated on the Cold War fusion of American nationalism and premillennial dispensationalist beliefs to push a political ideology that linked the imposition of fundamentalist morality with the continued survival of the nation. This new fundamentalist politics not only sought to save souls ahead of the apocalypse; it sought to establish fundamentalist beliefs as guiding principles of social and political action.

Falwell's initial refusal of worldly politics and later full-fledged embrace of religious political organizing bears witness not only to the influence of the establishment-or-outsider paradox on his religious development, but also his attempt to resolve it for himself and his followers. And while Falwell increasingly came to dominate the public face of fundamentalism, he was not alone. Falwell's rallies were simply the most visible representation of a broader movement by religious political entrepreneurs that had been taking place and was gathering steam. In the 1950s Bill Bright had founded Campus Crusade for Christ, and the following decade Pat Robertson got the Christian Broadcasting Network off the ground. In 1974 Ed McAteer founded the Christian Freedom Foundation. In 1975 Francis Schaeffer, C. Everett Koop, and Harold O. J. Brown formed the Christian Action Council.[56] The following year, Jimmy Carter would become the first self-identified "born-again" Christian to be elected president, shining a spotlight on new evangelicals and opening their political horizon of possibility.

In the middle and latter half of the decade, religious political entrepreneurs, led by Falwell, sought to take on the role of shepherding the fundamentalist flock into mainstream politics. But rather than return to a previous model of fundamentalist or evangelical politics that focused on either saving individual souls (the outsider model) or campaigning for social reforms (the establishment model), Falwell and his ilk sought to redefine the very nature of the American sociocultural establishment and craft the state in (what they believed to be) God's image.

Building Institutions to Build Ideas: The Production of a Conservative Protestant Coordinative Discourse

While Paul M. Weyrich, Richard Viguerie, Connaught Marshner, and other denizens of the New Right were busy building the New Right's coordinative discourse, the Reverend Jerry Falwell was building a fundamentalist coordinative discourse of his own. By pioneering the use of new media and fundraising technologies, facilitating institutional growth via church planting, constructing an ideological justification for coalitions, and mobilizing an identity of victimhood, Falwell mirrored the developments on the CNR and prepared the ground for CPs to join forces with their conservative Catholic counterparts.

During the mid- to mid-late 1970s, Falwell implemented what, in hindsight, looks a lot like a strategic plan for political organizing. In 1980 Ed Dobson, Ed Hindson, and Jerry Falwell published *The Fundamentalist Phenomenon*, an insider's guide to the "Resurgence of Conservative Christianity."[57] The same year, Falwell published a book titled *Listen, America!* that included a "Biblical Plan of Action." In both, Falwell identifies what he sees as the critical next steps for fundamentalists to take, with the former focusing on institutional developments and the latter largely on the need for prayer, "national repentance," and identifying "the national sins" that "moral Americans need to be ready to face": abortion, homosexuality, pornography, humanism, and the fractured family.[58] While *Listen, America!* advanced a theological justification for Falwell's seemingly newfound politics, *The Fundamentalist Phenomenon* was a how-to manual, with the final chapter of the book concretely identifying a three-prong organizing plan, centered on "church planting," "Christian education," and "national revival."

Christian Education

In the 1930s and 1940s, fundamentalists focused on building colleges and other institutions, but these tended to be regional rather than national in scale and scope.[59] Liberty Baptist College, which Falwell founded in 1972, was started with the intention of training students to "go out in all walks of life to impact this world for God." "Young people would come to Lynchburg, study with us, be a part of America's fastest growing church, see it expanding, see it growing," Falwell explained. At Liberty, they would "learn how it's done, catch the vision, carry the vision to their own home-towns," and then they would "translate what God was doing in Lynchburg to church[es] in every state of the union and every country of the world."[60] In short, the college was to serve as a site of ideological production and to facilitate the educational relationship necessary for the production of cultural hegemony.

The idea of producing a new generation of politicized CPs was not the exclusive provenance of Falwell. For example, Bill Bright's Campus Crusade for Christ actively sought to recruit college students to Christ and conservatism throughout the 1960s.[61] (We might also draw parallels to other conservative youth organizations, such as Young Americans for Freedom and the Young Republicans, which sought to inculcate conservative political values and train the next generation of conservative activists.) However, the aims and scope of Falwell's educational program, which included a primary and secondary school alongside Liberty College, surpassed that of his predecessors. With Liberty, Falwell would not have to compete with outside secular forces for the loyalty and allegiance of the youth; rather, he would be able to have a community of ready and willing soldiers for Christ come to him.

Church Planting

Falwell also understood Liberty's mission in terms of "church planting," which he effectively transformed into a form of grassroots political organizing. Looking to the future, Falwell explained:

> Church planting must be a major priority on our agenda for the eighties. *We must establish thousands of new Bible-believing churches committed to practical evangelism and political activism.* Our goal at Liberty Baptist College is to train pastors who can effectively explain the Scriptures, preach the word with power and conviction, and lead their congregations as sincere men of God. We must turn America around at the grassroots, local-church level.[62]

Church planting is an evangelist process that relies on starting a new church to bring God's word to a specific community that is deemed to be underserved. The founders of the church may or may not come from within the community, and the church may or may not be an independent or unaffiliated entity. While church planting can take many forms, ministry experts Craig Van Gelder and Dwight J. Zscheile explain that the process has regularly taken its cues "more from business entrepreneurship and institution-building than from the practices of cultivating discipleship, discernment, and witness."[63] If we understand church planting as a process that creates decentralized, local-level organizations whose members have a shared identity and belief system, its utility as a social and political organizing tool is immediately recognizable. Church planting, and the associated practice of educating Christian pastors, should be understood as part of a sophisticated institutional strategy for producing not only a particular kind of discipleship but also a particular kind of fundamentalist political ideology. Falwell essentially sought to create an inward-facing religious community in relative isolation from the world around it, so that the community could storm the ramparts of secular politics and revolutionize the outside world.

National Revival

Falwell was uniquely willing to form unexpected coalitions, much like his New Right counterparts, and he sought to ally with other Bible-believing Christians, Catholics, and even Jews. As a fundamentalist, he was initially wary of working with nonfundamentalists, but over time he evolved to believe that "evangelical Christians have a tendency to pride themselves on their intelligent comprehension and defense of the faith. Fundamentalists tend to pride themselves on their strong, uncompromising stand for the faith. We must have both! We must stop polarizing each other by constant and unnecessary attacks on 'straw men.'"[64] The "straw man" Falwell referred to could quite possibly have been himself, as some isolationist preachers, like Bob Jones, attacked him for weakening fundamentalism. Anticipating that critique in *Listen, America!*, Falwell expressed support for maintaining denominational difference, writing, "Our freedoms have given us the privilege and luxury of theological disagreement. I would not for a moment encourage anyone to water down his distinctive beliefs." But he also advanced there was a pressing need for broad-based, interdenominational coalition building because "When the entire issue of Christian survival is at stake, we must be willing to band together on at least the major moral issues of the day."[65] To get to a place where he could theologically justify working in concert with nonfundamentalists, Falwell turned to Francis Schaeffer, a fundamentalist theologian who had developed a theory of "co-belligerency."[66] Borrowing from Schaeffer, Falwell began espousing the theory of co-belligerency, which justified forming coalitions with nonfundamentalists to move beyond the high wall of fundamentalist separation that had kept the former socially and politically isolated.

Schaeffer, whose writing on abortion was touched on in chapter 1, operated a fundamentalist ministry, L'Abri, in the Swiss Alps and was something of an "evangelical star" by the mid-1970s. Unique for his robust engagement with secular philosophy and emphasis on intellectualism, Schaeffer was a prolific author and responsible for making two films that galvanized the conservative Protestant base, particularly around the issue of abortion.[67] Following Schaeffer, we can define a co-belligerent as "a person with whom I do not agree on all sorts of vital issues, but who, for whatever reasons of their own, is on the same side in a fight for some specific issue of public justice." Schaeffer applied this theory to the problem of evangelical and fundamentalist coalition building, urging strategic unity: "Separatists stress holiness. Evangelicals stress love. Both are essential. Fundamentalists must learn not only to act in love but to act so as to show their love. The Evangelicals must learn to confront. Fundamentalists and Evangelicals mutually confront opponents of Biblical positions when problems face them."[68] Two years later, at a 1982 meeting held to bridge the evangelical-fundamentalist divide, Schaeffer and Falwell plainly spoke about the need for increasing and strengthening the religious coalitions being built by the Moral Majority in terms of adopting co-belligerency as an organizing strategy.[69]

This was met with no small measure of opprobrium from hardline Baptists, whom Falwell labeled "Bob Jones Fundamentalists," and were represented by groups like the Fundamental Baptist Fellowship. In 1985 the Fellowship warned against the "pseudo-fundamentalism" of Falwell and "Denounce[d] all attempts to pave the way for unity between Roman Catholicism and bible-believing Christianity."[70] But Falwell took Schaeffer's message to heart, and he believed "that there is no Biblical mandate against evangelical Christians joining hands for political and social causes as long as there was no compromise of theological integrity."[71] Rather than capitulate to isolationist pressure from hardline fundamentalists, Falwell doubled down on his commitment to resolve the "establishment-or-other" paradox in favor of creating a new establishment.

What makes Falwell's approach to revival unique is that he, along with Schaeffer, transformed theology into political ideology. A biblical case can certainly be made for ecumenism and/or interfaith cooperation, but Schaeffer and Falwell's framing of co-belligerent cooperation places it squarely within the realm of secular politics. Biographer Sean Michael Winters argues that Falwell inadvertently secularized religious morality "by reducing religion to ethics."[72] I would add to this that beginning in the early 1970s, when Falwell first turned his attention to reviving the moral fabric of the nation, he also inadvertently began reducing religion to political coalition building. Falwell's embrace of the theory of co-belligerency, and his subsequent communication of it to the fundamentalist base, served as a "constitutive moment" that set fundamentalists on the path of broad-based conservative coalition building and toward the creation of the Religious Right.[73]

Creating Victims

Falwell did not only use the threat of apocalyptic financial ruin to encourage donations; he also drew on the Manichean conception of the political that mirrored the New Right's strategy of embracing single-issue politics. In the mid-1970s, as Falwell toured the country holding "I Love America" rallies, his sermons had taken on an increasingly political tenor as he warned of the imminent destruction of the nation as a result of Americans' sinful behavior. Throughout 1977 and 1978, Falwell became increasingly active in politics, preaching against the sin of homosexuality and the "threat" of gay people. In 1977 Falwell explicitly dove into politics when he joined Anita Bryant in Dade County, Florida, to fight a gay rights ordinance. High off the win in Dade County (the ordinance was overturned), Falwell turned his attention to California and the Proposition 6 campaign, which would have banned lesbians and gay men from teaching in public schools.

While Prop 6 was a direct attack on gays and lesbians, a flier for a rally Falwell held in support of the measure framed the issue in terms of "protecting" Christians from the threat of homosexuals. Prop 6 would "protect children," who would otherwise be subjected to "homosexuals influencing [them] to adopt the 'gay' lifestyle," and it would "protect" parents' right to shape the worldview of their children. Those who would be harmed by the legislation, that is, gay and lesbian teachers, were appointed as perpetrators, while those who sought to harm them were assigned the status of victims. A subsequent fundraising letter dated November 3, 1978, warned of the imminent peril Christians faced: "In the years that lie ahead, I believe that we will be in a constant battle for our lives. This experience called Proposition Six in California is only one chapter in the book. This is just the beginning. We must never give up. America is worth saving."[74] By constructing Bible-believing Christians as victims of an unjust and illegitimate secular humanist agenda, Falwell helped cultivate an ideology of victimhood that supported Christian supremacist policies and an ideology of Christian supremacism.

Concluding Thoughts

Given the robust participation of fundamentalists in shaping Cold War politics and leading anticommunist crusades, and their growing experience as grassroots activists, it is unrealistic to think fundamentalists were incapable of developing a resistant politics until Paul Weyrich came along. As a group, fundamentalists, with Jerry Falwell at their helm, rose up to meet cultural changes; they were not passive before coming into contact with CNR activists, and they were not merely acting in self-defense. Throughout the early and mid-1970s, Falwell and other fundamentalist faith leaders came to embrace many of the trappings of "modernism" even as they condemned its influence. As fundamentalist believers became increasingly politically active and organized at the grassroots level, fundamentalist leaders turned their attention to institution-building and political organizing. Falwell and his fundamentalist brethren developed an outward-facing politics of their own accord as they began to envision becoming the establishment rather than merely fighting it.

The institutions that Falwell created in the 1960s and early 1970s provided one foundation for the NCR's rapid rise to national prominence. Reenvisioning the role of radio broadcasts employed by previous generations of fundamentalist preachers, Falwell built his ministry using technology, beginning with radio broadcasts (1956), expanding to local television (1957), national television (1970s), and eventually, after the acquisition of Jim and Tammy Faye Bakker's Praise The Lord network, twenty-four-hour satellite coverage (1987). In conjunction with new religious educational institutions, this technologically advanced media empire was used to communicate a nascent political ideology to a mass audience of observant followers.[75] Falwell's vision of what fundamentalism would accomplish and how it would do so—through ideological coalition building, church planting, technological innovation, and education—fits comfortably within the framework of coordinative discourse production. This coordinative discourse operated along multiple temporal registers: immediate and short-term change was pursued through policy advocacy on issues like Proposition 6, while Christian education and co-belligerency provided a framework for advancing midrange programmatic ideas. At the same time, the long-term project of national revival sought to provide Bible-believing Christians with a new means of understanding the American political system and their place in it. Through his ministry, Falwell essentially created a plan for fundamentalist and evangelical political activism that demanded full-frontal engagement with the outside world. At the same time, the Bible-believing Christian framework of Falwell's institutions helped solidify the identity of his followers as self-identified fundamentalists, who were nevertheless building bridges to other evangelicals, as well as with other "moral" conservatives. In sum, Falwell sought to create a system for both producing and enacting a new political fundamentalism.

As fundamentalists resolved the establishment-or-outsider paradox in favor of engaging with and transforming the secular political and cultural establishment, they found themselves in a unique position as the decade drew to a close. They possessed ample economic resources, a large, readily mobilized base, and political will, but they lacked both the political capital (in the form of established institutions) and cultural capital (in the form of intellectual traditions that could be used to substantiate their religious claims) necessary to fully enter mainstream politics. Beginning in 1979, they would tap into these resources by joining forces with the New Right.

5

PRO-FAMILY POLITICS AND THE POLITICAL CONVERGENCE OF CONSERVATIVE CATHOLICS AND PROTESTANTS ON THE AMERICAN RIGHT

Well, first of all, from our point of view, this is really the most significant battle of the age-old conflict between good and evil, between the forces of God and forces against God, that we have seen in our country. We see the antifamily movement as an attempt to prevent souls from reaching eternal salvation, and as such we feel not just a political commitment to change this situation, but a moral and, if you will, a religious commitment to battle these forces. I don't mean to be simplistic about it, but there is no other way to view what is happening, especially if you read, believe in and understand Holy Scripture. And I think any other interpretation of it misses the point.

—Paul Weyrich

The family is under vicious assault.

—Jerry Falwell

We have together, with the Protestants and the Catholics, enough votes to run the country. And when people say, "We've had enough," we are going to take over.

—Pat Robertson

In 1976 the nation elected its first openly born-again, evangelical Protestant as president. A peanut farmer from Georgia, Jimmy Carter not only brought new attention to American Protestantism but also promised to restore some measure of morality to an executive branch tarnished by the venal behavior of Richard Nixon. While on the campaign trail in 1976, Carter expressed genuine concern about the challenges facing American families and had pledged to hold a national conference, the White House Conference on Families (WHCF), to address the changing social, cultural, and economic welfare of American families. Carter's interest and investment in the family stemmed from his complicated relationship with and genuine commitment to his Baptist faith. It was also an expression of his attempts to negotiate the tension between the conservative social values he held on a personal level and his broader commitment to liberal political ideals. But by championing the WHCF, Carter inadvertently created an opening for the convergence of conservative Catholics and Bible-believing Protestants. By the end of his term, conservative religious activists had wrested all control over the discourse of "the family" from Democrats and had successfully used it to facilitate the process of building a New Christian Right (NCR) coalition.

As we have seen, throughout the 1970s, White conservative Protestants (CPs) and Catholic New Right (CNR) political entrepreneurs were organizing on parallel tracks. Both groups were developing and refining their political positions and establishing institutional, organizational, and grassroots support. As the decade drew to a close, both groups had identified the benefits of undertaking concerted political activism while also coming to recognize the limitations of their respective strategies. Independently of one another, each came to a point where they acknowledged the need for ecumenical coalition-building. On the CP side, this was facilitated by the development of the doctrine of co-belligerency. On the part of CNR activists, poor electoral returns created a new sense of urgency when it came to broadening their coalition. By 1979 these two groups were poised to converge. They just needed a consolidated discourse to knit together the plurality of issues that were, on one hand, galvanizing the Bible-believing grassroots and, on the other hand, promoted by the New Right. This discourse would center on the protection and preservation of the "traditional family."

Surveying the religious-political landscape, Connie Marshner and Paul Weyrich began to see a convergence between their interests and those of fundamentalist and evangelical Protestants in harnessing the coercive power of the state to regulate and structure social relations. It was this shared commitment to imposing Christian values through family policy that formed the basis of an alliance between conservative Catholic and Protestant elites. Seizing on increased attention to the composition and place of the family in American society, CNR elites developed a comprehensive "pro-family agenda," which formed the basis for the explosive mobilization of the NCR and helped reshape the American electorate.

There is much to be said about the discourse of "the family" in American political discourse during this time.[1] However, my interest here is not in the family per se, but rather in how the development of "pro-family" politics was spearheaded by and bore the imprint of the CNR. The creation and adoption of a pro-family political agenda asks us to take a closer look at the links between CNR and evangelical/fundamentalist Christian Right actors, as the latter relied extensively on the help of their Catholic counterparts in crafting the pro-family agenda. As Michael Lienesch has observed, New Right actors "set much of the agenda for their politically less sophisticated recruits."[2] I elucidate these connections to draw out how conservative Catholics and Bible-believing Protestants forged a coalition that diminished the theological and political distance between them.

This chapter, therefore, details how CNR activists helped their CP counterparts launch the NCR movement with Falwell's Moral Majority at the helm. It begins by examining how both the successes and failures of the parallel organizing strategies undertaken by CNR and CP activists in the middle of the decade enabled a coalition to take shape in 1979 and 1980. A recognition of the similarities between these groups—and of the respective limitations of their individual strategies—pushed the CNR to pivot from a single-issue coalition strategy to the promulgation of an ideologically cohesive, multi-issue "pro-family" platform. From the end of 1979 through Ronald Reagan's election in November 1980, CNR activists turned their attention to building the Moral Majority into a successful movement, providing the latter movement with organizational, institutional, and ideological support. Using the WHCF as a springboard, CNR activists, most notably Connie Marshner, are shown to have been the architects of a cohesive political platform premised on defending the "traditional" family. In turn, this platform enabled the NCR to inject itself into the fray of national politics.

By November 1980, when Reagan rode a wave of conservative support to sweep the presidential election, the NCR had come into its own as a movement, "pro-family" politics had become the rallying cry of the right, and abortion, as an issue that was discursively constructed as a violent assault on the family, became one of the pivotal issues—if not *the* pivotal issue—for judging the conservative bona fides of elected officials. But the NCR did not stop with the election of Reagan; rather, the movement sought to advance "pro-family" policies that would transform American social relations. By way of demonstrating this process, the chapter concludes with an examination of how the Family Protection Act of 1981 sought to use the "traditional family" of a mythical past to justify the implementation of social policies in the present that would prefigure a White Christian supremacist political future—or, in the words of Pat Robertson, how conservative Catholics and Protestants sought to "take over" the nation.

A "Very Convenient Sink": The New Right Sees an Opening

Carter's proposal to convene a national conference to discuss American families was made in an already politically charged environment. More than a decade prior, the 1965 Moynihan Report had pathologized Black families and thrust discussion of family policy into the national spotlight. That same year, the Supreme Court legalized access to oral contraception for women in *Griswold v. Connecticut*. Over the next decade, the Court extended the right to unmarried women (*Eisenstadt v. Baird*, 1972) and legalized abortion (*Roe v. Wade* and *Doe v. Bolton*, 1973). At the same time, state legislatures moved to adopt no-fault divorce laws, and the 1964 Civil Rights Act transformed the status of people of color and women in the workforce by prohibiting discrimination in employment and education. This is to say nothing of a growing hostility among conservatives toward social welfare programs. As Melinda Cooper explains, "It was rather the growing realization that welfare was making women *independent* of individual men and freeing them from the obligations of the private family that turned a generation of social reformers against the welfare state tout court."[3] To wade into the waters of family policy, therefore, necessitated an engagement with questions of race, class, and gender as the family was both a site for enforcing and contesting White and male supremacism.

Throughout the 1970s, Paul Weyrich and other New Right activists had worked to mobilize single-issue coalitions that targeted abortion alongside other conservative issues. But the abortion agenda, as with other New Right single-issue agendas, was pursued by loosely affiliated and largely autonomous single-issue groups. By the mid-1970s the New Right had successfully built a network of think tanks and PACs and had articulated a political strategy—premised on ruthless pragmatism and ad hoc coalitions—in lieu of a cohesive political ideology. The nonhierarchical and diffuse structure of the New Right both enabled and required that single issues remain atomized. The benefit of this strategy was that it allowed Weyrich, and other conservative Catholics in the New Right, to aggressively support anti-abortion politics and a host of other issues without committing the identity of their movement to any one particular issue. But the strategy also suffered from limitations, as it failed to result in a cohesive and reliable conservative electorate, a fact driven home by the 1976 election, when conservatives not only lost the presidency to a Democrat but also failed to gain any seats in the House.

We might read Carter's election as reflecting an electorate—and a conservative movement—in transition as White Southern democrats began to migrate to the Republican Party and partisan identities crystallized. Despite 1976 being labeled "The Year of the Evangelical" by *Newsweek*, Carter's win was not the result of overwhelming Protestant support. Nixon's "southern strategy" had already begun the process of siphoning White union and religious voters from the Democratic Party. Four years prior, in 1972, the conservative pollster Arthur Finkelstein predicted, "Richard Nixon is going to be re-elected President in perhaps the greatest electoral landslide since James Monroe."[4] Finkelstein's projection was based on polling data that suggested Nixon would "carry the band of working middle-income people that surround these core cities," which Finkelstein referred to as "the Peripheral Urban Ethnics (PUE)." Finkelstein described the PUE as encompassing working- and middle-class ethnic Whites, who were in "large measure Catholic" but should not be considered "in terms of a Catholic vote."[5] Rather than being united around a shared religious identity, this swath of the electorate was defined by a shared identity formed in relation to "threat, control, power, security, respect and alienation." That November, Finkelstein's prediction came to fruition, as Nixon won the electoral college vote in forty-nine states, and 52 percent of the Catholic vote swung to him.[6] But just four short years later, Carter received a strong majority of the Catholic vote (57%) even as he failed to win a majority of the Protestant vote (securing only 46%).[7] While underway in the mid-1970s, the realignment of conservative White Protestants *and* Catholics to the Republican Party was not yet complete. The CNR could not reliably turn out the conservative Catholic vote or mobilize a broad-based coalition on the basis of a "conservative" political identity. The movement found itself in need of coalition partners if it wanted to have a sustained impact on national elections. Thus, the Catholic New Right set its sights on conservative Protestants.

In the lead-up to the 1978 election, Weyrich and Marshner identified a new groundswell of anti-abortion sentiment within the CP grassroots. Memos from the time, such as one titled "Democrats Fear Single-Issue Groups," detail the success of anti-abortion groups who "distributed three hundred thousand anti-Clark leaflets in Iowa churches on the Sunday before the November 7 election."[8] Randall Balmer remarks that "the correspondence surrounding the 1978 election fairly crackled with excitement," as Weyrich "stumbled on the issue—abortion—that would motivate politically conservative evangelical voters."[9] But family issues were already of central concern to the Protestant grassroots, which had proven itself to be a formidable force in local campaigns and elections focused on resisting the threat of government overreach through the imposition of federally mandated programs, like school busing and sexual education, and "secular humanist" progressive curriculums. Much like the New Right, the Protestant grassroots lacked a cohesive political platform to stitch together these disparate issues. While abortion would be central to this platform, it would not form the basis of it. Instead, the "family" would.

Against this backdrop, in January 1978 Carter announced that planning for the WHCF would commence—and the political hazards that would trip up the conference immediately became apparent.[10] As early as December 1978, Carter's aides began suggesting that he shelve the conference. A handwritten note addressed to Kathy Cade, Mrs. Carter's director of projects, urged Carter to abandon the conference before it could become "a very convenient 'sink' into which all political opposition (if they are clever and no matter what their persuasion) can pour all kinds of distortions, stimulating fears, misrepresentations, exaggerated misinterpretations about his intentions, and his plans for interfering with communities and that 'sacred of sacreds' the mythical American family."[11] With the economy faltering and conservative forces—both religious and secular—gathering at the ramparts, the WHCF was increasingly viewed as a political liability by Democrats and a political opportunity by conservatives.

After the 1978 midterm elections, when Republicans gained three Senate seats and fifteen House seats, mounting recognition of the importance of abortion developed into an increasing awareness of the political potential for a broad array of "family issues," elements of which CNR actors had been legislatively championing for the past decade. While there were Christian religious justifications for opposing abortion, the issue also came to encapsulate the fears of more secular conservatives over the perceived degradation of the family and the corrosive effects of feminism. By affording women the agency to chart their own paths in life, access to safe and legal abortion was a conduit for women's economic and social emancipation from their husbands and the family. Thus, the legalization of abortion at a federal level could be cast not only as the sanctioning of murder but also as an assault on "traditional" gender roles and the family. By early spring 1979, Paul Weyrich was jubilant about "great changes taking place in the political process," as a result of a meeting with "leaders of various Christian education and morality groups" to organize around the danger of federal "government intrusion into the family.[12]

As the summer of 1979 heated up, Connie Marshner got to work developing a "pro-family" platform and movement. In July of that year, she launched Library Court, a "fairly close-knit coalition of over 20 nationwide groups whose leaders meet every other Thursday morning to discuss tactics."[13] Chaired by Marshner, Library Court members worked together to share information, strategize, and volunteer for explicitly political "assignments"—including lobbying elected representatives, launching letter-writing campaigns, and drumming up press—to spur the pro-family agenda onward.[14] Interestingly, members of Library Court went to great lengths to assert the group's independence, with Gary Potter, the president of Catholics for Christian Political Action, stating, "I don't like the label 'conservative' because I think a lot of conservatives lack spiritual vision, and they represent the right wing of liberalism. At Library Court, we are concerned with political issues serious enough to be moral issues." *Conservative Digest* took great pains to drive home the point, also quoting Jim Wright, the head of the Christian Coalition for Legislative Action, as saying, "The pro-family movement is not a subset of the conservative movement," and noting that another unnamed member remarked, "The New Right influences the pro-family movement only to the extent that it shares the movement's God-centered views and that the movement needs the New Right's technical guidance."[15] Given Marshner and Weyrich's active involvement in creating Library Court and their deep personal religiosity, there is something disingenuous about the denial of the New Right's influence on the coalition.

But distinguishing Library Court, and by extension the nascent "pro-family" movement, from the New Right served an important purpose: it enabled the individual coalition partners to deflect criticism directed at their allies. As John "Terry" Dolan explained at a Religious Roundtable gathering of pro-family activists several years later,

> It is my belief, and our polling data confirms this, that there is at the very least a subconscious effort on the part of some in the media—I would say without hesitation that this applies to the three networks—to tie us all together, to use the negatives that each one of us may have as part of this coalition to beat the other to death, and to attempt to stunt our growth. Therefore, I would make the point over and over that your movement is separate, that your motivations are vastly different than mine and the people I represent. Now, that does not mean we are not allies. We certainly are.[16]

This strategy of maintaining the discrete identity of coalition members was made possible by the New Right's pioneering use of ad-hoc single-issue coalitions, which were diffuse and horizontally organized. But it also had another effect, which may or may not have been intentional: it obscured the influence of conservative Catholic thought on the development of the NCR, which was fronted by Bible-believing Protestants.

The New Christian Right: The New Right Helps Build a Behemoth

Around the time the Library Court coalition was forming, Weyrich and Howard Phillips set out to turn the Reverend Jerry Falwell into a political activist. They found Falwell, and other CP elites, more than eager to become co-belligerents for the conservative cause. The work Falwell and others had already put into building their televangelist empires ensured that Bible-believing Protestant leaders were well-funded and had ready access to a mass audience, while the newly popular strategy of co-belligerency had primed them for coalition work across denominational lines and within the sphere of secular politics. Moreover, single-interest issues, like sex education curricula and the preservation of tax-exempt status for segregation academies, had galvanized the interest of the Bible-believing grassroots.

Despite their full coffers and energized base, Bible-believing Protestants lacked access to the political networks and institutions necessary to fully participate in mainstream electoral politics. Fundamentalist hostility to modernity and liberalism, coupled with the faith group's establishment/ outsider oscillation, had cut off most roads to power. This position of relative political weakness was only reinforced by a Protestant theology that had historically encouraged emotive faith above reason and eschewed the development of institutionalized knowledge production. Put simply, Bible-believing Protestants needed the New Right's institutional and intellectual support as well as their political know-how and Washington, DC, insider access.

It is well known that NR activists were instrumental in having recruited Falwell to found the Moral Majority at a meeting facilitated by Bob Billings, the founder of the National Christian Action Coalition.[17] Weyrich is even said to have coined the name Moral Majority, playing off Nixon's use of the term "silent majority," which implied conservatives were a victimized majority. While they may appear contradictory on their surface, parallel claims to the occupation of majority and victim statuses in the 1970s and early 1980s were not in themselves paradoxical. Rather, these claims worked together: by couching their political agenda in terms of self-defense (or "backlash") against progressive attacks on "tradition," conservative Christian actors asserted the right of conservative Christians to have their voices heard in the public sphere while simultaneously manufacturing new fears to help mobilize the grassroots. In doing so, they effectively obscured the proactive nature of their political ideology and helped birth a narrative that views the American right as always and necessarily reactionary.

The launch of the Moral Majority in August 1979 was just the beginning of a wave of Christian Right political advocacy groups. Ed McAteer, a former field director for the Conservative Caucus, founded the Religious Roundtable just weeks later in September. Alongside Robert Grant's Christian Voice, Timothy LaHaye's Family America, and Bob Billings's National Christian Action Coalition, these groups formed the core of the Christian Right zeitgeist that swept the nation in the fall and winter of 1979–1980. The Religious Roundtable played a key role in fostering the growth of the NCR coalition by providing Christians with "an educational forum for political issues."[18] Christian Voice introduced evangelicals to

K Street and pioneered the production and use of religious voter scorecards (which ranked elected officials' voting records based on a Christian morality scale).[19] In his comprehensive history of the movement, William Martin quotes Weyrich as having said the Moral Majority "was by no means the most important of the groups that had been formed." [20] Nonetheless, it garnered the most media attention and came to represent the movement as a whole. In many ways Falwell's Moral Majority came to be synonymous with the NCR in the 1980s.

Drawing on his expansive "Old Time Gospel Hour" television and radio empire, Falwell turned his millions of followers on to politics, channeling their political energies into a national C-4 lobbying organization, Moral Majority Inc., with state-level affiliates, and a C-3 Moral Majority PAC.[21] As founder and spokesperson for the Moral Majority, a political coalition aimed at registering voters, endorsing candidates, and influencing public discourse and governmental policy, Falwell not only helped create the NCR political movement; he became its public face. As the spokesman for the movement, Falwell amplified conservative Christians' claims to represent the body politic. The very name of his organization suggested that social conservatives could demand a seat at the head of the political table because, as the majority of the nation's electorate, they were entitled to shape public policy.

Falwell and others were responding to a very real desire and demand for concerted political action on the part of the conservative Christian grassroots. And many of the NCR's pioneers—Falwell chief among them, but no less Pat Robertson, Oral Roberts, and James Robison—arrived on the scene with captive audiences from their radio and television ministries. The Christian Right had no shortage of foot soldiers ready to do battle for America and Christ. But while CPs possessed two key elements for social movement mobilization—a grassroots base and significant fundraising prowess—neither factor directly translated into political know-how or the presence of necessary organizational leaders.[22] For this, Bible-believing Protestants needed the New Right.

In the first months after the public emergence of the NCR, the movement's reliance on and debt to the New Right was a source of near-constant attention, both in conservative and mainstream media. A pamphlet written by Connie Marshner's husband, Dr. William H. Marshner,[23] stated, "To a remarkable extent, these Christian activists have found skilled allies in one and only one place, among one and only one group of organizations—the group loosely known as the 'New Right.'"[24] Itself reflecting the close relationship between the two groups, William Marshner's pamphlet was first published by Weyrich's CSFC before being reprinted by the Religious Roundtable.

Similarly, the August 1979 issue of *Conservative Digest*, a New Right publication, was dedicated almost entirely to the birth of the Moral Majority and the growth of the Christian Right. In addition to noting the size and potential scope of the Moral Majority, the magazine highlighted its close ties to New Right political entrepreneurs:

> The bedrock of the Moral Majority will be fundamentalist Protestants and, in particular, the estimated 15 million Americans who watch Falwell's "Old Time Gospel Hour" regularly. (Falwell already has 2 million names on his "Gospel Hour" mailing list.) But Falwell intends to build a coalition of far more than his own religious following, and he hopes to persuade leading Catholics, Mormons and Jews to join his board. Indeed, New Right leaders Paul Weyrich, an Eastern Rite Catholic, and Howard Phillips, a Jew, worked closely with Falwell in setting up the Moral Majority.[25]

Recognition of the closeness between these two groups was not limited to New Right publications. An AFL-CIO's legislative alert warned about the "*use* of religion" at the hands of New Right operatives and drew linkages from the John Birch Society through Falwell to Weyrich and Howard Phillips.[26] It was no secret then that the New Right had a hand in bringing the Christian Right to the political table.

It would, however, be a mistake to view the New Right as a secular fairy godmother or to read Weyrich as a religiously disinterested political broker in this coalition. Weyrich was, first and foremost, a conservative Catholic. When discussing the convergence of conservative Catholics and Protestants, Weyrich used the first-person plural, interpellating himself as a *Catholic* activist embedded in the movement: "Unite Protestant fundamentalists and Catholic ethnics into a political bloc by emphasizing emotional 'family' issues?" an August 1979 article in *Time* asked, before answering with a quote from Weyrich, "A year or two ago nothing was happening. . . . Now we're moving.'"[27] In stressing the ecumenical nature of the coalition, Weyrich again identified as a part of it:

> This is no false unity based on papering over doctrinal differences. . . . *Our* very right to worship as we choose, to bring up *our* families in some kind

of moral order, to educate *our* children free from the interference of the state, to follow the commands of the Holy Scripture and the Church are at stake. These leaders have decided it is better to argue about denominational differences at another time. Right now, it is the agenda of those opposed to the Scriptures and the Church which has brought *us* together (emphasis added).[28]

Put simply: Weyrich and his fellow CNR activists were themselves a part of the NCR coalition, and the coalition was a vehicle for advancing not only the positions of Bible-believing Protestants but also those held by conservative Catholics.

In his column in *Conservative Digest*, Weyrich captured the reciprocal nature of the CNR/CP Christian Right coalition:

Each part of the coalition brings something useful. The fundamentalist/ evangelical Protestants bring knowledge of and devotion to the Bible which no politician can shake. In addition, they have mastered the use of television and radio for their efforts, and this will make communications easier. The Catholics and Eastern Orthodox bring philosophical underpinnings which can help make the coalition impervious to attack, so that this alliance will not be swept away as happened earlier in the century. The Catholics also bring with them their rich cultural traditions from places like Ireland and Italy which can serve well during these times of attack on the family.[29]

For Weyrich, Bible-believing Protestants brought mastery of the media to the table, while Catholics brought the philosophical and intellectual heft needed to avoid another embarrassing Scopes debacle. Leaving little question that the coalition was a two-way street, Weyrich's formulation nevertheless suggests that CPs had more to gain from allying with conservative Catholics. While this is true from an organizational and strategic standpoint, it downplays the importance of the coalition for the CNR. Allying with Protestant religious conservatives allowed CNR activists to import their "philosophical underpinnings" into a new coherent conservative ideology and socially conservative political identity.

Given the political outsider status of fundamentalist and evangelical Protestants, the New Right's transfer of institutional knowledge and political leadership was invaluable for the growth of the NCR as a political movement. But CNR brokers did something else for the NCR: they constructed an ideologically cohesive policy platform, rhetoric, and political identity for the latter movement to coalesce around and glom onto. In short, the CNR were the architects of both the communicative and coordinative discourses employed by the NCR.

Developing the Pro-Family Platform

Drawing on their socially conservative single-issue positions and Catholic natural law traditions, CNR brokers utilized the politically charged signifier of the family to generate new coalitions and produce a vehicle for the NCR to ride into the mainstream of American politics via Republican Party incorporation. This is not to suggest CPs entered into the Christian Right coalition without a politics of their own and without strong judgments on issues like homosexuality and sex education curricula. Rather, it is to highlight the influence of conservative Catholic thought and CNR political activists on the development of the "pro-family" platform.

This assertion echoes that of the political scientist Timothy A. Byrnes, whose work is centrally concerned with the role Catholic bishops played in creating the pro-life movement and in connecting abortion to American partisan electoral politics. Byrnes credits Paul Weyrich and Richard Viguerie, in conjunction with abortion activists Judy and Paul Brown of the Life Amendment Political Action Committee, with expanding abortion from a single issue into a broader platform by "associating the phrase 'right-to-life' with a much broader social agenda" that encompassed a broad array of family "rights."[30] "The 'brilliant innovation' of the new right," Byrnes writes, "was to expand the 'pro-life' agenda into a 'pro-family' one." Doing so "allowed them to incorporate opposition to abortion into a broader political agenda and to channel that opposition into coordinated and conservative political action."[31] While there is no denying the importance of abortion to the Catholic leaders of the New Right, "pro-family" politics neither began nor ended with abortion. Rather, the "pro-family" position embraced by the CNR reflected an all-encompassing worldview and policy agenda that sought to structure everything from gender roles and familial relations to the economy and role of the state.

From her first days in Washington, Connie Marshner was committed to advancing a conservative policy agenda to use federal legislative policy to impose her conservative Catholic view of appropriate gender and family social relations. Her successful campaign to oppose universal childcare in the early 1970s (discussed in detail in chapter 3) was just the beginning of her "pro-family" activism. Marshner was, therefore, primed and ready to take on the WHCF long before the Carter administration was ready to host the conference. In 1978 she drafted a memo outlining a preliminary strategy to oppose the conference, which outlined the following steps: "generate interest among traditionalist individuals and parents to apply for the Advisory Committee"; "encourage traditionalist individuals or parents, and political conservatives with family 'angles' to seek those positions"; "consider the desirability/feasibility/advisability of staging our own conference, maybe in late 1979, to strongly state a defense of the traditional family and a critique of the socialist schemes for 'family intervention.'"[32]

These steps were intended to help advance the "pro-family" platform, which focused on six core elements that, in turn, formed the basis of the "pro-family" position more broadly adopted by the NCR. The "pro-family" platform was premised on: (1) normatively defining the family as a heterosexual unit comprised of a father, mother, and children, and affirming the family as the basic unit on which society and, by extension, the government is founded; (2) opposing abortion, because to do so was to protect ("preborn") children; (3) opposing the legal equality of women by ensuring the failure of the Equal Rights Amendment; (4) supporting the passage of the Family Protection Act (discussed in detail later); (5) advocating on behalf of "family rights," that is, defending parental rights and opposing the ascription of rights to children; and (6) advancing tax policies that would benefit the family and "traditional" gender roles within it.[33] Meeting agendas from Library Court largely mirror these planks and also reflect early and consistent hostility for homosexuality and gay rights, as well as a recurring focus on targeting Planned Parenthood and influencing judicial nominations.

Concern over so-called family issues was nothing new for either conservative Catholics or Protestants. What was new about the "pro-family" platform was the way in which it sought to reshape the state in line with conservative Christian ideas about the family. Thus, "pro-family" politics went beyond those policies that most directly affected families to include a political vision for the state. The desire to subjugate the state to the family is suggested in a "Pro-Family Position Paper," which asserted:

> Families are strong when they have a function to perform. A government which, regardless of the benevolence of its intentions, attempts to take over the family's job of providing for the needs of its members, is laying the groundwork for the destruction of the family unit. . . . Government policies

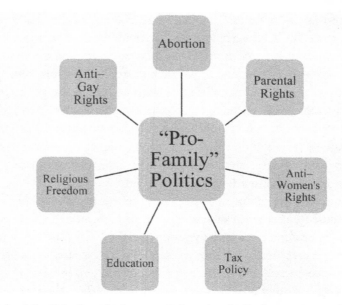

"Pro-family" politics formed a big-tent ideological umbrella that encompassed most, if not all, of the New Right's socially conservative single-issue constituents and provided the common ground on which a Catholic/Protestant coalition could be built.

which disregard the synergistic nature of families, and which run rough-shod over the moral concerns of ordinary parents and families have got to be corrected. . . . Yet today, the government is on a collision course with the Judaeo-Christian morality, on which the nation was founded, and to which a majority of citizens still adhere. Government must not be allowed to undermine the morality of the nation; such policies must be corrected.[34]

While the "traditional" family supersedes the state, it nonetheless requires the state's help to reassert its primacy. It should then come as no surprise that the position paper proposed a host of reforms to the media, social services, church-state separation, employment law, tax policy, welfare policy, education, and health insurance, among others. Many of these proposals spoke to the "red flag" single issues promoted by the New Right throughout the 1970s. But the "pro-family" platform did not only strategically bene-fit from the work of CNR political actors; it also substantively bore the intellectual imprint of conservative Catholic thought. The Catholic influ-ence is particularly evident in the definition of the family adopted by the "pro-family" platform and its embrace of the principle of subsidiarity, which asserts the family is the main building block of society and government.

The position paper defines the family as "the most important unit in society," responsible for "determin[ing] the vitality and moral life of society." As the basis of all social relations, "the family is the best and most efficient 'department of health, education, and welfare.'" This definition mirrors the argument advanced by the Catholic juridical scholar John Finnis in his 1979 treatise *Natural Law and Natural Rights*. Finnis posited that the family must be at the center of any society directed toward the common good. The principle by which the family should be organized, according to Finnis, is "subsidiarity," defined as "assistance" in relation to its "Latin root *subsidium*." Subsidiarity, Finnis wrote, "affirms that the proper function of association is to help the participants help themselves, or, more precisely, to constitute themselves through the individual initiatives of choosing commitments ... and of realizing these commitments through personal inventiveness and effort in projects."[35] Developing along this vein, the "Pro-Family Position Paper" asserts that "wherever possible, the principle of subsidiarity must be observed: the level of government closest to the individual and lowest in the chain of government should be the government of first resort in the provision of social services, as in everything else." Thus, we arrive at a theory of government that is ordered on principles drawn from Catholic philosophy: on the basis of the natural law, "traditional" gender and familial roles are necessary for the maintenance of society and the pursuit of the good, and social welfare should, ideally, be relegated to the familial and community level. At the same time, government can still play a role in structuring social relations and ordering social welfare. And so, instead of CP hostility to government, we begin to see hints of an approach that seeks to use the state to coerce behavior.

Launching the Pro-Family Movement

Behind the wheel of the "pro-family" car was Connie Marshner, who took advantage of the opening created by the White House Conference on Families to put the "pro-family" discourse into action. Marshner was a committed conservative Catholic and a dyed-in-the-wool social conservative. But she also was a sly and strategic political activist. While she certainly did not act alone, receiving support both from other CNR activists and Bible-believing religious leaders, like Falwell and Tim and Bev LaHaye, Marshner was instrumental in developing the pro-family platform. And it was this platform that transformed American political discourse and enabled the NCR to influence the Republican Party.

In support of the "pro-family" agenda, over the span of a year and a half Marshner launched a number of "pro-family" coalitions and working groups, including Library Court and the National Pro-Family Coalition, "an umbrella organization for about 150 anti-abortion, anti-Equal Rights Amendment groups,"[36] and began publishing the *Family Protection* newsletter. She also sent a trained army of social conservative activists to swamp the WHCF delegate selection process in order to ensure there would be representation of the "pro-family" platform at the WHCF.

The opening shots in what would become an all-out war over the family were fired less than three months after the formation of the Moral Majority, on November 14, 1979, when a group of ostensibly grassroots conservatives, loosely organized under a pro-family umbrella, upended a bureaucratic convening in Virginia. At what was expected to be Virginia's run-of-the-mill statewide meeting for selecting delegates to attend the national White House Conference on Families, a battle ensued over the definition of the family, family values, and the government's place in family life. An ambitious project, the WHCF was conceived of as not a single conference but rather three regional conferences—to be held in Baltimore, Minneapolis, and Los Angeles in the summer of 1980—which would bring together the voices and concerns of "ordinary" Americans from all fifty states.[37]

To represent the concerns of everyday Americans adequately and accurately, delegates would be selected by each state to attend the national conference. Writing for the *Washingtonian*, Lewis Z. Koch reported, "Marshner decided to billet her baggage at the various state conferences, where, beginning last November, delegates and issues for the national conferences were chosen by ballot. To stampede the state sessions with her troops, Marshner deliberately raised the issues of abortion and homosexuality. Unless her people were elected, she warned, those causes would be advanced at the national conference."[38]

While Marshner personally opposed both legal abortion and rights for homosexuals, she acknowledged that these single issues were incorporated into the "pro-family" platform because of their volatility. Koch reported that Marshner remarked, "In a political battle, first you have to polarize people in order to get their attention, in order to get people to talk about

issues. . . . If you polarize, people either agree with you or they don't. Polarization is an essential political tool."[39] And polarize the people she did.

In Virginia, over three hundred individuals dedicated to a conservative interpretation of the family swamped the delegate selection process;
this "Pro-Family Coalition" succeeded in electing twenty-two out of the
twenty-four available delegates and produced a statement of principles
that articulated a socially conservative vision of what the American family should look like. Cast as a spontaneous grassroots mobilization by the
New Right organizer JoAnn Gasper,[40] *The New Right Report* let slip that
the victory was perhaps not the product of an organic and spontaneous
outpouring of conservative sentiment: "Conservative leaders such as Morton Blackwell, Mrs. JoAnn Gasper, Dr. Onalee MacGraw, and Virginia
delegate-elect Larry Pratt masterminded a successful conservative takeover of the Virginia Conference on Families."[41] Pro-family forces continued
to gain momentum, sweeping the delegate selection process in Oklahoma
and Minnesota in the following months.[42] Throughout this time, Marshner worked through the pages of *The Family Protection Report* and *Conservative Digest* to keep New Right members informed and enraged about the
imminent danger the WHCF posed to the traditional family.

Crafting a Pro-Family Communicative Discourse

While the WHCF provided a useful political opening for social conservative activists, the strength of "pro-family" politics as a political ideology
stemmed not only from its fortuitous timing but also from its deployment
of narratives of victimization and construction of the "traditional." For the
"pro-family" platform to succeed, it needed to be communicated in a way
that would: (1) defend its necessity; (2) minimize its radicality; and (3) galvanize conservative Christians and ensure their buy-in. Building on their
earlier successes in cultivating an ideology of victimhood, they promoted
"pro-family" politics using the discourse of backlash to construct a new
"traditional family" to defend.

As seen in the epigraphs to this chapter, both Paul Weyrich and Jerry
Falwell framed "pro-family" politics in the starkest of possible terms: the
"traditional" family was under violent attack. At stake was no less than the
everlasting souls of good Christians, Protestant and Catholic alike. Or, as
Weyrich put it, "pro-family" forces were part of an "age-old conflict between
good and evil." Christians were, therefore, victims, motivated purely by a

desire to hold the line against the radical agenda of a Godless left hellbent on the destruction of the family and society. Writing to conservative WHCF delegates, Marshner struck a strident tone, urging them to see themselves as participants in a battle that was bigger than any one individual:

> The defense of the traditional family at the White House Conference will depend on you and other pro-family delegates. The situation will not be pleasant; in fact the days you spend at the Conference may be among some of the most unpleasant of your life. But you will not be alone, either: other pro-family activists throughout the country are planning and working to see to it that the White House Conference reacts to *our* agenda for the American family, and not that of the enemies of the traditional family.[43]

In the summer of 1980, the "pro-family" movement succeeded at forcing the Carter administration and, more importantly, the Republican Party to react to its agenda by inserting its planks into delegate discussions, staging a walk-out of the Baltimore WHCF, and hosting a conference, pointedly named America's Pro-Family Conference, of their own.[44]

The Pro-Family Conference was made possible by Marshner and other CNR actors, who promoted the pro-family agenda heavily in New Right publications and brought their significant organizational skills to the table to help make it happen. And yet, promotional materials for America's Pro-Family Conference suggested the (Protestant) Christian Right had taken the lead on "pro-family" issues. It is here that we see the "pro-family" agenda and ideology developed by the CNR become the "pro-family" platform of the NCR.

Represented by speakers from the National Christian Action Coalition, the Moral Majority, Campus Crusade for Christ, the Eagle Forum, and the National Right to Life, America's Pro-Family Conference aggressively asserted that a new political day was dawning. A brochure for the conference circulated by the Moral Majority stated, "A new term has appeared in our lexicon: pro-family. It describes a political philosophy, based on the sanctity of life, the worth of an individual, and the importance of traditional family life as the cornerstone of American society."[45] The movement's claims to uphold "traditional family life" served to tether modern Christian conservatism to the country's (imagined) past. Furthermore, by claiming ownership over the nation's traditions and founding, the NCR asserted it represents the nation's rightful majority.

Echoing a 1980 "Family Issues Voting Index," published by the National

Christian Action Coalition,[46] the Moral Majority pamphlet implies that, at some undefined point in the past, "pro-family" ideology was hegemonic. Recent changes, however, threatened the "traditional" family:

> The "New Deal" brought new definitions of responsibility. Uncle Sam re-placed dad as a provider of food and clothing. We have witnessed the "Great Society" of the Sixties, and the bloated Welfare programs it spawned in the Seventies. Today's society is characterized by "planned parenthood," the pill, no-fault divorce, open marriages, "gay rights," "palimony," test-tube babies, women's liberation, uni-sex, day-care centers, child advocates, and abortion on demand. A man is no longer responsible for his family; a woman need not honor and obey her husband. God has been kicked out, and Human-ism enthroned.[47]

In order to construct the past as the halcyon days of "traditional" family values, the argument must render invisible the material realities of the fam-ily and the conditions that necessitated the development of social welfare policies. Moreover, by invoking a normatively coded good "before" and an evil "after," it reifies the "traditional" and venerates the past supremacy of (White) Christian men. By focusing on the protection of vulnerable sub-populations, specifically women and families, whom it alleges are harmed by secular humanism, the NCR was able to claim represent the victims of liberal aggression. And, while not explicitly addressing the civil rights movement or feminism, it implied that the perpetrators of this aggression were feminists, homosexuals, and people of color.

The pamphlet's reference to the New Deal and the Great Society clearly draws on Cold War discourses that equate government action with the evils of communism/socialism, while also promoting slippage between the threats posed by communism and (secular) humanism. This slippage can also be found in Marshner's notes, as reflected by a handwritten comment she jotted at the top of a summary of family legislative proposals, which reads, "Family is in crisis—what cause + solution depend on whether Xian or secular humanist/socialist."[48] The universal boogeyman of "secular hu-manism," which could be held responsible for everything from abortion, feminism, and gay rights to desegregated schools and sex education cur-ricula, was conjured to give a singular form to the multiplicity of threats perceived by religious conservatives.

CNR activists both injected a conservative Catholic worldview into the "pro-family" platform and brought conservative Catholic and Protestant social issues under a common umbrella. Having done so, the "pro-family" movement deployed a communicative discourse that cast Christians as a victimized majority in order to both sell its political program to the Christian grassroots and deflect criticism by claiming the mantle of self-defense. By constructing a common enemy out of secular humanism, conservative Christian activists helped create a shared identity of victimhood for Catholics and Protestants alike. At the same time, CNR and NCR elites used the myth of a "traditional" past to rhetorically justify advocacy for social policies in the present. If enacted, these policies would, in turn, prefigure new social relations that would form the foundation for manifesting an illiberal political.

Advancing a Pro-Family Coordinative Discourse

On July 17, 1980, less than a week after America's Pro-Family Conference, Ronald Reagan accepted the Republican nomination for president. The platform developed at the 1980 Republican National Convention reinforced the perception that conservatives were victims of a progressive agenda, highlighting the perceived threats to women: "We reaffirm our belief in the traditional role and values of the family in our society. The damage being done today to the family takes its greatest toll on the woman. Whether it be through divorce, widowhood, economic problems, or the suffering of children, the impact is greatest on women. The importance of support for the mother and homemaker in maintaining the values of this country cannot be over-emphasized."[49] While the Republican Party had not yet fully incorporated the NCR, it was clear from its platform that conservative Christian discourses were having an impact.

On October 1, 1980, the Reagan campaign formed a Family Policy Advisory Board (FPAB), chaired by Connie Marshner and tasked with establishing a "pro-family" strategy for the Reagan campaign (and, after November, the incoming Reagan administration). The Family Policy Advisory Board worked to create a broad sociopolitical platform for Reagan, which included the passage of (1) a human life amendment; (2) prayer in schools; (3) tuition tax credits; and (4) the Family Protection Act. The group also proposed that Reagan abolish the Department of Education and appoint Phyllis Schlafly to one of three roles: Supreme Court justice, undersecretary of defense, or secretary of education.[50] That fall, the FPAB advised Reagan on how to campaign on the "pro-family" platform, urging him to court the segregation academy and Catholic votes by pressing tuition tax credits. Weyrich also contributed to the effort, drafting a memo that urged Reagan to "unleash a strong attack on the White House Conference on Families," which would be directed to a "grass-roots or religious audience, possibly in the south."[51]

While there were behind-the-scenes tensions between Reagan and New Right activists who thought he was not doing enough to solicit religious voters and were concerned he would not be conservative enough,[52] Reagan nonetheless won over "pro-family" voters in November—and conservative Christians won over the Republican Party. By the fall of 1980, the NCR had moved into the mainstream of American politics, with the process of incorporation into the Republican Party underway and the movement termed a "civil rights group," at least in the conservative press run by Viguerie:

> The New Right Christians may be called a civil rights group, not in the sense, as in the case of blacks, that certain rights have been denied them, but in the important psychological sense common to all civil rights groups, that they have been shut out of politics and are now ignored. Feeling so oppressed, they have now become aggressors. The members of the Moral Majority, Religious Roundtable, National Christian Action Coalition, Eagle Forum, National Pro-Family Coalition, Catholics for Christian Political Action, Christian Voters Victory Fund, American Life Lobby, Christian Family Renewal, Concerned Women for America, and still other groups are asking, as blacks, women and other groups have done, for recognition, for status in the polity.[53]

That same month, *Conservative Digest* remarked on the changing status of religious conservatives, writing: "Until this year, the only political group in America to associate with these Christians was the New Right. . . . This year, however, the Republican Party proved to be the first major party hospitable to the New Right Christians. . . . The alliance of the Republican Party with the New Right Christians is understandable, given the ideological shaping of the Democratic Party."[54] Contributing to the sense that the Religious Right had integrated itself into electoral politics, Falwell claimed the Moral Majority registered three million *new* voters in advance of the presidential election.[55]

Nonetheless, movement activists sought to keep the pressure on and pushed for the reintroduction and passage of the Family Protection Act (FPA), a bill that closely echoed family policy proposals first sketched by

Marshner in 1974. Originally introduced by the New Right Republican senator Paul Laxalt in 1979, the FPA thrust a deeply conservative interpretation of the "family" into congressional political debate.[56] After the legislation failed to pass in the Ninety-Sixth Congress, it was reintroduced by Senator Roger Jepsen and Representative Albert Lee Smith in the Ninety-Seventh Congress with minor revisions.[57]

As reported by the Congressional Research Service, the legislation was divided into "six titles: 1) family preservation, 2) taxation, 3) education, 4) voluntary prayer and religious meditation, 5) rights of religious institutions and educational affiliates, and 6) miscellaneous."[58] In a concept summary of the bill, produced by Jepsen's office, the following core "pro-family" elements contained within Title I were highlighted:

+ Expansion and codification of parental rights as applied to determining the "religious and moral upbringing of their children";
+ Parental notification requirement for minors receiving contraception or abortion services from any organization that receives federal funding;
+ Limits the power of the federal government and legislates the supremacy of state statutes in matters pertaining to juvenile delinquency, child abuse, and spousal abuse;
+ Prohibits the Legal Services Corporation from undertaking litigation in support of abortion, divorce, and homosexual rights;
+ Mandates automatic payment of "dependent's allowance" for military personnel stationed away from their families;
+ Prohibits any federal funding for organizations that support gay rights.[59]

The bill's other provisions were no less in line with the "pro-family" platform: Title II, concerning taxation, "would make it more difficult for the Internal Revenue Service to deny or revoke exemption of a private school on grounds of discrimination,"[60] and aimed to amend the tax code to encourage "traditional" two-parent single-earner households by creating new tax-exemptions and deductions. Title III, focused on education reforms, would empower parents to have increased access to and influence over their children's public education and limit the federal government's power to regulate public education. Title IV would override the Supreme Court's decision in *Engle v. Vitale* and reintroduce school prayer, while Title V would exempt religious organizations from federal oversight.

Were the Family Protection Act to be enacted into law, it would effectively redefine the family and the place of people of color, women, homosexuals, and children in society. The FPA would undermine desegregation efforts, weaken the federal government's power to advance protections for historically underrepresented groups, and reassert the supremacy of (White) Christian men. Thus, the FPA was a comprehensive piece of legislation that sought to simultaneously limit the power of the state while also harnessing its coercive capacity to prescribe a particular set of social relations premised on the new definition of the "traditional" family. In a newspaper editorial, James A. Autry critically summarized the act as "a thinly veiled conservative manifesto, an omnibus of objectives established in the past few years by ideologues of the right, intended not so much to protect families as to impose an agenda of concerns on the rest of the citizens."[61] But the fact that it was an attempt to "impose an agenda" on the country was, perhaps, its greatest selling point for social conservatives.

While the "pro-family" movement's communicative discourse used backlash discourse to define the movement as being on the defensive, its coordinative discourse was defined in terms of its proactive nature. In a series of handwritten notes, seemingly penned by Marshner in preparation for a speech, the proactive nature of the FPA was stressed. the "FPAct [is] beginning to give us an *offensive*. Pornography, abortion, ERA, domestic violence. We've always been 'against.' Now there's something we can be 'for.'" [62] Senator Jepsen reiterated the proactive nature of the FPA in a letter to the conservative reporter James Kilpatrick, who criticized the bill in his column, writing, "It was imperative for conservatives to provide an alternative to the WHCF version of federalism. The Family Protection Act fulfilled that need. It was a positive measure instead of merely a reaction to liberal programs; supporters could be for something instead of constantly in opposition."[63]

The "FPAct will only go somewhere if PFM [Pro-Family Movement] goes somewhere," Marshner's notes continue, as the act is "the outgrowth of the movement as well as the cutting edge of the movement."[64] Thus, on the one hand, the FPA reflected the coordinative—or policy—discourse of the "pro-family" movement, as it was drawn from the "pro-family" platform. On the other hand, the FPA formed the basis of the "pro-family" coordinative discourse as it was the means by which the movement could advance its ends. The "pro-family" coordinative discourse also included specific proposals for constitutionally banning abortion (Human Life Amendment) and injecting prayer into public education (School Prayer Amendment), as well as reversing no-fault divorce in the states. It also, as Melinda Cooper's work on the convergence of neoconservatism and neoliberalism has shown, sought to use welfare reform as a means of actively producing social relations premised on a conservative Christian worldview.[65] The FPA and the "pro-family" platform promoted a comprehensive set of policies that would reach into all areas of Americans' lives. Marshner was clear that "pro-family" issues were not isolated. Rather, the family was a conduit for attacking feminism, homosexuality, and desegregation, on one hand, and transforming public education, the tax code, welfare, and the criminal law, on the other hand.

The family was also the basis for raising an army composed of Christian soldiers who would go forth and do battle for God. Toward the end of a set of handwritten speech notes (presumably written by Marshner), the tone turns martial. In the left margin, there are a series of bullet points under the heading "What can you here in _____ do?" that read: "strategy; united front → linkages; neg + positive; offensive → FPAct; truth-or-consequences; principle." To the right, the text reads: "Succeed only if army behind us. That army has to be felt in Congress. Reward friends + punish enemies. Army will have respect only if world knows loud + clear that it stands for principle first, last, + always, + doesn't play national politics. There are tough things to be said—you, or the p-fm [pro-family movement], have to say them. . . . No one else defending family—if not you, who? Psalm 52:15 Green Olive Tree." Thus, the "pro-family" position was framed as both the basis for and the battle call of the NCR army.

By seeking to transform the relationship between the state and the family, the FPA aimed to comprehensively prefigure a *new* set of social relations on the basis of protecting the "traditional." The policy changes it sought to produce would have defined new embodied roles for and relations between men, women, and children and restructured the ways in which individuals related to one another in both the public and private spheres. Through the imposition of these new embodied roles, the FPA further sought to entrench a hierarchical social order premised on conservative Christian ideals. To do so would be to undo the secular foundations of America's liberal democratic institutions. Thus, the NCR did not merely want to stem the tide of cultural change; it wanted to reshape the country's politics by proactively advancing policies that took aim at the very foundations of the liberal political order.

Reconceptualizing the Success of the Catholic New Right

The "pro-family" platform enabled the large, easily mobilized evangelical grassroots base to become fused with the Republican Party. While the CNR crafted the pro-family umbrella in large part on the basis of its own political and religious beliefs, American Catholics do not represent a unified voting bloc, and the diffuse nature of the conservative movement meant the New Right did not have a cohesive grassroots base that could be easily mobilized. CNR actors, therefore, recognized early on the power of the CP grassroots and saw that the pro-family platform could be more effectively used to mobilize a voting base that would support their interests if it was publicly represented by the NCR. This is not to suggest that NCR leaders or the CP grassroots were without agency in this relationship; CPs entered into this coalition as a result of changes within their faith system and on the basis of their own political beliefs. Rather, it is to stress the enduring influence of the CNR in shaping the future of conservative Christian politics and the American political landscape.

When Ronald Reagan won the 1980 election, it seemed the NCR would have unprecedented access to mainstream political power. Phyllis Schlafly was eager to claim that at least partial credit for this success went to pro-family forces: "Ronald Reagan won both the nomination and the election because he rose the rising tides of the pro-family movement and the conservative movement. Reagan articulated what those two separate movements want from government, and therefore he harnessed their support and rode them into the White House like an athlete rides the ocean waves on a surfboard."[66] But the New Right and the NCR were not content to have sent Reagan to the White House; they wanted a seat at the political table, and they wanted the power to enact "pro-family" platform into law.

After Ronald Reagan's inauguration in 1981, the New Right and the NCR jockeyed for positions that would guarantee them access to power. The New Right was largely shut out of the new administration, with only one operative, Morton Blackwell, appointed to Reagan's cabinet. Hyperbolic outrage ensued, and the New Right lashed out, dedicating an entire issue of *Conservative Digest* to airing its fears about Reagan's appointments and cabinet being too moderate.[67] Christian Right leaders fared slightly better with appointments,[68] and they remained less vocal in their criticism of the president, preferring to apply softer pressure on Reagan to uphold his campaign promise to focus on social issues rather than delay in order to address economic issues first.[69] Even James Robison, one of the more outspoken Bible-believing critics of Reagan, was tempered in his criticism, noting he was "going to continue to speak forcefully but I'm going to knock gently."[70]

Initially, the New Right and the NCR both vacillated between outright criticism of and collaboration with the Republican president. Early on, Reagan told conservative Christians that he would turn his attention to social issues once his economic agenda was enacted. However, just six months into his first term, his decision to nominate Sandra Day O'Connor to the Supreme Court immediately frustrated both the New Right and NCR, as both groups feared she would not be conservative enough on social issues, particularly abortion. At first, conservative political entrepreneurs chose their words carefully, wary of alienating the new administration. Thus, while Weyrich and Howard Phillips went on the offensive, Weyrich pulled his punches when talking to the media: "I think the decision (to nominate Mrs. O'Connor) was made without all the cards in the deck. . . . I think when he (Reagan) has all the facts—if they are true—he may change his mind."[71] But the New Right was never much for pulling its punches, and that same month a headline in the *Washington Post* blared, "For Reagan and the New Right, the Honeymoon is Over." The article continued, "For some of the most vocal leaders of the New Right movement, the nomination was the latest in a series of slights and insults they have suffered from Reagan advisers which raise questions in their minds about whether the president really is their kind of conservative."[72]

NCR leaders were less vocal in their criticism but nonetheless expressed their frustration with the president delaying action on his campaign promises to them as a means of compelling the administration to act. And so began a recurring pattern: when Reagan repeatedly failed to sufficiently throw his weight behind socially conservative policies, the NCR would threaten to break with the president. The president would then endorse a policy promoted by conservative Christians, such as constitutional amendments on school prayer and abortion. In short, the president was willing to endorse the "pro-family" platform and, when push came to shove, he could be pressured into throwing social conservatives a bone. This pattern, of conservative Christian activists going hot and then cold on the president, persisted throughout Reagan's first term and into his second. Meanwhile, ever eager to play the role of insurgent and radical outsider movement, the

New Right more decisively broke with the Reagan administration, threatening to launch a "new third party called the Populist Conservative Party," and comparing Reagan to "Neville Chamberlain, the British Prime Minister who ceded Central Europe to Adolf Hitler."[73]

That the New Right was shut out of the Oval Office and continued to operate as an insurgent outsider group, while the NCR moved increasingly into mainstream politics, has given rise to the historical narrative that the latter was the more successful movement. In *When Movements Anchor Parties*, Daniel Schlozman proposes that within the context of American politics, some social movements are so important they "have redefined the fundamental alignments of political parties and, in turn, the organizable alternatives in national politics." These movements, which he terms "anchoring groups," are those that gain incorporation into a political party "when winning coalitions of partisan and movement elites accept the bulk, albeit not the totality, of each other's priorities, and when movements wield legitimate vetoes, over partisan priorities in Congress and presidential nomination, that reorient the party's long-term ideological trajectory."[74] In Schlozman's view, the NCR is one such anchoring group. The acceptance of the pro-family platform by the Republican Party signaled the NCR's incorporation as it gained mainstream political access and cemented socially conservative issues as a core part of the party's platform. American politics was fundamentally altered by this realignment, as the platform of the GOP and its enduring reliance on White evangelicals to win local and national elections over the past forty years has demonstrated.

Schlozman holds that Weyrich and his New Right colleagues spearheaded the formation of the NCR but that, in an ironic twist, "the movement that sought to supersede the Republican Party ultimately defined and strengthened it. The search for a durable conservative majority brought together the single-issue groups, and forged ideological commonalities across their particular stances."[75] In short, Schlozman holds that the incorporation of the NCR was a defeat for the New Right because "rather than behaving as a set of ad hoc single issue groups putting pressure on elected officials, the Christian Right became a centerpiece of a new Republican coalition."[76] And yet, the vehicle CP leaders rode into Washington was built by the New Right's conservative Catholic political entrepreneurs. As President Reagan's adoption of the pro-family platform is frequently signposted as a marker of the NCR's influence on and incorporation into the Republican Party, it seems worthwhile to ask why the CNR activists who built the

pro-family platform did not pursue party incorporation. We must, therefore, ask: did the New Right fail where the NCR succeeded? Was party
incorporation the aim? Or, perhaps, were CNR activists after something
else and, if so, did they succeed in other, perhaps less obvious, ways?

The answer to this question, I propose, is that Republican Party incorporation was never the aim of the movement—fundamentally changing
the American political landscape was. And CNR entrepreneurs were able
to do so by propelling their socially conservative agenda into the political
mainstream while they continued to pursue a more brutalist and insurgent
politics of disruption from the outside. The New Right left the indelible
imprint of Catholic thought on not only the NCR but right-wing politics
writ large, and it was able to secure a place for Catholic intellectuals within
the conservative movement that has held to the present.[77]

In sum, rather than view the New Right's failure to incorporate into
the GOP as a failure, I propose we understand its promulgation of the
"pro-family" platform and sponsorship of the NCR as a unique success.
Rather than learn and adopt its strategies from the modern left, the New
Right borrowed a trick from antiquity: it used the NCR as a Trojan horse
to incorporate the religiously inspired social issues of its platform into the
Republican Party without having to sacrifice the movement's independence
or bend to an established party's will.

Concluding Thoughts

The "pro-family" platform served as a vehicle for the convergence of conservative Catholic and Protestant political elites. On one hand, we can attribute the success of the "pro-family" platform to the NCR's deployment
of a communicative discourse predicated on the construction of the "traditional" and the mobilization of an ideology of victimhood. CNR and
Bible-believing Protestant elites constructed a false narrative of historical
"tradition" and manufactured the "threat" of secular humanism in order to
frame the NCR movement as reactionary and in terms of self-defense. In
other words, the NCR operationalized backlash discourse as a means of
constructing a "before" to which Americans should aspire to "return." In
doing so, the radical and prefigurative nature of the "pro-family" platform
was obscured, and the responsibility for the development of the NCR was
shifted onto the threat of "secular humanism."

In turn, "secular humanism" encompassed not only the older threat of communism but also the threat posed by the extension of rights to people of color, women, and members of the LGBTQ+ community. Engaging in a battle against "secular humanism," rather than addressing issues of equality and discrimination head-on, enabled the movement to advance White, Christian, and male supremacist ideologies while also coopting the liberal discourse of rights-based claims from historically marginalized communities. Instead of women having a right to reproductive autonomy, the conversation became one about the "right to life" of the fetus. The battle for equal rights for women was refashioned as a battle to preserve the rights of wives. LGBTQ+ advocates were not advancing gay rights but rather stripping parents of their rights. By co-opting the discourse of rights, and claiming it sought a return to "traditional" liberal values, the NCR aligned itself with the liberal tradition. But, as Gary Gerstle has observed, while liberalism is an elastic ideology, it cannot depart from "three foundational principles: emancipation, rationality, and progress. Indeed, liberalism's evolution can be understood as a series of efforts to reinterpret these principles in light of unexpected historical developments." Those who reject these principles have "effectively renounced the earlier liberal hope of universal emancipation."[78] In short, the "pro-family" movement assumed the language of liberal rights even as its policies demanded a radical—and fundamentally illiberal—departure from the liberal tradition and the positive valuation of individual autonomy and agency.

And so, on the other hand, we can attribute the success of the CNR and NCR to the development of a "pro-family" coordinative discourse that sought to use the promise of a "return" to an imagined past to justify using the state to impose new forms of illiberal social relations. The CNR and NCR did not merely seek entrance to liberal democratic institutions; they sought to refashion them and make the American polity anew. Their aim was to bring about a Christian theocratic future by constructing an imagined past that would serve as the justification for using the state to impose prefigurative social policies in the present. Through the construction of an imagined past, social conservatives effectively framed the prefigurative development of a theocratic politics as a return to "tradition."

EPILOGUE

———◆———

WHO IS IT THAT OVERCOMES THE WORLD?

The New Right, with which I have been associated over the past twelve years, was unprepared for its political success. Consequently, we had in a sense a trivial agenda. Don't misunderstand me. It is not that I believe abortion and school prayer are not important. They are. But the sad fact is that in today's culture the enactment of corrective Constitutional Amendments, and the rest of our agenda, would not change things much at all. In today's culture, Constitutional Amendment or no Constitutional Amendment, abortion and abandonment of prayer would not stop because these are only symptoms of a larger problem. That problem is cultural, and it is rooted in the instant-gratification society. We need to attack this in a larger context.

—Paul Weyrich

By the mid-1980s, Paul Weyrich had begun referring to the New Right's agenda as "trivial." The "pro-family" aims of the movement, he suggested, were too limited and did not go far enough. Instead of advancing a "pro-family" politics, the job of conservative Christians was to remake the culture. Cultural conservatism, Weyrich asserted, would be the most important "political idea" of the decade, and it would be the key to building a "powerful national constituency." In language that foreshadows the ideology of Western chauvinism adopted by the Proud Boys and other right-wing groups of the 2020s, Weyrich defined cultural conservatism as the belief:

> that there is an unbreakable link between traditional Western, Judeo-Christian values and the secular success of Western societies. These values, which include definitions of right and wrong, and ways of thinking and living, have brought about the prosperity, liberty, and opportunity for fulfillment that Western societies have offered their citizens. These will be lost if we abandon these issues.[1]

Implicit in this definition is the assertion that the "traditional" authors of "Western, Judeo-Christian values" were White Christian men. To embrace cultural conservatism, then, is to embrace the inherent supremacism of the West/Whiteness, the masculine/male, and Christianity.

The cultural conservative platform was laid out in a slim volume titled *Cultural Conservatism: Toward a New National Agenda*, authored by William S. Lind and Connie Marshner's husband, the theologian William H. Marshner, and published by the Institute of Cultural Conservatism at the Free Congress Foundation. Together, Lind and William Marshner set out a comprehensive agenda for understanding "society and government as forces acting in support of traditional values and culture, not as legislative bullies, but with funding and advocacy."[2] While Lind and William Marshner argue the institutional design of government should be brought in line with the principle of subsidiarity, they nonetheless contend the government should act on the following policy areas in order to bring them in line with culturally conservative values: the family, education, the economy, social welfare, and the police (among others). Within each arena, they propose reforms that would have the effect of limiting individual rights, imposing checks on the free market, and strengthening the government's coercive capacities. In short, the cultural conservative agenda is premised on exercising the levers of government control to craft policies that will enforce a particular and singular vision of American culture that takes Christian values and families as its building blocks.

Take, for example, Lind and William Marshner's agenda for welfare. Unlike "some conservatives" who believe "if a free economy leaves some people destitute—so be it," cultural conservatives "accept the obligation to the less fortunate."[3] But welfare must go "beyond providing the bare means of living," to include "cultural welfare." Cultural welfare, they explain, "is a recognition that the underclass can only be transformed into a normal, productive part of society by transforming its culture. Its dysfunctional values must be replaced by functional values, that is, by traditional values: delayed gratification, work and saving, commitment to family and to the next generation, education and training, self-improvement, and rejection of crime drugs, and casual sex."[4]

How, one might ask, will cultural conservatives transform "the underclass . . . into a normal, productive part of society"? By using the state to coerce compliance with "traditional" behaviors. "Under cultural welfare," we are told, "subsidies must be structured to uphold and reward traditional values."[5]

To achieve this goal, Lind and Marshner suggest refusing welfare support to anyone "who has not graduated from high school," limiting case benefits to "intact families," and excluding benefits to anyone under age twenty-one "unless they live with one or both parents." At the same time as they suggest using the government to coerce poor people into nuclear families, they recommend incentivizing government workers to get people off welfare by providing early retirement for those who clear their welfare rolls, creating an education voucher system to "facilitate the establishment of alternative, high-quality inner-city schools, characterized by strong discipline," and establishing "inner-city enterprise zones, with government subsidies for firms locating in such zones who hire poverty-level male heads of household." These "firms would be permitted to pay a competitive sub-minimum wage from company funds, with government subsidy added to raise wages for male heads of household to a 'family wage' level—the level necessary to support a family." Lest the gendered aims of the proposal are not clear, Lind and Marshner elaborate, "The object would be not merely to bring jobs to the inner city, but to rebuild the functional role of underclass males as heads of households and family providers."[6] But the "traditional" economic and social roles invoked by Lind and William Marshner are not grounded in the historical record.

In what past America, which was shaped from the beginning by the horrors of slavery, were men of color allowed to be the heads of their household? In what past was domestic violence not a threat within the home? In what past was there an expectation that all Americans would receive, let alone complete, a high school education? The "traditional" America Lind and Marshner claim to be seeking a return to can only be manufactured through the prefiguration of a new set of social relations that are, in turn, imposed coercively by the state.

In many ways, the cultural conservative welfare policy agenda reflects the marriage of Christian Right and neoliberal worldviews.[7] In Melinda Cooper's formulation, social conservatives have succeeded in substituting the family as the basic unit of social organization rather than the individual. Having done so, they seek to use the state to manufacture the "traditional" family. As Cooper explains, "The neoconservatives are under no illusion that the traditional family will simply reassert itself of its own accord, absent government intrusion." Subsequently, "They see the primary function of the state as that of sustaining the family, the foundation of all social order, if necessary through the use of force," making it "the task of neoconservative welfare reform . . . to 'reinvent tradition' by actively inculcating a culture of abstinence, monogamy, and marriage among the poor."[8] Cooper further highlights how neoconservatism and neoliberalism are mutually reinforcing ideologies, which are dependent on one another, as "In extremis, neoliberals must turn to the overt, neoconservative methodology of state-imposed, transcendent virtue to realize their dream of an imminent virtue ethics of the market."[9] To my mind, Cooper's account presents a stunningly accurate analysis of what *has* occurred since the inception of the NCR. It does not, however, consider what the NCR *wanted* to occur.

Over the course of the preceding five chapters, I have sought to examine the influence of conservative Catholic political entrepreneurs on the development of ideas within the Christian Right. In short, drawing on a rich trove of archival material, I have strived to show what happened. But I have also sought to gesture to what the CNR and NCR *wanted* to make happen, which is to say, I have emphasized how these actors sought to use the past to impose policies in the present that would shape the direction of the future. For this reason, it seems fitting to conclude with a discussion of not what has transpired, but what was wished for. And what has been wished for goes far beyond the imposition of social conservative/neoliberal policies premised on the family. Rather, what the CNR and NCR has wished for is the death of liberalism.

While couched in the language of a return to the "traditional," cultural conservatism proposes nothing short of a complete disavowal of the ideological commitment to liberal individual rights and free-market capitalism that underpins American political institutions. At the same time, it is the very ideology of liberalism that creates the conditions of possibility for the articulation of cultural conservatism. Thus, in closing, I want to propose that we read the NCR as a fundamentally liberal movement that has fundamentally illiberal aims.

There is no doubt in my mind that the development of the NCR was dependent on the existence of a liberal order. The New Right's single-issue politics strategy and the embrace of a "Culture War" framing presupposes the existence of a liberal and pluralist political order in which competition over interests can occur. Moreover, conservative Catholics and Protestants coopted the discourse of rights, claiming to advocate on behalf of the rights of the family, parental rights, the rights of the unborn, and religious freedom rights, among others. In *The Rights Turn in Conservative Christian Politics*, Andrew Lewis persuasively details how the Christian Right has embraced the rhetoric of rights. But Lewis goes a step further, arguing in the introduction to his book that "Evangelicals, and their Christian Right allies, have been baptized into political liberalism." This assertion is premised on the assumption that "rights learning" and "rights claiming" may potentially result in "rights extending," which is to say that it presupposes that the use of rights discourse reflects an acceptance of the liberal political order.[10] But I would caution against conflating the use of liberalism with an acceptance of liberalism.

It might be helpful to step back here and ask: what is the liberal political order? The conservative Catholic theorist Patrick Deneen opens his book *Why Liberalism Failed* with the following definition: "Liberalism conceived humans as rights-bearing individuals who could fashion and pursue for themselves their own version of the good life. Opportunities for liberty were best afforded by a limited government devoted to 'securing rights,' along with a free-market economic system that gave space for individual initiative and ambition."[11]

Following from this definition, "pro-family" rights are not individual rights. The "pro-family" platform is not a liberal platform. For the CNR and NCR, there is only one version of the good life and only one path to religious and political salvation. Afterall, "Only the one who believes that Jesus is the Son of God" will overcome the world.[12] Therefore, the role of government is not to preserve individual rights and manage competing interpretations of the good but to impose and enforce a singular conception of the good through the regulation of social relations.

But if not political liberalism, then what? Asked another way, what does it mean to suggest that what the CNR and the NCR *wanted* was to produce an illiberal state? At its most basic level, it means to take the Christian

Right at face value: the aim was, and continues to be, to define the state in relation to Christianity. To conceive of the state in this way demands we disavow liberalism as a structuring principal philosophy as the goal of state is transformed from upholding liberty to imposing conformity.

We can see this desire at work in recent calls for a revitalized "Christian nationalism" movement, which openly rejects the basic tenets of liberal pluralism on the grounds that America was founded as a Christian nation. In seeking to rewrite America's past and its founding traditions as the basis for imposing new social policies in the present, Christian nationalists are actively engaged in prefiguring the past with the intent of creating a Christian political system in the future. The forward to *Christian Nationalism: A Biblical Guide for Taking Dominion and Discipling Nations* makes this clear, asserting:

> Then, after we have attained enough Christians in our nation, we are obliged to peacefully order our state governments in such a way as to help Christianity grow and flourish in our states without restrictions. This is in obedience to our Lord and his command. The purpose of government, from a Christian perspective, is to preserve and protect the Christian understanding of civilization, otherwise known as Christendom (Prov. 8:15, Dan. 2:21, Dan. 4:17, Rom. 12:21, Rom. 13:1–2), as opposed to such things as the Marxist understanding of civilization or the Islamic understanding.[13]

Here, we see the subsuming of the state to the advancement of Christian ideology. The purpose of government is transfigured from protecting individual rights to protecting the rights of Christians.

Lest we be tempted to call the system proposed by Christian nationalists a theocracy, in the next breath the authors assert, "Christians are integralists not theocrats, in that we have always favored two separate institutions, one for religion (the church) and one for government (the state)." Never mind that they continue, "When a certain activity or behavior is found to be a danger to [Christian] society, and such dangerous activity can be mitigated by law, without the risk of creating a police state (which itself is unchristian), Christians have the moral duty to act, bringing the force of government to bear."[14] In this conception, government becomes the agent of imposing Christian values through the regulation of social relations and activity. Call it what you will, the system of government Christian nationalists seek to call into being is antithetical to liberal pluralist democracy.

Why then do we persist in misrecognizing the Christian Right as a liberal movement? The answer to this question, I would suggest, is twofold. On one level, we have accepted the false narrative of backlash and enabled the movement to adopt and instrumentalize an ideology of victimhood. Doing so has enabled it to claim it is acting within a liberal framework to defend and uphold the "rights" of Christians. Subsequently, we have failed to accept the (Catholic and Protestant) Christian Right for what it has told us it is from the very beginning: radical, revolutionary, and in the words of Jerry Falwell, Ed Dobson, and Ed Hindon, the "militant opposition of liberalism." Thus, on a second level, we have failed to identify how the Christian Right has and continues to prefigure the past in order to shape the future of America. The aim has never been to merely make America great again, but rather always to make America anew.

NOTES

Preface

1. Sarah Palin, *Going Rogue: An American Life* (New York: Harper, 2009).

2. Martin Griffin, "The Anti-Catholic Spirit of the Revolution," *American Catholic Historical Researches* 6, no. 4 (October 1889): 146–178; William M. Shea, *The Lion and the Lamb: Evangelicals and Catholics in America* (Oxford: Oxford University Press, 2004); Robert Wuthnow, *The Restructuring of American Religion* (Princeton, NJ: Princeton University Press, 1988).

3. Brief of 250 American Historians as Amici Curiae in Support of Planned Parenthood of Southeastern Pennsylvania, 1992.

4. Tisa Wenger, *Religious Freedom: The Contested History of an American Idea* (Chapel Hill: University of North Carolina Press, 2017).

5. Angela M. Lahr, *Millennial Dreams and Apocalyptic Nightmares: The Cold War Origins of Political Evangelicalism* (New York: Oxford University Press, 2007).

6. Neil J. Young, *We Gather Together: The Religious Right and the Problem of Interfaith Politics* (New York: Oxford University Press, 2016).

7. Quoted in Lahr, *Millennial Dreams and Apocalyptic Nightmares*, 105–106.

8. "Evangelicals and Catholic Together: The Christian Mission in the Third Millennium," *First Things*, May 1994, https://www.firstthings.com/article/1994/05/evangelicals-catholics-together-the-christian-mission-in-the-third-millennium.

9. The perceived threat to conservative Christians is inextricably tied up with concerns about immigration, changing racial and ethnic demographics, and "White replacement." This trend is represented, in part, by the redirection of bias toward other racialized groups, most notably immigrants from Central and South America and Muslims, as White Catholics have become more fully assimilated. See Una Cadegan, "Catholic Immigrants Didn't Make It on Their Own, *Washington Post*, April 18, 2017, https://www.washingtonpost.com/posteverything/wp/2017/04/18/catholic-immigrants-didnt-make-it-on-their-own-they-shouldnt-expect-others-to/; Camila Domonoske, "Hate Crimes Rose in 2015, with Religious Bias a Growing Motivation, FBI Data Shows," NPR, November 14, 2016, https://www.npr.org/sections/thetwo-way/2016/11/14/502036699/hate-crimes-rose-in-2015-with-religious-bias-a-growing-motivation-fbi-data-shows; "The 'Great Replacement' Theory, Explained," *National Immigration Forum*, December 2021, https://immigrationforum.org/wp-content/uploads/2021/12/Replacement-Theory-Explainer-1122.pdf. On a

related but distinct note, Jason Bruner importantly adds an international dimension to this conversation by focusing on the complex interplay between events affecting Christians overseas and the development of American political and religious identities. For his account of how US Catholics and Protestants have embraced a limited ecumenicism based on a shared conception of victimhood, see chap. 3 of *Imagining Persecution: Why American Christians Believe There Is a Global War against Their Faith* (New Brunswick, NJ: Rutgers University Press, 2021), 65–107.

10. For an overview of why Protestants have tended to shy away from natural law theory, see Jennifer Herdt, "Natural Law in Protestant Christianity," in Tom Angier, ed., *The Cambridge Companion to Natural Law Ethics* (Cambridge: Cambridge University Press, 2019); see also Carl E. Braaten, "Protestants and Natural Law," *First Things*, January 1992, https://www.firstthings.com/article/1992/01/protestants-and -natural-law.

11. Adam D. Sheingate, "Political Entrepreneurship, Institutional Change, and American Political Development," *Studies in American Political Development* 17, no. 2 (October 2003): 185–203; and "Institutional Dynamics and American Political Development," *Annual Review of Political Science* 17, no. 1 (December 2013): 461–477.

12. While American conservatism takes both secular and religious forms, at its root, it adopts a Burkean avowal of morality predicated on natural law, a veneration of the "traditional," and a tendency to view social and political change with skepticism and/or hostility. Russell Kirk has identified six basic tenets of conservatism that serve as a useful intellectual foundation, as they are intelligible in both less and more religious contexts. They may be paraphrased as follows: (1) a belief in a "transcendent order," in which religious morality is at the center of society; (2) a general resistance to the belief that society should be explained by recourse to rationalism; (3) a desire to impose order through the maintenance of hierarchy and social classes; (4) a deep and abiding conviction that private property is necessary and the belief that it is intrinsically linked to freedom; (5) a belief that custom and traditions are necessary for the maintenance of order; and (6) a corresponding distrust of social and political change. Russell Kirk, *The Conservative Mind from Burke to Eliot*, 7th ed. (Washington, DC: Regnery Publishing, 2001, 8–9; Jonah Goldberg, "When We Say Conservative, We Mean . . ." *National Review*, June 20, 2015, http://www.nationalreview.com/article/420055/con servatism-definition-difficult-produce.

13. See, for example, Randall Balmer, *Thy Kingdom Come: An Evangelical's Lament* (New York: Basic Books, 2006); Robert B. Horwitz, *America's Right: Anti-establishment Conservatism from Goldwater to the Tea Party* (Cambridge: Polity Press, 2013); Daniel K. Williams, *God's Own Party* (Oxford: Oxford University Press, 2010).

14. Alan Crawford, *Thunder on the Right* (New York: Pantheon Books, 1980); Thomas J. McIntyre with John C. Obert, *The Fear Brokers* (Boston: Beacon Press, 1979); John S. Saloma III, *Ominous Politics* (New York: Hill & Wang, 1984); Richard Viguerie, *The New Right: We're Ready to Lead* (Falls Church, VA: Viguerie Company, 1981).

15. William Martin, *With God on Our Side: The Rise of the Religious Right in America* (New York: Broadway Books, 1996); Williams, *God's Own Party*.

16. See also Sara Diamond, *Not by Politics Alone: The Enduring Influence of the Christian Right* (New York: Guilford Press, 1998); and *Spiritual Warfare: The Politics of the Christian Right* (Boston: South End Press, 1989); Dan Gilgoff, *The Jesus Machine* (New York: St. Martin's Griffin, 2007); Esther Kaplan, *With God on Their Side* (New York: New Press, 2004); Robert C. Liebman and Robert Wuthnow, eds., *The New Christian Right* (New York: Aldine , 1983); David G. Bromley and Anson Shupe, eds., *New Christian Politics* (Macon, GA: Mercer, 1984); Gary Wills, *Heart and Head: American Christianities* (New York: Penguin Press, 2007).

17. For an excellent overview of this literature, see Axel Schäfer, *Countercultural Conservatives* (Madison: University of Wisconsin Press, 2011), introduction.

18. Single-issue politics are those that, while focusing on a single political question, are framed as representing a larger moral or ethical worldview. The issues around which single-issue groups organize tend to have emotional valence, are framed as "questions of principle," and members "couch much of their support (or in some cases their opposition) in terms of what is right and just public policy." Sylvia Tesh, "In Support of 'Single-Issue' Politics," *Political Science Quarterly* 99, no.1 (Spring 1984): 29.

A Note on Terminology

1. L. Benjamin Rolsky, "Producing the Christian Right: Conservative Evangelicalism, Representation, and the Recent Religious Past," *Religions* 12, no. 3:171 (March 2021): 2, https://doi.org/10.3390/rel12030171.

2. Rolsky, "Producing the Christian Right," 8.

3. National Association of Evangelicals, "What Is an Evangelical?," n.d., https://www.nae.net/what-is-an-evangelical/.

Introduction

1. "Interview with Beverly and Tim LaHaye," 1995–1996, William Martin Religious Right collection, Woodson Research Center, Rice University [hereafter WM], Box 73.

2. Gabriella Borter and Sharon Bernstein, "Factbox: U.S. State Abortion Legislation to Watch in 2023," Reuters, May 3, 2023, https://www.reuters.com/world/us/us-state-abortion-legislation-watch-2023-2023-05-03/; see also "State Legislation Tracker," Guttmacher Institute, https://www.guttmacher.org/state-legislation-tracker.

3. "What Anti-trans Bills Passed in 2023?," Trans Legislation Tracker, https://translegislation.com/bills/2023/passed.

4. Equality Maps, Movement Advancement Project, 2023, https://www.lgbtmap.org/equality-maps/.

5. Equality Maps, Movement Advancement Project.

6. CRT Forward, UCLA School of Law, 2023, https://crtforward.law.ucla.edu/.

7. See chapter 4 for a more extensive discussion of secular humanism.

8. Megan Messerly, "Thousands lose Medicaid in Arkansas: Is This America's future?," *Politico*, June 14, 2023, https://www.politico.com/news/2023/06/13/medicaid-insurance-coverage-arkansas-00101744.

9. Katie Bergh and Dottie Rosenbaum, "Debt Ceiling Agreement's SNAP Changes Would Increase Hunger and Poverty for Many Older Low-Income People; New Exemptions Would Help Some Others," Center on Budget and Policy Priorities, May 31, 2023, https://www.cbpp.org/research/food-assistance/debt-ceiling-agreements-snap-changes-would-increase-hunger-and-poverty-for.

10. For a discussion of the religious significance of and symbolism on display during the January 6, 2020, insurrection, see Bradley Onishi, *Preparing for War: The Extremist History of White Nationalism—and What Comes Next* (Minneapolis: Broadleaf Books, 2023), 5–26 and 159–177.

11. "Voting Laws Roundup: June 2023," Brennan Center for Justice, June 13, 2023, https://www.brennancenter.org/our-work/research-reports/voting-laws-roundup-june-2023?_ga=2.117393990.1560545562.1689609770–2045684559.1689609770&_gac=1.153346634.1689619289.CjwKCAjwsvujBhAXEiwA_UXnAMr25CY86g680c845K3eXdyQ9_CglusuZUGkBuoMpT4BWdShT7wZphoCIGAQAvD_BwE.

12. Tom McCarthy, "Trump's Judges: A Revolution to Create a New Conservative America," *The Guardian*, April 28, 2020, https://www.theguardian.com/us-news/2020/apr/28/donald-trump-judges-create-new-conservative-america-republicans.

13. Katherine Stewart, "How the Christian Right Took over the Judiciary and Changed America," *The Guardian*, June 25, 2022, https://www.theguardian.com/world/2022/jun/25/roe-v-wade-abortion-christian-right-america.

14. See *Trinity Lutheran Church of Columbia, Inc. v. Comer* 582 US___ (2017); *Espinoza v. Montana Department of Revenue* 591 US ___ (2020); *Carson v. Makin* 596 US _ (2022); and *Kennedy v. Bremerton* 597 US (2022).

15. Vivien A. Schmidt, "Britain-out and Trump-in: A Discursive Institutionalist Analysis of the British Referendum on the EU and the US Presidential Election," *Review of International Political Economy* 24, no. 2 (March 2017): 248–269; "Discursive Institutionalism: The Explanatory Power of Ideas and Discourse," *Annual Review of Political Science* 11, no. 1 (June 2008): 303–326; and "Taking Ideas and Discourse Seriously: Explaining Change through Discursive Institutionalism as the Fourth 'New Institutionalism,'" *European Political Science Review* 2, no. 1 (March 2010): 1–25.

16. Schmidt, "Britain-out and Trump-in," 249.

17. Schmidt, "Discursive Institutionalism," 304.

18. Within the discursive institutionalism framework, institutions are understood as (1) "embod[ying] the structures and constructs of meaning internal to agents whose 'background ideational abilities' enable them to create (and maintain) institutions . . . while their 'foreground discursive abilities' enable them to communicate critically about them so as to change (or maintain) them"; and (2) "represent[ing] the formal and

informal institutions external to actors that may be seen to constrain (or empower) them." Schmidt, "Britain-out and Trump-in," 252.

19. Francis Schaeffer, *The Church at the End of the 20th Century* (Westmont, IL: InterVarsity Press, 1970).

20. Schmidt, "Discursive Institutionalism," 310.

21. Schmidt, "Discursive Institutionalism," 310.

22. Angie Maxwell and Todd Shields, *The Long Southern Strategy: How Chasing White Voters in the South Changed American Politics* (New York: Oxford University Press, 2019).

23. "Anita Bryant's Crusade: Where Next?," *Conservative Digest*, August 1977.

24. Gillian Frank, "'The Civil Rights of Parents': Race and Conservative Politics in Anita Bryant's Campaign against Gay Rights in 1970s Florida," *Journal of the History of Sexuality* 22, no. 1 (January 2013): 127.

25. While elements of the ideology of victimhood can be traced to the first few centuries of the religion, so too can elements of Christian supremacism. In *Christian Supremacy: Reckoning with the Roots of Antisemitism and Racism*, the historian Magda Teter explains that early Christian theology "negated Judaism as it claimed to 'replace' it," and constructed a Christian identity premised on "theological superiority." Moreover, Christian supremacism is inextricably caught up with ideas of racial hierarchy and supremacy as contemporary US and European White supremacist ideologies are "built on the foundations of early Christian supersessionist theology." Magda Teter, *Christian Supremacy: Reckoning with the Roots of Antisemitism and Racism* (Princeton, NJ: Princeton University Press, 2023), 2–3.

26. Mitch Berbrier, "The Victim Ideology of White Supremacists and White Separatists in the United States," *Sociological Focus* 33, no. 2 (May 2000): 175–191.

27. Berbrier, "The Victim Ideology of White Supremacists," 176.

28. Berbrier, "The Victim Ideology of White Supremacists," 178–179.

29. Katherine Stewart, *The Power Worshippers* (New York: Bloomsbury Publishing, 2020); Andrew L. Whitehead and Samuel L. Perry, *Taking America Back for God: Christian Nationalism in the United States* (New York: Oxford University Press, 2020).

30. Berbrier, "The Victim Ideology of White Supremacists," 187.

31. As such, there has been sustained attention to how the Christian right uses victimhood. For more on the topic, see Arlene Stein, "Revenge of the Shamed: The Christian Right's Emotional Culture War," in Jeff Goodwin, James M. Jasper, and Francesca Polletta, eds., *Passionate Politics: Emotions and Social Movements* (Chicago: University of Chicago Press, 2009); Christopher Duerringer, "The 'War on Christianity': Counterpublicity or Hegemonic Containment?," *Southern Communication Journal* 78, no. 4 (September 2013): 311–325; Christopher Duerringer, *Crucified Christians, Marked Men, and Wanted Whites: Victimhood and Conservative Counterpublicity* (PhD diss., Arizona State University, 2011), https://repository.asu.edu/attachments/56508/content/Duerringer_asu_0010E_10424.pdf; R. Bennett Furlow, "Extremism and Victimhood in the U.S. Context," Report No. 1204, Arizona State University Center for

Strategic Communication, 2012; Alan Noble, "Why Do Evangelicals Have a Persecution Complex?," *The Atlantic*, August 4, 2014, https://www.theatlantic.com/national /archive/2014/08/the-evangelical-persecution-complex/375506/;LeeBebout,"Weaponizing Victimhood: Discourses of Oppression and the Maintenance of Supremacy on the Right," in Anthony Nadler and A. J. Bauer, eds., *News on the Right: Studying Conservative News Cultures* (Oxford: Oxford University Press, 2019); and Jason W. Alvis, "Christianities and the Culture (Wars) of Victimhood: Persecution, Purity, Patience," *Philosophy Today* 65, no. 4 (August 2021): 881–898.

32. International Christian Concern, "Violent Threats and Vandalism: An Attack on Pro-Life Organizations," June 30, 2022, https://www.persecution.org/2022/06/30 /violent-threat-and-vandalism/#.

33. Religious Freedom Institute, "Religious Pro-Life Americans under Attack," September 2022, https://religiousfreedominstitute.org/religious-pro-life-americans -under-attack/.

34. Onishi, *Preparing for War*, 18.

35. Katherine Stewart, "Opinion: Christian Nationalists Are Excited About What Comes Next," *New York Times*, July 5, 2022, https://www.nytimes.com/2022/07/05 /opinion/dobbs-christian-nationalism.html.

36. Quoted in Alan Crawford, *Thunder on the Right* (New York: Pantheon Books, 1980), 269.

37. Jerry Falwell, audio recording of "I Love America" rally in Austin, TX, 1980, WM.

38. I develop this concept in a chapter titled "Tomorrow's Past Today: The Prefigurative Construction of Christian Right Belonging," in Cody Musselman, Erik Kline, Dana Lloyd, and Michael J. Altman, eds., *American Examples: New Conversations about Religion* (Tuscaloosa: University of Alabama Press, 2024).

39. Carl Boggs, "Marxism, Prefigurative Communism, and the Problem of Workers' Control," *Radical America* 11 (November 1977): 99–122.

40. Paul Raekstad, "Revolutionary Practice and Prefigurative Politics: A Clarification and Defense," *Constellations* 25, no. 13 (September 2017): 359–372.

41. Flora Cornish, Jan Haaken, Liora Moskovitz, and Sharon Jackson, "Rethinking Prefigurative Politics: Introduction to the Special Thematic Section," *Journal of Social and Political Psychology* 4 (May 2016): 114–127.

42. CSPAN, "Q and A with Paul Weyrich and Brian Lamb," March 22, 2005, transcript, p. 4 of 17, http://www.c-span.org/video/transcript/?id=7958.

43. Connaught Marshner, "New Traditional Woman," Paul Weyrich Papers, American Heritage Center, University of Wyoming, Laramie [hereafter AHC], Box 82, Folder 18.

44. Whitehead and Perry, *Taking America Back for God*, x.

45. Loretta Ross, "White Supremacy in the 1990s," *Political Research Associates*, n.d., http://www.publiceye.org/eyes/whitsup.html.

46. Emily K. Carian, Alex DiBranco, and Chelsea Ebin, eds., preface to *Male*

Supremacism in the United States: From Patriarchal Traditionalism to Misogynist Incels and the Alt-Right (New York: Routledge, 2022), vii.

47. Robert O. Self, *All in the Family: The Realignment of American Democracy since the 1960s* (New York: Hill & Wang, 2012), 6.

Chapter 1. Problematizing Backlash

1. Interview with Paul Weyrich, WM, Box 76 (1995–1996), 19–20.

2. Thomas Edsall and Mary Edsall, *Chain Reaction: The Impact of Race, Rights, and Taxes on American Politics* (New York: Norton, 1992), 4.

3. See, for example, Lars Rensmann, "The Noisy Counter-Revolution: Understanding the Cultural Conditions and Dynamics of Populist Politics in Europe in the Digital Age," *Politics and Governance* 5, no. 4 (December 2017): 123–135; Axel Schäfer, *Countercultural Conservatives* (Madison: University of Wisconsin Press, 2011). The term "counterrevolutionary" can be understood in two distinct ways. On one hand, it can be taken to mean the revolution of B is intended to counter, or reverse, that of A. Understood in this way, counterrevolutionary is synonymous with backlash as it implies that B's motivations are caused by A's actions. If, however, we take it to mean A and B both seek revolutionary ends, and these ends are antithetical to one another, the term can be aptly used when describing the New Christian Right. Nonetheless, I'm wary of employing the term because of this slippage.

4. Daniel Martinez HoSang, *Racial Propositions: Ballot Initiatives and the Making of Postwar California* (Berkeley: University of California Press, 2010), 17.

5. Corey Robin, *The Reactionary Mind* (New York: Oxford University Press, 2011), 28, 16.

6. Robin, *The Reactionary Mind*, 34–35.

7. Robin, *The Reactionary Mind*, 18–19.

8. Robin, *The Reactionary Mind*, 17–18.

9. Cas Mudde, *The Far Right Today* (Cambridge: Polity Press, 2019), 7.

10. Robin, *The Reactionary Mind*, 22–23.

11. Martinez HoSang, *Racial Propositions*, 18.

12. Joseph Lowndes, *From the New Deal to the New Right* (New Haven, CT: Yale University Press, 2008), 4.

13. Natalia Molina, *How Race Is Made in America: Immigration, Citizenship, and the Historical Power of Racial Scripts* (Berkeley: University of California Press, 2014).

14. Suzanne Staggenborg, *Social Movements*, 2nd ed. (Oxford: Oxford University Press, 2016), 21. J. Craig Jenkins and Bert Klandermans define "political opportunities" as "the impact of the state and the political representation system on social movements." Building on work in social movement theory, including that of Charles Tilly and Theda Skocpol, they further assert: "More recently, the political context has also been shown to be of considerable importance for the mobilization and the impact of different types of social movements." The idea of a political opportunity structure emerges out of the need "for systematic analysis of the political context that mediates structural conflicts

given as latent political potentials." Jenkins and Klandermans, *Politics of Social Protest: Comparative Perspectives on States and Social Movements* (Minneapolis: University of Minnesota Press, 1995).

15. This formulation of backlash mirrors that put forward by Davina Cooper, who writes: "The concept of backlash is grounded in a three-part, chronological model of change: 1) time period A (society is in equilibrium but certain areas, such as education, are vulnerable to takeover or alteration by more radical forces); 2) time period B (through exerting their power, radical forces manage to win control over certain aspects of society); and 3) time period C (society becomes out of balance and forces of reaction mobilize to intervene)." Davina Cooper, "At the Expense of Christianity," in Leslie G. Roman and Linda Eyre, eds., *Dangerous Territories* (New York: Routledge, 1997), 45.

16. Frederick S. Lane, *The Court and the Cross: The Religious Right's Crusade to Reshape the Supreme Court* (Boston: Beacon Press, 2008), x.

17. Lane, *The Court and the Cross*, 77.

18. Adam Cohen, *Supreme Inequality: The Supreme Court's Fifty-Year Battle for a More Unjust America* (New York: Penguin Books, 2021); Michael J. Graetz and Linda Greenhouse, *The Burger Court and the Rise of the Judicial Right* (New York: Simon & Schuster, 2016).

19. See, for example, *Eisenstadt v. Baird* 405 US 438 (1972) concerning birth control and *Roe v. Wade* 410 US 113 (1973) concerning abortion.

20. See, for example, *Phillips v. Martin Marietta Corporation* 405 US 542 (1971) concerning gender-based employment discrimination.

21. Jerry Falwell, *If I Should Die Before I Wake* (Nashville, TN: Thomas Nelson, 1986); Frank Schaeffer, *Crazy for God* (Philadelphia: Da Capo Press, 2007).

22. Randall Balmer, "The Real Origins of the Religious Right," *Politico*, May 27, 2014, https://www.politico.com/magazine/story/2014/05/religious-right-real-origins-107133.

23. Daniel Schlozman, *When Movements Anchor Parties* (Princeton, NJ: Princeton University Press, 2015), 91–92.

24. See, for example, Michael Sean Winters, *Left at the Altar: How the Democrats Lost the Catholics and How the Catholics Can Save the Democrats* (New York: Basic Books, 2008), 73–4, 109, 116–120. See also K. Healan Gaston, explaining the pervasiveness of a narrative of school prayer backlash: "Some have identified school prayer as *the* original culture wars issue. They argue that outrage following the Supreme Court's 1962 *Engel v. Vitale* decision, banning school-sponsored prayer, helped launch the intertwined careers of the Christian right and its most effective champion, President Ronald Reagan. Engel and its 1963 successor *Abington School District v. Schempp*, which ruled out Bible lessons in public schools, fueled the belief among conservatives that a pious, Christian or Judeo-Christian majority labored under the oppressive yoke of a socialistic, anti-religious, anti-American left." K. Healon Gaston, "A Trumped-Up Controversy? School Prayer in Policy, History, and Ethics," *Berkley Forum*, George-

town University, February 13, 2020, https://berkleycenter.georgetown.edu/responses/a-trumped-up-controversy-school-prayer-in-policy-history-and-ethics.

25. One of several definitions given by Jane Mansbridge and Shauna L. Shames, "Toward a Theory of Backlash: Dynamic Resistance and the Central Role of Power," *Politics and Gender* 4, no. 4 (December 2008): 625.

26. Fred Barnes, "A New Issue for the Right Wing: The Politics of AIDS," November 4, 1985, Paul Weyrich Notebooks at the Library of Congress [hereafter LoC Weyrich], Box 15, Folder 5.

27. Tina Fetner has complicated a straightforward gay backlash narrative by demonstrating there was a reciprocal influence between the gay rights and Christian Right movements, as the Christian Right both mobilized in response to gay and lesbian rights gains and "the emergence of the [Christian Right] counter movement impacted the rhetorical strategies used by lesbian and hay activists on lesbian and gay rights, an issue which was contested by the anti-gay movement." Tina Fetner, "Working Anita Bryant: The Impact of Christian Anti-Gay Activism on Lesbian and Gay Movement Claims," *Social Problems* 48, no. 3 (August 2001): 411–428, 413. See also Tina Fetner, *How the Religious Right Shaped Lesbian and Gay Activism* (Minneapolis: University of Minnesota Press, 2008).

28. Gillian Frank, "The Civil Rights of Parents: Race and Conservative Politics in Anita Bryant's Campaign against Gay Rights in 1970s Florida," *Journal of the History of Sexuality* 22, no. 1 (January 2013): 126–160.

29. Didi Herman, "'Then I Saw a New Heaven and a New Earth': Thoughts on the Christian Right and the Problem of Backlash," in Leslie G. Roman and Linda Eyre, eds., *Dangerous Territories* (New York: Routledge, 1997), 65.

30. Cooper, "At the Expense of Christianity," 56.

31. "Interview with Beverly and Tim LaHaye," 1995–1996, WM, Box 73. Some punctuation added.

32. Ruth and David Collier explain the concept of critical junctures in the following manner: "Numerous scholars have focused on major watersheds in political life, arguing that these transitions establish certain directions of change and foreclose others in a way that shapes politics for years to come. Such transitions can, following Seymour Martin Lipset and Stein Rokkan, be called'critical junctures.'" Ruth Berins Collier and David Collier, *Shaping the Political Arena: Critical Junctures, the Labor Movement, and Regime Dynamics in Latin America* (2015), 27, retrieved from https://escholarship.org/uc/item/8qr1z7gc.

33. The prayer New York students were asked to recite was "Almighty God, we acknowledge our dependence upon Thee, and we beg Thy blessings upon us, our parents, our teachers and our Country." *Engel v. Vitale* 370 US 421 (1962), https://supreme.justia.com/cases/federal/us/370/421/#tab-opinion-1943886.

34. *Engel v. Vitale* 370 US 421 (1962), p. 370 US 430, https://supreme.justia.com/cases/federal/us/370/421/#tab-opinion-1943886.

35. While the legal prohibition was clear, researchers have found that school prayer

continued into the twenty-first century in some communities and geographic regions of the United States. Kevin T. McGuire, "Public Schools, Religious Establishments, and the US Supreme Court: An Examination of Policy Compliance," *American Politics Research* 37, no. 1 (January 2009): 50–74.

36. Kirk W. Elifson and C. Kirk Hadaway, "Prayer in Public Schools: When Church and State Collide," *Public Opinion Quarterly* 49, no. 3 (1985): 317–329.

37. President J. F. Kennedy, quoted in Angela M. Lahr, *Millennial Dreams and Apocalyptic Nightmares: The Cold War Origins of Political Evangelicalism* (New York: Oxford University Press, 2007), 65.

38. Michael D. Waggoner, "When the Court Took on Prayer and the Bible in Schools," *Religion and Politics*, June 25, 2012, http://religionandpolitics.org/2012/06/25/when -the-court-took-on-prayer-the-bible-and-public-schools/. For a nuanced and in-depth look at the complex and conflicting political and social identities of Christians in the 1960s, see chap. 3 of Schäfer's *Countercultural Conservatives*.

39. Lahr, *Millennial Dreams and Apocalyptic Nightmares*, 70.

40. The initial mixed response of conservative Protestants to the *Engel* decision also reflects an ideological struggle that took place within conservatism over the place of government in the everyday lives of people: while conservative Protestants were developing an orthodoxy that equated small government with good/Godly govern-ment, they were simultaneously struggling with the desire to use the government to impose and enforce their interpretation of morality on all Americans. This para-dox—of decrying big government while wanting the government to enforce conser-vative social regulations—could not be resolved within the radically individualistic logic of fusionist conservatism. Both the theoretical and abstract moralism of Buck-ley and Meyer—which was derived from natural law theology—and the race-baiting moralism of Goldwater were underwritten by a disavowal of statist intervention. In short, the Buckley/Goldwater incarnation of conservatism was defined by an ideolog-ical commitment to limited government. It could, therefore, not stretch and bend to accommodate a moralism that explicitly sought to enlist the state's enforcement and regulatory capacities. Such an accommodation would be made by the New Right two decades later, as we see in the final chapter and epilogue.

41. Lahr, *Millennial Dreams and Apocalyptic Nightmares*, 69–73. Following the *Engel* and *Abington* decisions, in 1964 and 1966, Congress responded to that senti-ment by holding hearings on a constitutional amendment that would allow prayer in government institutions and public schools. See "Congress Fails to Act on School Prayer Amendments," from the *Congressional Quarterly Almanac* (1964), for an ex-cellent overview of congressional action in response to the Court's decision and a survey of responses from a range of public officials, legal experts, religious organi-zations, and religious leaders, https://library.cqpress.com/cqalmanac/document .php?id=cqal64–1304697.

42. Douglas Laycock, "A Survey of Religious Liberty in the United States," *Ohio State Law Journal* 47, no. 2 (1986): 423.

43. Laycock, "A Survey of Religious Liberty," 418.

44. For an excellent discussion of convergence between Catholics and Protestants in response to an earlier school decision, *Everson v. School Board of the Township of Ewing* (1947), affirming church-state separation, and a shared rejection of secularism and embrace of what she calls "Judeo-Christian exceptionalism," see K. Healan Gaston, *Imagining Judeo-Christian America: Religion, Secularism, and the Redefinition of Democracy* (Chicago: University of Chicago Press, 2019), chap. 5.

45. Weyrich Interview, WM, Box 76, 18.

46. Alan Crawford, "Richard Viguerie's Bid for Power," *The Nation*, January 29, 1977, LoC Weyrich 1977, Box 6, Folder 3.

47. Quoted in Alan Erenhalt, "The Right in Congress: Seeking a Strategy," *Congressional Quarterly*, August 5, 1978, LoC Weyrich 1978, Box 7, Folder 1.

48. Robert G. Kaiser, "Nervous Liberals Eye 1980," June 1979, excerpted from the *Washington Post* and reprinted in *Conservative Digest*.

49. Reagan's proposed amendment was succinct: "Nothing in this Constitution shall be construed to prohibit individual or group prayer in public schools or other public institutions. No person shall be required by the United States or by any State to participate in prayer." 19 Weekly Comp. Pres. Doc. 370, Public Papers of the President, March 8, 1983, WM, Box 83.

50. Curtis J. Sitomer, "Why Reagan Grabbed the Initiative on School Prayer," *Christian Science Monitor*, May 10, 1982, https://www.csmonitor.com/1982/0510/051005 .html.

51. "Questions and Answers on the President's Proposed School Prayer Amendment," White House, May 6, 1982, AHC, Box 26, Folder 1.

52. 19 Weekly Comp. Pres. Doc. 370, Public Papers of the President, March 8, 1983, WM, Box 83.

53. The letter is dated November 15, 1979, and the report attached to it is titled "Christian America Under Attack: Special Report No. 5." Throughout the copy of the report found in the American Heritage Center archive there is extensive underlining accompanied by checkmarks in the margins that suggest whoever read the report approved of a number of key passages.

54. "Christian America Under Attack," AHC, Box 36, Folder 35.

55. For the institutional changes that facilitated the development of a conservative Catholic identity in the 1960s, see chapter 2. For an examination of the development of American Protantism and changes between Bible-believing Protestants, particularly those facilitated by Francis Schaeffer and Jerry Falwell's adoption of the justificatory schema of co-belligerency the following decade, see chapter 4.

56. Cooper, "At the Expense of Christianity," 56.

57. Herman, "Then I Saw a New Heaven and a New Earth," 65.

58. Kristina Peterson, "House Republicans Now Unanimous in Opposing Abortion Rights," *Wall Street Journal*, March 21, 2019, https://www.wsj.com/articles /house-republicans-now-unanimous-in-opposing-abortion-rights-11553172954.

59. Jeffrey M. Jones, "Abortion Poised to Be a Bigger Voting Issue Than in Past," Gallup.com, June 6, 2022, https://news.gallup.com/poll/393263/abortion-poised-bigger-voting-issue-past.aspx; Lydia Saad, "Abortion Remains a Potent Issue for Pro-Choice Voters," Gallup.com, June 21, 2023, https://news.gallup.com/poll/507527/abortion-remains-potent-issue-pro-choice-voters.aspx.

60. As seen in reports produced by the conservative pollster Arthur Finklestein in the 1980s, abortion ranked low among issues self-identified Republicans cared about. A 1981 report produced for the Republican National Committee (RNC) and based on a survey of contributors to the RNC, highlights the following polling results: RNC donors view the "Economy and Inflation" as "the single most important problem facing the United States," followed by concerns over "Military/Defense and Foreign Affairs." "Conspicuous by its absence," the report continues, "is any significant concern with 'New Right' religious-moral issues. There is little doubt that RNC contributors are not Jerry Falwell–Moral Majority enthusiasts, but rather conservatives of a more traditional ilk. This conclusion is reinforced by the response to many other questions on the survey and will be elaborated upon subsequently in this report." This further elaboration shows, "In the Social-Moral category, Reducing Crime is by far the most important issue goal. Bringing Morality Back to Government and Restoring Capital Punishment are each somewhat important, but Prohibiting Abortion, Returning Prayer to Public Schools, Banning Pornography, and Stopping Prostitution are all accorded low priority." "Summary and Analysis of Sample Survey of Contributors to the Republican National Committee," Data Collection: October 9 through November 2, 1981, 8–10, Arthur J. Finkelstein Papers at the Library of Congress [hereafter LoC Finkelstein], Box 54. But just five years later, a poll conducted in the fall of 1985 and surveying "Registered Republicans, Republican Primary Voters, a Metromail List, and Subscribers to Conservative Publications," found that "Overall, tax issues were the top mention followed by environmental concerns and abortion, respectively. Abortion was the most frequently cited issue by registered Republicans." "List Survey Results," October 31, 1985, LoC Finkelstein, Box 54.

61. Howard Ball, *The Supreme Court in the Intimate Lives of Americans* (New York: New York University Press, 2002), 93–94. For an explanation of the "seamless garment" doctrine, see Mark Shea, "The Seamless Garment: What It Is and Isn't," *National Catholic Register*, June 14, 2014, https://www.ncregister.com/blog/the-seamless-garment-what-it-is-and-isn-t.

62. While my interest is in the role of religious political entrepreneurs, it should be noted that there is disagreement within the scholarly community concerning the strength of anti-abortion attitudes among the Protestant grassroots. Of particular interest is Neil A. O'Brian's work, which asserts that the Protestant grassroots was more firmly opposed to abortion than previously recognized. Neil A. O'Brian, "Before Reagan: The Development of Abortion's Partisan Divide," *Perspectives on Politics* 18, no. 4 (December 2020): 1031–1047.

63. Linda Greenhouse and Riva B. Siegel, *Before Roe v. Wade*, Creative Commons, 2012, 71–73, https://papers.ssrn.com/sol3/papers.cfm?abstract_id=2131505.

64. Randall Balmer, *Thy Kingdom Come: An Evangelical's Lament* (New York: Basic Books, 2006), chap. 1.

65. Mark J. Rozell, "Political Marriage of Convenience," in Kristin E. Heyer, Mark J. Rozell, and Michael A. Genovese, eds., *Catholics and Politics: The Dynamic Tension between Faith and Power* (Washington, DC: Georgetown University Press, 2008), 28.

66. ERLC Staff, "5 Facts about the History of the SBC and the Pro-Life Cause," Ethics and Religious Liberty Commission of the Southern Baptist Convention, https://erlc.com/resource-library/articles/5-facts-about-the-history-of-the-sbc-and-the-pro-life-cause/.

67. Barry Hankins, *Francis Schaeffer and the Shaping of Evangelical America* (Grand Rapids, MI: William B. Eerdmans, 2008), 187–191.

68. Francis Schaeffer and Everett C. Koop, *Whatever Happened to the Human Race?* (N.p.: L'Abri Publishing, 1979), 24.

69. Schaeffer and Koop, *Whatever Happened to the Human Race?*, 25.

70. Schaeffer and Koop, *Whatever Happened to the Human Race?*, 32.

71. Carol Mason, "Created Equal, but Equal in No Other Respect: Opposing Abortion to Protect Men," in Emily K. Carian, Alex DiBranco, and Chelsea Ebin, eds., *Male Supremacism in the United States: From Patriarchal Traditionalism to Misogynist Incels and the Alt-Right* (Abingdon, UK: Routledge, 2022).

72. Schaeffer and Koop, *Whatever Happened to the Human Race?*, 33.

73. Sean Michael Winters, *God's Right Hand: How Jerry Falwell Made God a Republican and Baptized the American Right* (New York: HarperOne, 2012), 99.

74. Winters, *God's Right Hand*, 99, 102–104; Randall Balmer notes that the first abortion sermon was not until 1978; see Balmer, "Jimmy Carter and the Evangelical Divide," *HuffPost*, June 9, 2014, https://www.huffingtonpost.com/randall-balmer/jimmy-carter-evangelical-_b_5473456.html.

75. Jerry Falwell, *Strength for the Journey* (New York: Simon & Schuster,1987), 337.

76. Williams, *God's Own Party*, 172.

77. The strategy of co-belligerency can be summarized in brief as one that justified overlooking doctrinal and denominational differences between Protestants for the purpose of politically working together to oppose the scourge of secular humanism. Schaeffer's development of the theory of co-belligerents is discussed in more detail in chapter four.

78. Michael Martin interview with Kristin Kobes Du Mez, "How Abortion Became a Mobilizing Issue among the Religious Right," All Things Considered, NPR, May 8, 2022, https://www.npr.org/2022/05/08/1097514184/how-abortion-became-a-mobilizing-issue-among-the-religious-right.

79. After the introduction of the birth control pill in the early 1960s, sexual norms changed rapidly and state laws criminalizing contraception increasingly conflicted with

people's lived experiences and social expectations. In 1965 the Supreme Court weighed in and recognized a married woman's right to contraception (*Griswold v. Connecticut*). The Court's decision in *Griswold* was premised on the explicit recognition of a constitutional right to privacy. Writing for the majority, Justice William O. Douglas explained the Court's logic in terms of its precedents: "The foregoing cases suggest that specific guarantees in the Bill of Rights have penumbras, formed by emanations from those guarantees that help give them life and substance. See *Poe v. Ullman*, 367 US 497, 367 US 516–522 (dissenting opinion). Various guarantees create zones of privacy." Griswold v. Connecticut, 381 US 479 (1965), p. 381 US 4040, Accessed at https://supreme.justia.com/cases/federal/us/381/479/. The decision, which was followed by a 1972 decision extending birth control access to unmarried women (*Eisenstadt v. Baird*), had a transformative impact on both individual women's lives and American society. As Linda Gordon has written, the Pill became the "'moral property' of millions of women," and "women made it a tool for autonomy, freedom, and higher aspirations." Linda Gordon, *The Moral Property of Women* (Champaign, IL: University of Chicago Press, 2007), 288. The Court's recognition of a right to privacy opened the door to subsequent decisions affecting sexual behavior and bodily autonomy, including the legalization of abortion. Howard Ball, *The Supreme Court in the Intimate Lives of Americans* (New York University Press, 2002), 47.

80. For an excellent and in-depth account of the development of Protestant theology as it concerns the place of women, see Beth Allison Barr, *The Making of Biblical Womanhood* (Grand Rapids, MI: Brazos, 2021).

81. Balmer, "The Real Origins of the Religious Right." My archival research lends support to Balmer's emphasis on desegregation as a—if not the—key motivating issue for Christian Right religious and political entrepreneurs. My findings also lend support to Balmer's claim that abortion was, at least in part, an instrumental issue for religious entrepreneurs. In a closed-door meeting of evangelical and fundamentalist leaders in 1982, aimed at finding ways of creating ecumenism in the interest of forging a religious right majority, Falwell asserted that the issue of abortion could bridge denominational rifts and had wide appeal. His comments were summarized in the meeting notes as, "He [Falwell] and [Senator] Mark Hatfield [R-OR] accept each other as fellow believers. They work together even though they disagree. Abortion is one such issue on which they can agree. To win people you have to speak strongly and simply. You can't always append a long list of scholar's footnotes to every statement you make. So it is with the questions of pornography and of Isreal." "Meeting of Fundamentalists and Evangelicals in Response to the Invitation Given by Jerry Falwell in His Volume, The Fundamentalist Phenomenon," February 1, 1982, Fal 3–2 s1 Fundamentalist Evangelical Meeting of 1982, Jerry Falwell and Moral Majority Archives at Liberty University [hereafter Moral Majority].

82. Balmer, "The Real Origins of the Religious Right."

83. Randall Balmer, "The Historian's Pickaxe: Uncovering the Racist Origins of the Religious Right," 3, https://www.sas.upenn.edu/andrea-mitchell-center/sites/www

.sas.upenn.edu.andrea-mitchell-center/files/Balmer%20-%20Historian%27s%20
Pickaxe.pdf.

84. O'Brian, "Before Reagan: The Development of Abortion's Partisan Divide."

85. Gerald Rosenberg, *The Hollow Hope: Can Courts Bring About Social Change?*,
2nd ed. (Chicago: University of Chicago Press, 2008), chap. 1.

86. Rosenberg, *The Hollow Hope*, 47.

87. Rosenberg, *The Hollow Hope*, 48.

88. Anthony M. Champagne, "The Segregation Academy and the Law," *Journal of
Negro Education* 42, no. 1 (Winter 1973): 58–66; Olatunde C. A. Johnson, "The Story
of Bob Jones University v. the United States: Race, Religion, and Congress' Extraordinary Acquiescence," in William Eskridge, Philip P. Frickey, and Elizabeth Garrett,
eds., Columbia Law School Public Law and Legal Theory Working Paper No. 10–
229 (2010), https://scholarship.law.columbia.edu/faculty_scholarship/2523/?utm
_source=scholarship.law.columbia.edu%2Ffaculty_scholarship%2F2523&utm
_medium=PDF&utm_campaign=PDFCoverPages.

89. Johnson, "The Story of Bob Jones University," 4.

90. Johnson, "The Story of Bob Jones University," 5–6.

91. I have altered the language in this quote to read "n—s." In the original, the word
is written in full. Champagne, "The Segregation Academy and the Law," 63.

92. Johnson, "The Story of Bob Jones University," 6.

93. A decade after it began, the legal controversy was finally resolved by the Supreme
Court's decision in *Bob Jones University v. United States* 416 US 735 (1983), which de-
termined that the IRS could continue to penalize private schools for their failure to desegregate. For a more detailed explanation of the controversy, see Balmer, "Historian's
Pickaxe;" Neal Devins, "On Casebooks and Canons or Why Bob Jones University Will
Never Be Part of the Constitutional Law Canon," William and Mary Law School Scholarship Repository Faculty Publications, Paper 363 (2000); David Kurlander, "'We Want
Them Burned': The 1978 Controversy over Discriminatory Schools," *The Cafe*, February 17, 2022, https://cafe.com/article/we-want-them-burned-the-1978-irs-controversy
-over-discriminatory-schools/; Martha Minnow, "Should Religious Groups Be Exempt
from Civil Rights Laws?," *Boston College Law Review* 48 (2007): 781–849.

94. Balmer, "The Real Origins of the Religious Right."

95. See "Discrimination and Christian Conscience," quoting from the 1943 statement, Catholic Bishops of the United States Pastoral Letters, November 14, 1958,
https://www.usccb.org/issues-and-action/cultural-diversity/african-american/re
sources/upload/Discrimination-Christian-Conscience-Nov-14-1958.pdf.

96. "On Racial Harmony," Catholic Bishops of the United States, August 23, 1963,
https://www.usccb.org/issues-and-action/cultural-diversity/african-american/re
sources/upload/On-Racial-Harmony.pdf.

97. Roy Reed, "Parochial School Desegregation Asked by Catholics in Louisiana,"
New York Times, July 6, 1970, https://www.nytimes.com/1970/07/26/archives/pa
rochial-school-desegregation-asked-by-catholics-in-louisiana.html.

98. James Charles Moses, "Desegregation in Catholic Schools in the Archdiocese of Chicago, 1964–1974, Including a Case Study of a Catholic High School" (PhD diss., Loyola University, 1977), 1748, 6, https://ecommons.luc.edu/luc_diss/1748.

99. James T. Hannon, "The Influence of Catholic Schools on the Desegregation of Public School Systems: A Case Study of White Flight in Boston," *Population Research and Policy Review* 3, no. 3 (October 1984): 222, http://www.jstor.org/stable/40229701.

100. Tisa Wenger, *Religious Freedom: The Contested History of an American Idea* (Chapel Hill: University of North Carolina Press, 2017), 1.

101. Wenger explains, "they [Catholics] reconfigured those hierarchies to rank (white) Catholics and (white) Protestants as equals. In other words, they pushed to replace the Anglo-Saxon at the top tier of the American racial order with the somewhat broader category of whiteness, a category that could include European immigrants who happened to be Catholics within its scope." Wenger, *Religious Freedom*, 39.

102. For an examination of how school prayer mobilizations aim to assert Christian privilege, see Daniel Tagliarina, "Power, Privilege, and Prayer: Christian Right Identity Politics and Mobilizing for School Prayer" (PhD diss., University of Connecticut–Storrs, 2014), 525, https://opencommons.uconn.edu/dissertations/525.

103. Anthea Butler, *White Evangelical Racism* (Chapel Hill, NC: University of North Carolina Press, 2021).

104. Sophie Bjork-James, "White Sexual Politics: The Patriarchal Family in White Nationalism and the Religious Right," *Transforming Anthropology* 28, no. 1 (March 2020): 58–73.

105. Herman, "'Then I Saw a New Heaven and a New Earth,'" 65.

106. Cooper, "At the Expense of Christianity," 54.

107. Cooper, "At the Expense of Christianity," 53.

108. "ABC report on the New Conservatism," n.d., AHC, Box 20, Folder 2.

Chapter 2. Paul Weyrich: 1968 and the Roots of a (Catholic) Radical

1. Paul Weyrich Roast, CSPAN, April 1, 1991, https://www.c-span.org/video/?17380-1/paul-weyrich-roast.

2. Adam D. Sheingate, "Political Entrepreneurship, Institutional Change, and American Political Development," *Studies in American Political Development* 17, no. 2 (October 2003): 185–203, 188.

3. Richard Viguerie was a pioneer of direct mail fundraising strategies for the New Right; Howard Phillips founded the Conservative Caucus in 1974, an organization aimed at mobilizing the grassroots; and John Terry Dolan was the head of the National Conservative Political Action Committee (NCPAC, founded in 1975), the New Right's most effective political campaign organization. Alongside Weyrich's Committee for the Survival of a Free Congress (CSFC, founded in 1974), and with funding from Viguerie's direct mailers as well as conservative donors like Joseph Coors, these three organizations formed the basis of the New Right's institutional power structure in the early to mid-1970s. In addition to these organizations, each of these men was

involved in half a dozen other ad hoc committees, boards, and so on. Their outsized roles and virtual omnipresence in the leadership of the New Right gave rise to the moniker "Gang of Four." Alf Tomas Tønnessen, *How Two Political Entrepreneurs Helped Create the American Conservative Movement, 1973–1981* (Lampeter, UK: Edwin Mellen Press, 2009), 76.

4. See, for example, David G. Bromley and Anson Shupe, eds., *New Christian Politics* (Macon, GA: Mercer, 1984); Robert C. Liebman and Robert Wuthnow, eds., *The New Christian Right* (New York: Aldine, 1983); William Martin, *With God on Our Side* (New York: Broadway Books, 1996); Daniel Schlozman, *When Movements Anchor Parties* (Princeton, NJ: Princeton University Press, 2015); and Daniel K. Williams, *God's Own Party* (Oxford: Oxford University Press, 2010).

5. For more on "pro-family" politics, see J. Brooks Flippen, *Jimmy Carter, the Politics of Family, and the Rise of the Religious Right* (Athens: University of Georgia Press, 2011); Leo P. Ribuffo, "Family Policy Past as Prologue: Jimmy Carter, the White House Conference on Families, and the Mobilization of the New Christian Right," *Review of Policy Research* 23, no. 2 (March/April 2006): 311–338; and Robert O. Self, *All in the Family: The Realignment of American Democracy since the 1960s* (New York: Hill & Wang, 2012).

6. Paul M. Weyrich Scrapbooks, 1942–2009, LoC Weyrich.

7. Letter petitioning for transfer to Byzantine-Slavonic Rite (1968), LoC Weyrich, Box 3, Folder 7.

8. It is commonly asserted that Weyrich worked on the Goldwater campaign, but I found no evidence of this in the archives.

9. Personal documents and ephemera from 1942–1964, LoC Weyrich, Boxes 1–2, Vols. 1–6.

10. CSPAN Q and A with Paul Weyrich and Brian Lamb, March 22, 2005, transcript, p. 4 of 17, accessed at http://www.c-span.org/video/transcript/?id=7958.

11. Paul Weyrich, "A Forgotten American Catholic Speaks Out," *The Wanderer*, 1969, LoC Weyrich, Box 3, Folder 10, Vol. 11.

12. The definition of American conservatism has historically been up for grabs. While the term has more well-defined and concrete meanings in relation to specific historical periods, it often functions as a vessel into which Americans pour their changing values and beliefs. Rather than preemptively impose the definition of conservatism that the New Right operationalized in later years, in this instance I am relying on Weyrich's early writings to describe *his* conception of what it meant to be an American (and religious) "conservative" at this time. For alternative historically grounded expositions of conservatism in America, see Daniel Bell, *The Radical Right* (Piscataway, NJ: Transaction, 2001); Brian Farmer, *American Conservatism: History, Theory and Practice* (Cambridge: Cambridge Scholars Publishing, 2005); and George H. Nash, *The Conservative Intellectual Movement* (Wilmington, DE: Intercollegiate Studies Institute, 2006).

13. Nash, *The Conservative Intellectual Movement*, 265.

14. Nash, *The Conservative Intellectual Movement*, 267–268.

15. Quoted in Nash, *The Conservative Intellectual Movement*, 268.

16. Jack Anderson, "Conservatives Court Working Man," *Conservative Digest*, May 1978, LoC Weyrich, Box 7, Folder 3, Vol. 23.

17. Weyrich, "A Forgotten American Catholic Speaks Out."

18. Weyrich, "A Forgotten American Catholic Speaks Out."

19. *Casti Connubii*, encyclical of Pope Pius XI on Christian marriage, https://w2.vatican.va/content/pius-xi/en/encyclicals/documents/hf_p-xi_enc_19301231_casti-connubii.html; see also Leslie Woodcock Tentler, *Catholics and Contraception: An American History* (Ithaca, NY: Cornell University Press, 2004), 7.

20. Tentler, *Catholics and Contraception*, 74.

21. Joseph A. Komonchak, "Interpreting the Council," in Mary Jo Weaver and R. Scott Appleby, eds., *Being Right: Conservative Catholics in America* (Bloomington: Indiana University Press, 1995), 18.

22. Mark S. J. Massa, *The American Catholic Revolution: How the Sixties Changed the Church Forever* (New York: Oxford University Press, 2010), 7.

23. Weaver and Appleby, *Being Right: Conservative Catholics in America*, ix.

24. Paul Weyrich, "The Groppi Agape," *The Wanderer*, 1969, LoC Weyrich, Box 3, Folder 10, Vol. 11.

25. The Catholic Traditionalist Manifesto, December 31, 1964, http://www.latinmass-ctm.org/about/charter.htm.

26. William D. Dinges, "We Are What You Were," in Weaver and Appleby, *Being Right: Conservative Catholics in America*, 243.

27. Dinges, "We Are What You Were."

28. Flier, 1967, LoC Weyrich, Box 3, Folder 4, Vol. 9.

29. Flier, 1968, LoC Weyrich, Box 3, Folder 5, Vol. 10; for more information, see http://www.latinmass-ctm.org/about/origin.htm.

30. Letter petitioning for transfer to Byzantine-Slavonic Rite, 1968, LoC Weyrich, Box 3, Folder 7, Vol. 10.

31. Kenneth R. Himes, "Vatican II and Contemporary Politics," in Paul Christopher Manuel, Lawrence C. Reardon, and Clyde Wilcox, eds., *The Catholic Church and the Nation-State* (Washington, DC: Georgetown University Press, 2006), 24.

32. Himes, "Vatican II and Contemporary Politics," 22.

33. Ted Jelen, "The American Church," in Manuel, Reardon, and Wilcox, *The Catholic Church and the Nation-State*, 76.

34. Komonchak, "Interpreting the Council," 24.

35. "An Open Letter to Gov. Burns of Hawaii," 1970, LoC Weyrich, Box 3, Folder 11.

36. Komonchak, "Interpreting the Council," 19.

37. William Martin, *With God on Our Side: The Rise of the Religious Right in America* (New York: Broadway Books, 1996), 170.

38. Weyrich was particularly critical of school busing programs. Paul Weyrich, "A

Chance to Save the Now Generation," *The Wanderer*, November 5, 1970, LoC Weyrich, Box 3, Folder 11.

39. In a "Washington Report" press release from Senator Allott's office, conducted shortly after MLK was assassinated, Weyrich asks if there's a "connection between violence and the assassination?" Allott says only as "pretense," before going on to condemn student protests and praise the University of Colorado for its handling of the protests and for the "swift expulsion" of student activists. 1968, LoC Weyrich, Box 3, Folder 7, Vol. 10.

40. Petition and attached article "Catholics Receive Episcopalian Communion for Dr. King," 1968, LoC Weyrich, Box 3, Folder 7, Vol. 10.

41. Petition and attached article "Catholics Receive Episcopalian Communion for Dr. King."

42. Pope Paul VI, *Nostra Aetate*, October 28, 1965, http://www.vatican.va/archive/hist_councils/ii_vatican_council/documents/vat-ii_decl_19651028_nostra-aetate_en.html.

43. It is worth noting here that, as a religiously faithful White man from the Midwest, Paul Weyrich was not alone in opposing the civil rights movement. In 1968 the sociologist Milton Rokeach found that among White people, increased religiosity corresponded to decreased support for civil rights. Among 1,400 respondents, "Those who felt Dr. King had 'brought it on himself' or who had responded to the assassination with 'fear' ranked *salvation* fourth on the average, and those who responded with 'sadness,' 'anger,' or 'shame' cared considerably less for salvation, ranking it anywhere from ninth to fourteenth." Rokeach reported his findings in stark terms: "For lack of space I will not discuss all of these results in detail but instead content myself to point out that on all civil rights issues, which concern open occupancy, fair employment, education, dating, intermarriage, race difference in intelligence, and the black struggle for equality, a high value for *salvation* was indeed significantly related to civil rights position but in a negative position, that is, those who opposed equal rights for blacks placed a higher value on *salvation* than those who favored equal rights." Milton Rokeach, "Part II: Religious Values and Social Compassion," *Review of Religious Research* 11, no. 1 (Autumn 1969): 24–39.

44. Fliers and news clippings, 1968, LoC Weyrich, Box 3, Folder 7, Vol. 10.

45. James A. Sullivan, "Catholics United for the Faith," in Weaver and Appleby, *Being Right: Conservative Catholics in America*, 107.

46. CUF Declaration of Purpose, 1968, LoC Weyrich, Box 3, Folder 7, Vol. 10.

47. Linda Gordon, *The Moral Property of Women: A History of Birth Control Politics in America* (Champagne, IL: University of Chicago Press, 2007).

48. Donald Critchlow, *Intended Consequences: Birth Control, Abortion, and the Federal Government in Modern America* (New York: Oxford University Press, 2008), 112–115.

49. Gordon, *The Moral Property of Women*, 288. See also Matthew Connelly, *Fatal

Misconception: The Struggle to Control World Population (Cambridge, MA: Harvard University Press, 2008), 158–159.

50. Gordon, *The Moral Property of Women*, 282.

51. Gordon, *The Moral Property of Women*, 279–280, 284.

52. Karl Sax, *Standing Room Only: The Challenge of Over Population* (Boston: Beacon Press, 1955).

53. See, for example, Jon Gjerde, *Catholicism and the Shaping of Nineteenth-Century America*, ed. S. Deborah Kang (Cambridge : Cambridge University Press, 2012); Katie Oxx, *The Nativist Movement in America: Religious Conflict in the 19th Century* (London: Routledge, 2013).

54. Melissa Wilde identifies 1930 as a critical year for noting the difference in Protestant and Catholic attitudes toward artificial contraception: "The Roman Catholic Church condemned 'artificial means' of birth control in 1930, the same year Anglicans announced that they had approved the use of contraceptives. . . . This view was different from that of the majority of mainline Protestants, who did not distinguish between artificial and natural methods of contraception." Melissa Wilde, *Vatican II: A Sociological Analysis of Religious Change* (Princeton, NJ: Princeton University Press, 2007), 117.

55. Critchlow, *Intended Consequences*, 17.

56. Paul Weyrich, "A Chance to Save the Now Generation," *The Wanderer*, November 5, 1970, LoC Weyrich, Box 3, Folder 11, Vol. 12; AHC, Folder 10, Box 82.

57. Tentler, *Catholics and Contraception*, 4, 246–247.

58. Tentler, *Catholics and Contraception*, 230.

59. Wilde, *Vatican II*, 116.

60. Tentler, *Catholics and Contraception*, 230.

61. Tentler, *Catholics and Contraception*, 236–237.

62. Thomas J. Fleming, "Confrontation in Washington: The Cardinal vs. the Dissenters," *New York Times Magazine*, November 24, 1968, LoC Weyrich, Box 3, Folder 7, Vol. 10.

63. "Rally, Vigil to Dramatize Clash on O'Boyle Stance," *Evening Star*, November 9, 1968, LoC Weyrich, Box 3, Folder 7, Vol. 10.

64. Russell Chandler, "Suspension, Dissent Raise Question of Right to Speak," *Washington Star* (undated), LoC Weyrich, Box 3, Folder 7, Vol. 10.

65. Quoted in Tentler, *Catholics and Contraception*, 230.

66. "Lay Group to Rally Support for Pope," *Catholic Standard*, September 19, 1968, LoC Weyrich, Box 3, Folder 7, Vol. 10.

67. Russell Chandler, "Suspension, Dissent Raise Question of Right to Speak," *Washington Star* (undated; 1968), LoC Weyrich, Box 3, Folder 7, Vol. 10.

68. *Apostolicam Actuositatem*, http://www.vatican.va/archive/hist_councils/ii_vatican_council/documents/vat-ii_decree_19651118_apostolicam-actuositatem_en.html.

69. Thomas J. Fleming, "Can the 'Catholic Revolution' Succeed?," *Redbook Magazine*, May 1969, LoC Weyrich, Box 3, Folder 8, Vol. 11.

70. *The Wanderer* is a Roman Catholic weekly journal, published by laymen, and *Eastern Catholic Life* is a newspaper affiliated with the Eastern Catholic Church of the Byzantine Rite. Both publications have a conservative political bias and advocate for what they hold is religious orthodoxy.

71. "Our Odyssey to the East," *Eastern Catholic Life*; and "CUF Stops Dissidents from Church Takeover," *The Wanderer*, 1969, LoC Weyrich, Box 3, Folder 8, Vol. 11.

72. See, for example, the previously referenced "An Open Letter to Gov. Burns of Hawaii," published in *The Wanderer*, which lambasted Burns for not vetoing legislation that made abortion broadly accessible to women in Hawaii.

73. In a fascinating editorial, Weyrich condemned an anti-abortion direct action led by Leo Brent Bozell. Weyrich, "Militancy and Responsibility," *Eastern Catholic Life*, June 28, 1970, LoC Weyrich, Box 4, Folder 1, Vol. 12.

74. "Anti-Life Forces Continue Gains," *The Wanderer*, 1970, LoC Weyrich, Box 4, Folder 1, Vol. 12.

75. See especially chap. 4 of Timothy A. Byrnes, "The Bishops, Abortion, and a 'New Majority,'" in *Catholic Bishops and American Politics* (Princeton, NJ: Princeton University Press, 1991), 54–67. Byrnes writes, "The bishops' involvement with abortion as a political issue began in earnest shortly after the close of the Second Vatican Council when the American Law Institute's Model Penal Code called for liberalization of the various state laws governing abortion. At a series of meetings in 1967, the bishops decided to denounce the code and actively oppose legal abortion," 54.

76. "A Story of the Real Beautiful People," *The Wanderer*, 1970, LoC Weyrich, Box 3, Folder 11, Vol. 12.

77. "Anti-Life Forces Continue Gains," *The Wanderer*, 1970, LoC Weyrich, Box 4, Folder 1, Vol. 12.

78. Weyrich expresses no such displeasure that the youth surveyed are overwhelmingly opposed to affirmative action and busing for the purpose of racial integration. "A Chance to Save the Now Generation," *The Wanderer*, November 5, 1970, LoC Weyrich, Box 4, Folder 2, Vol 12.

79. "Catholic Power," *The Wanderer*, LoC Weyrich, Box 4, Folder 3, Vol. 13.

80. Michael W. Cuneo, *The Smoke of Satan: Conservative and Traditionalist Dissent in Contemporary American Catholicism* (Baltimore: John Hopkins University Press, 1999), 23–25.

81. Massa, *The American Catholic Revolution*, 12, 156.

82. Mark S. J. Massa, *The Structure of Theological Revolutions* (New York: Oxford University Press, 2018), 24–25.

83. William J. Lanouette, "The New Right—'Revolutionaries' Out after the 'Lunch-Pail' Vote," *National Journal*, January 21, 1978, LoC Weyrich, Box 6, Folder 7.

84. Weaver and Appleby, *Being Right: Conservative Catholics in America*, 38.

Chapter 3. Building the New Right and the New Traditional Woman

1. Nicholas von Hoffman, "The Breaking of Richard Nixon" (reprinted from *Penthouse Magazine*), *Conservative Digest*, May 1977.

2. Kevin Phillips, "The Conservative Revolt against Nixon," King Features Syndicate (for release June 28, 1971), LoC Weyrich, Box 4, Folder 3, Vol. 13.

3. Vivien Schmidt, "Discursive Institutionalism: The Explanatory Power of Ideas and Discourse," *Annual Review of Political Science* 11, no. 1 (June 2008): 310.

4. Vivien Schmidt, "Britain-out and Trump-in: A Discursive Institutionalist Analysis of the British Referendum on the EU and the US Presidential Election," *Review of International Political Economy* 24, no. 2 (March 2017): 251.

5. Vivien Schmidt, *Handbook of Critical Policy Studies* (Cheltenham, UK: Edward Elgar, 2015), 9.

6. See Morris P. Fiorina and Samuel Abrams, "Americans Aren't Polarized, Just Better Sorted," *Washington Post*, January 21, 2014, https://www.washingtonpost.com /news/monkey-cage/wp/2014/01/21/americans-arent-polarized-just-better-sorted/, for a straightforward explanation of "the sorting of partisans into parties with clearer identities" over time.

7. Connie Marshner Curriculum Vitae, AHC Box 79, Folder 5.

8. Most notably, an interview with Connie Marshner by John Rees, titled "Profamily Leader Connie Marshner," in *Review of the News*, January 21, 1981, AHC Box 81, Folder 13.

9. Extrapolating from memos in the archives, it seems Joy worked for first Congressman Philip Crane and later Senator James Buckley in the early to mid-1970s.

10. William Roth, "The Politics of Day Care: The Comprehensive Child Development Act of 1971," December 1976, 1, https://www.irp.wisc.edu/publications/dps /pdfs/dp36976.pdf. The report was written for the Institute for Research on Poverty at the University of Wisconsin-Madison with funds from the Department of Health, Education, and Welfare (HEW).

11. Roth, "The Politics of Day Care," 5.

12. "Record Number of Women in the U.S. Labor Force," Population Reference Bureau, February 2001, https://www.prb.org/resources/record-number-of-wom en-in-the-u-s-labor-force/#:~:text=(February%202001)%20Over%20the%20 past,were%20in%20the%20labor%20force.

13. "Current Population Reports: Consumer Income," U.S. Department of Commerce/Bureau of the Census, May 7, 1971, https://www2.census.gov/library/publi cations/1971/demographics/p60-77.pdf.

14. Annelise Orlick, *Rethinking American Women's Activism* (New York: Routledge, 2015).

15. Dan Joy, "Memorandum for the Record," November 1,1971, AHC, Box 18, Folder 27. Of note is the difficulty Marshner, Joy, and Weyrich faced when trying to secure a statement from the Catholic hierarchy. There are repeated references to failed

attempts to get a member of the Catholic Church to go on record opposing the legislation in this folder.

16. Dan Joy, Paul Weyrich, and Connie Coyne, "Memorandum for the Record," December 2, 1971, AHC, Box 18, Folder 27.

17. Leo P. Ribuffo, "Family Policy Past as Prologue: Jimmy Carter, the White House Conference on Families, and the Mobilization of the New Christian Right," *Review of Policy Research* 23, no. 2 (March/April 2006): 325.

18. Connie Coyne, "Memorandum for the Record: Subject Child Development Operation," May 24, 1972, AHC, Box 18, Folder 27.

19. Connie Coyne, "Memorandum for the Record: Subject Child Development Operation," April 19, 1972, AHC, Box 18, Folder 27.

20. Connie Coyne, "Notes toward the Memo Paul Asked For," June 1, 1973, AHC, Box 19, Folder 1.

21. Connie Coyne, "Memorandum for the Files," Legal Services in the House, February 14, 1974, AHC, Box 19, Folder 1.

22. Richard Nixon, "387—Veto of the Economic Opportunity Amendments of 1971," December 9, 1971, https://www.presidency.ucsb.edu/documents/veto-the-economic-opportunity-amendments-1971.

23. See, for example, Catherine Rymph, *Republican Women: Feminism and Conservatism from Suffrage through the Rise of the New Right* (Chapel Hill: University of North Carolina Press, 2006); and Ronnee Schreiber, *Righting Feminism: Conservative Women and American Politics* (New York: Oxford University Press, 2008).

24. Rebecca E. Klatch, *Women of the New Right* (Philadelphia: Temple University Press, 1987), 9.

25. A notable exception to this trend is Klatch's work and Carol Mason's book *Reading Appalachia from Left to Right: Conservatives and the 1974 Kanawha County Textbook Controversy* (Ithaca, NY: Cornell University Press, 2009).

26. Marshner, "Notes toward the Memo Paul Asked For."

27. 1972 Scorecard Vote, OSHA exemptions, https://scorecard.lcv.org/roll-call-vote/1972-653-osha-exemptions.

28. Paul Weyrich, "Memo for the Record. Subject: Operation '72—the Weeks Ahead," July 24, 1972, AHC, Box 18, Folder 27.

29. Paul M. Weyrich, CSFC Statement before the Republican Platform Committee, August 10, 1976, LoC Weyrich, Box 6, Folder 1, Vol. 19.

30. Weyrich, CSFC Statement before the Republican Platform Committee.

31. Klatch, *Women of the New Right*, chap. 2.

32. Klatch, *Women of the New Right*, 46–7.

33. Klatch, *Women of the New Right*, 128–129, 30.

34. Anita Creamer, "Missionary Leaves Home to Preserve, Protect, Defend American Family," *Dallas Herald*, May 3, 1984, AHC, Box 27, Folder 4.

35. Creamer, "Missionary Leaves Home to Preserve, Protect, Defend American Family."

36. Donald T. Critchlow, *Phyllis Schlafly and Grassroots Conservatism: A Woman's Crusade* (Princeton, NJ: Princeton University Press, 2008); David Farber, *The Rise and Fall of Modern American Conservatism: A Short History* (Princeton, NJ: Princeton University Press, 2012); Klatch, *Women of the New Right*; Lisa McGirr, *Suburban Warriors: The Origins of the New American Right* (Princeton, NJ: Princeton University Press, 2015).

37. Phyllis Schlafly, "The Phyllis Schlafly Report," February 1972, Sara Diamond collection on the US Right, BANC MSS 98/70 cz, Bancroft Library, University of California, Berkeley [hereafter Diamond], Carton 13, Folder 11.

38. Jane Mansbridge, *Why We Lost the ERA* (Chicago: University of Chicago Press, 1986).

39. Connie Marshner, "The New Traditional Woman," AHC, Box 82, Folder 18, n.d.; Klatch also references this text, identifying it as a speech Marshner gave at the Family Forum II Conference in 1982.

40. Gillian Frank, "'The Civil Rights of Parents:' Race and Conservative Politics in Anita Bryant's Campaign against Gay Rights in 1970s Florida," *Journal of the History of Sexuality* 22, no. 1 (January 2013): 126–160.

41. Andrew R. Lewis, *The Rights Turn in Conservative Christian Politics: How Abortion Transformed the Culture Wars* (Cambridge: Cambridge University Press, 2017).

42. John S. Saloma III, *Ominous Politics: The New Conservative Labyrinth* (New York: Hill & Wang, 1984).

43. New Right opposition was especially fierce when it came to the first 1972 Strategic Arms Limitation Talks/Treaty (SALT I).

44. Richard A. Viguerie, *The New Right: We're Ready to Lead*, rev. ed. (Falls Church, VA: Viguerie Company, 1981), 81.

45. Viguerie also oversaw the publication and distribution of *Conservative Digest*, a monthly magazine dedicated to promoting conservative issues and candidates, as well as facilitated the distribution of other conservative media, such as *The Right Report*.

46. "Conservative Fund-Raisers: New Hope for 1974," Political Report, *Congressional Quarterly*, LoC Weyrich, Box 5, Folder 3, Vol. 16–17.

47. Viguerie, *The New Right*, 84, 88.

48. Weyrich quoted in "'New Right' Plans Move to Change Congress," *Congressional Quarterly*, 1976, LoC Weyrich, Box 6, Folder 2, Vol. 19.

49. John Chamberlain, "Conservative Groups Mushroom," February 1978, *Conservative Digest*.

50. Paul M. Weyrich, "Weyrich from Washington: Organizing the Conservative Movement," *Conservative Digest*, July 1979, LoC Weyrich, Box 7, Folder 7, Vol. 25.

51. "'New Right' Puts Cash into Conservative Campaigns: Congress Is the Major Target," *Congressional Quarterly*, 1976, LoC Weyrich, Box 6, Folder 2, Vol. 19.

52. "Conservative Fund-Raisers: New Hope for 1974," *Congressional Quarterly*, Political Report, 1974, LoC Weyrich, Box 5, Folder 3, Vol. 16–17.

53. Richard Viguerie, *Conservative Digest*, April 1977.

54. After the November 1976 election, journalist James Perry reported that conservative candidates had received an average of nine cents for every dollar donated through fundraising campaigns operated by Viguerie. James M. Perry, "The Right Wing Got Plucked," 1976, LoC Weyrich, Box 6, Folder 2, Vol. 19.

55. Connie Marshner, "Right On: Right to Life: Grounds for Decision," n.d., AHC, Box 88, Folder 8.

56. Cass R. Sunstein and John M. Olin, "The Law of Group Polarization," preliminary draft, University of Chicago Law School, December 1999, 20–21, https:// chicagounbound.uchicago.edu/cgi/viewcontent.cgi.

57. Robert Michels, Political Parties, trans. Eden and Cedar Paul (Kitchener, Ontario: Batoche Books, 2001); Günes Murat Tezcür, "The Moderation Theory Revisited." Party Politics 16, no. 1 (August 2009): 69–88.

58. James Davison Hunter, Culture Wars: The Struggle to Define America (New York: Basic Books, 1991), 49.

59. Jack Anderson, "Conservatives Court Working Man," 1978, LoC Weyrich, Box 7, Folder 1, Vol. 23.

60. Alf Tomas Tønnessen, How Two Political Entrepreneurs Helped Create the Conservative Movement, 1973–1981 (Lampeter, UK: Edwin Mellen Press, 2009), 6.

61. Clay F. Richards, "Coalition Name of Game for New Right," Boston Herald American, September 10, 1978, LoC Weyrich, Box 7, Folder 2, Vol. 23 (May–December).

62. Alan Crawford, "Richard Viguerie's Bid for Power," The Nation, January 29, 1977, LoC Weyrich, Box 6, Folder 3, Vol. 20.

63. Kevin Phillips, "New Right and the Two Party System," Florida Times Union, October 10, 1978, LoC Weyrich, Box 7, Folder 2, Vol. 23.

64. Crawford, "Richard Viguerie's Bid for Power."

65. "The New Activists," National Affairs, 1977, LoC Weyrich, Box 6, Folder 5–6, Vol. 21.

66. Connie Marshner, "Brainstorming for a 'Family Consolidation Act,'" 1974, AHC, Box 19, Folder 2.

67. Jerome L. Himmelstein, "The New Right," in Robert C. Liebman and Robert Wuthnow, eds., The New Christian Right: Mobilization and Legitimation (New York: Aldine, 1983), 14.

68. "Project Survival" Plan, AHC, Folder 29, Box 23. I base the assertion that Project Survival never got off the ground on the basis of it not appearing anywhere else in my extensive review of New Right archives or in the secondary literature on the New and Religious Rights.

69. Morton C. Blackwell, "How to Organize Conservatives," reprinted in Conservative Digest, July 1978.

70. Clay F. Richards, "Coalition Name of Game for New Right," Boston Herald American, September 10, 1978, LoC Weyrich, Box 7, Folder 2, Vol. 23.

71. The New Right Report, November 20, 1978.

72. Viguerie, The New Right, 83.

Chapter 4. Jerry Falwell: A Fundamentalist Phenomenon Rises Up to Meet the Grassroots

1. Ed Dobson, Ed Hindson, and Jerry Falwell, quoting Milton Rudnick, "Fundamentalism Is Alive and Well!," in *The Fundamentalist Phenomenon: The Resurgence of Conservative Christianity*, 2nd ed. (Grand Rapids, MI: Baker Book House, 1981), 3.

2. Frank Mead, Samuel S. Hill, and Craig D. Atwood, *Handbook of Denominations in the United States*, 13th ed. (Nashville, TN: Abingdon Press, 2010), 273.

3. See, for example "What Is an Evangelical?," National Association of Evangelicals, https://www.nae.net/what-is-an-evangelical/.

4. Barry Hankins, *Jesus and Gin: Evangelicalism, the Roaring Twenties, and Today's Culture Wars* (New York: Palgrave Macmillan, 2010), 65.

5. George M. Marsden, *Fundamentalism and American Culture*, 2nd ed. (Oxford: Oxford University Press, 2006), 7.

6. The way Marsden periodizes evangelicalism and fundamentalism draws attention to the slipperiness of the terms being used and the malleability of what can seem like rigid religious identities. In reality, there has been considerable movement between the two groups, and as a result there is some fluidity in distinguishing between evangelicals and fundamentalists. On the whole, to avoid this confusion and to encompass the theologically and politically conservative evangelicals and fundamentalists who comprised the New Right, I alternately use the terms "conservative Protestant" and "Bible-believing Protestant" to refer to what Marsden terms "Fundamentalistic Evangelicalism." In the following sections, however, the terms "evangelical," "fundamentalist," and "new evangelical" are used with more precision to refer to specific identities that existed at particular times in relation, and often opposition, to one another.

7. Marsden, *Fundamentalism and American Culture*, 125–126, 82–83.

8. For an accessible breakdown of pre- and postmillennialist thought, see Garry Wills, *Under God: Religion and American Politics* (New York: Simon & Schuster, 1990), 127–175.

9. Randall Balmer, *Bad Faith: Race and the Rise of the Religious Right* (Grand Rapids, MI: Wm. B. Eerdmans, 2021), 9.

10. See, for example, Chris Hedges, *American Fascists* (New York: Free Press, 2008), or Michelle Goldberg, *Kingdom Coming: The Rise of Christian Nationalism* (New York: W. W. Norton, 2006). Both offer a simplified view of postmillennial thought as it relates to political action.

11. Marsden, *Fundamentalism and American Culture*, 211.

12. Hankins, *Jesus and Gin*, 104.

13. Angela M. Lahr, *Millennial Dreams and Apocalyptic Nightmares: The Cold War Origins of Political Evangelicalism* (New York: Oxford University Press, 2007), 12; Daniel Williams, *God's Own Party: The Making of the Christian Right*, 1st ed. (New York: Oxford University Press, 2010), introduction and chap. 1.

14. Mark Taylor Dalhouse, *An Island in the Lake of Fire: Bob Jones University,*

Fundamentalism, and the Separatist Movement (Athens: Georgia University Press, 1996), 57.

15. Hankins, *Jesus and Gin*, 64–65.

16. Dobson et al., *The Fundamentalist Phenomenon*, 3.

17. Dobson et al., *The Fundamentalist Phenomenon*, 5.

18. My interest here lies in summarizing the internal development of conservative Protestant identities during this period. I do not, therefore, take into account corresponding changes within liberal Protestantism. For such an analysis, see K. Healon Gaston, *Imagining Judeo-Christian America: Religion, Secularism, and the Redefinition of Democracy* (Chicago: University of Chicago Press, 2019). In it, Gaston tells a much more complicated story about the relationship between Protestants, Catholics, Jews, and secularists during World War II and the Cold War. Her work expertly details a complex set of negotiations between these groups as they all sought to lay claim to the nation's political institutions and assert ownership over its democratic values.

19. Steven P. Miller, *Billy Graham and the Rise of the Republican South* (Philadelphia: University of Pennsylvania, 2009), 14.

20. Lahr, *Millennial Dreams and Apocalyptic Nightmares*, 32.

21. Anthea Butler, *White Evangelical Racism* (Chapel Hill: University of North Carolina Press, 2021), 41.

22. See Clyde Wilcox, "Support for the Christian Right Old and New: A Comparison of Supporters of the Christian Anti-Communism Crusade and the Moral Majority," *Sociological Focus* 22, no. 2 (May 1989): 87–97; Clyde Wilcox, "Popular Backing for the Old Christian Right: Explaining Support for the Christian Anti-Communism Crusade," *Journal of Social History* 21, no. 1 (Autumn 1987): 117–132; and Clyde Wilcox, "Sources of Support for the Old Right: A Comparison of the John Birch Society and the Christian Anti-Communism Crusade," *Social Science History* 12, no. 4 (Winter 1988): 429–449.

23. Lahr, *Millennial Dreams and Apocalyptic Nightmares*, 7, 43.

24. Irvin D. S. Winsboro, "Religion, Culture, and the Cold War: Bishop Fulton J. Sheen and America's Anti-Communist Crusade of the 1950s," *Historian* 71, no. 2 (June 2009): 209–233.

25. Marsden, *Fundamentalism and American Culture*, 239.

26. Jerry Falwell, *Strength for the Journey: An Autobiography* (New York: Pocket Books, 1987), 69.

27. Daniel K. Williams, "Jerry Falwell's Sunbelt Politics: The Regional Origins of the Moral Majority," *Journal of Policy History* 22, no. 2 (March 2010): 126.

28. Sean Michael Winters, *God's Right Hand: How Jerry Falwell Made God a Republican and Baptized the American Right* (New York: HarperOne, 2012), 33. See also Falwell, *Strength for the Journey*.

29. Winters, *God's Right Hand*, 83–84.

30. Falwell, *Strength for the Journey*, 276. See also Falwell's March 1964 sermon

"Ministers and Marches," Moral Majority (digital collection), https://liberty.con tentdm.oclc.org/digital/collection/p17184coll4/id/4691.

31. Lisa McGirr's history of the development of a new right in the late 1950s and early 1960s, *Suburban Warriors: The Origins of the New American Right* (Princeton, NJ: Princeton University Press, 2002), begins with an exposition of the ideological overlap between the John Birch Society (JBS) and the anticommunist crusades, and traces how a new right developed with the institutional support of local media, churches, and businessmen and through grassroots organizing and targeted local campaigns. Eschewing the most extreme conspiracy theories promulgated by the JBS, these grassroots activists retained and refined organizing strategies learned from the group, particularly those that relied on in-home meetings and word-of-mouth education. For another version of the argument about the fusion of social and economic conservatism, see Williams, "Jerry Falwell's Sunbelt Politics."

32. WM, Box 83; William Martin, *With God on Our Side* (New York: Broadway Books, 1996), 103, 117–118.

33. Parents' Action Guide, n.d., WM, Box 83. The guide is undated and does not have a clearly identified author. However, it follows a letter in the William Martin Archive stating, "Enclosed please find photocopies of material related to the sex education controversy which brought national attention to Anaheim in the 1960s. Included are items distributed by the Citizens Committee of Calif., Inc." A pitch at the end of the guide to order a companion guide directs readers to contact the Citizens for Excellence in Education in Costa Mesa, CA. Between this and the placement of the guide in the collection, it is probable the guide was part of the Anaheim parents' movement to oppose sex education.

34. Assorted media in WM, Box 83.

35. Lawrence J. Haims, "Problems Associated with the Implementation of Sex Education Programs," *Sex Education and the Public Schools: A Multidimensional Study for the 1970s* (Lexington, MA: Lexington Books: 1973), WM, Box 83.

36. Haims, "Problems Associated with the Implementation of Sex Education Programs."

37. Carol Mason, *Reading Appalachia from Left to Right: Conservative and the 1974 Kanawha County Textbook Controversy* (Ithaca, NY: Cornell University Press, 2009), 91.

38. Martin, *With God on Our Side*, 119.

39. John Egerton, "The Battle of the Books," *The Progressive*, 1974, WM, Box 80.

40. Kanawha Chronology, WM, Box 80; Martin, *With God on Our Side*, 128–130.

41. The controversy came to an anticlimactic end when the school board voted four against Moore's one to keep the books but required parents to submit "written permission for their children to be assigned the books." Martin, *With God on Our Side*, 126–132, 136.

42. Memo, 1975, AHC, Box 19, Folder 15.

43. Mason, *Reading Appalachia from Left to Right*, 9.

44. Clayton L. McNearney, "The Kanawha County Textbook Controversy," 534–535, WM, Box 80.

45. Mason, *Reading Appalachia from Left to Right*, 104.

46. Mason, *Reading Appalachia from Left to Right*, 110.

47. Susan Friend Harding, *The Book of Jerry Falwell* (Princeton, NJ: Princeton University Press, 2000), 109.

48. Winters, *God's Right Hand*, 98.

49. Falwell, *Strength for the Journey*, 300; Dirk Smillie, *Falwell Inc.* (New York: St. Martin's Press, 2008), 79.

50. Smillie, *Falwell Inc.*, 79–80.

51. Falwell, *Strength for the Journey*, 300.

52. Smillie, *Falwell Inc.*, 88.

53. Frances FitzGerald, "A Disciplined, Charging Army," *New Yorker*, May 18, 2007, https://www.newyorker.com/magazine/1981/05/18/a-disciplined-charging-army.

54. Falwell, *Strength for the Journey*, 330.

55. Falwell, *Strength for the Journey*, 331.

56. J. Brooks Flippen, *Jimmy Carter, the Politics of Family, and the Rise of the Religious Right* (Athens: University of Georgia Press, 2011), 58.

57. Dobson et al., *The Fundamentalist Phenomenon*, 157–164.

58. Jerry Falwell, *Listen, America!* (New York: Doubleday, 1980).

59. Dobson et al., *The Fundamentalist Phenomenon*,; see especially chap. 4, "The Aftermath," 79–112.

60. Jerry Falwell, *An Autobiography* (Lynchburg, VA: Liberty House Publishers, 1997), 333.

61. See, for example, Martin, *With God on Our Side*, 91–95.

62. Falwell, "An Appeal," *Fundamentalist Phenomenon*, 159 (emphasis added).

63. Craig Gelder and Dwight J. Zscheile, *The Missional Church in Perspective: Mapping Trends and Shaping the Conversations* (Grand Rapids, MI: Baker Academic, 2011), 162.

64. Dobson et al., *The Fundamentalist Phenomenon*, 158.

65. Falwell, *Listen, America!*, 256.

66. Falwell, *An Autobiography*, 386.

67. Barry Hankins, *Francis Schaeffer and the Shaping of Evangelical America* (Grand Rapids, MI: Williams B. Eerdmans, 2008).

68. Francis Schaeffer, *Plan for Action: An Action Alternative Handbook for "Whatever Happened to the Human Race?"* (Grand Rapids, MI: Fleming H. Revell, 1980), 68.

69. Moral Majority, Fal 3–2 s1 Fundamentalist Evangelical Meeting of 1982.

70. Moral Majority, Resolutions of the 65th Anniversary Meeting of Fundamental Baptist Fellowship (1985).

71. Falwell, *An Autobiography*, 386.

72. Winters, *God's Right Hand*, 10.

73. Elisabeth S. Clemens and James M. Cook explain, "Historical analyses

demonstrates how choices among institutional arrangements may be 'constitutive moments' or branching points that channel subsequent political and economic developments." Elisabeth S. Clemens and James M. Cook, "Politics and Institutionalism: Explaining Durability and Change," *Annual Review of Sociology* 25 (1999): 447.

74. Moral Majority, Fal 5–2 Correspondence 1978–1979.

75. Smillie, *Falwell Inc.*, 61–66.

Chapter 5. Pro-Family Politics and the Political Convergence of Conservative Catholics and Protestants on the American Right

1. Carter's missteps concerning the family, and the importance of pro-family politics for the Christian Right and the Reagan Revolution, have been detailed elsewhere, notably in J. Brooks Flippen's history of the period. J. Brooks Flippen, *Jimmy Carter, the Politics of Family, and the Rise of the Religious Right* (Athens: University of Georgia Press, 2011), 62.

2. Quoted in Flippen, *Jimmy Carter*, 23.

3. Melinda Cooper, *Family Values: Between Neoliberalism and the New Social Conservatism* (Princeton, NJ: Zone Books, 2017), 97.

4. Arthur Finkelstein, untitled memo, LoC Finkelstein Papers, Box 11, "Committee to Re-elect the President," Folder 1 or 3 (1972–1973).

5. Arthur Finkelstein, untitled memo, LoC Finkelstein Papers, Box 11, "Committee to Re-elect the President," Folder 1 or 3 (1972–1973), Library of Congress.

6. Jeffrey M. Jones, "The Protestant and Catholic Vote," Gallup.com, June 8, 2004, https://news.gallup.com/poll/11911/protestant-catholic-vote.aspx.

7. "Gallup Election Polls: Vote by Group 1976–1980," Gallup.com, https://web.archive.org/web/20171010174814/news.gallup.com/poll/9460/election-polls-vote-groups-19761980.aspx.

8. Frank Van Der Linder, "Memo: Democrats Fear Single-Issue Groups," November 20, 1978, AHC, Box 23, Folder 16.

9. Balmer, "Jimmy Carter and the Evangelical Divide," *Huffington Post*, June 9, 2014, https://www.huffingtonpost.com/randall-balmer/jimmy-carter-evangelical-_b_5473456.html. See also Balmer, "The Historian's Pickaxe: Uncovering the Racist Origins of the Religious Right," 3, https://www.sas.upenn.edu/andrea-mitchell-center/sites/www.sas.upenn.edu.andrea-mitchell-center/files/Balmer%20-%20Historian%27s%20Pickaxe.pdf.

10. Leo P. Ribuffo, "Family Policy Past as Prologue: Jimmy Carter, the White House Conference on Families, and the Mobilization of the New Christian Right," *Review of Policy Research* 23, no. 2 (March/April 2006): 324.

11. Carter Archives, Note from S. P. Herse M. D. to Kathy Cade, First Lady's Office-Projects, ERA—Rosalynn Carter's ERA Activities through Friendship Force-Board Meetings [2].

12. Paul Weyrich, "Memo to the Committee," March 27, 1979, AHC, #10138, Box 19, Folder 12.

13. "Library Court, the Washington Hub," *Conservative Digest*, May-June 1980.

14. "Library Court, the Washington Hub," *Conservative Digest*, May-June 1980.

15. "Library Court, the Washington Hub," *Conservative Digest*, May-June 1980.

16. "Religious Right Urged to Fight Harder on the Issues to Achieve Their Goals," *Conservative Digest*, February 1981.

17. The story of this meeting is told in countless places. A representative example can be found in Billings's obituary, "Robert Billings, Religious Activist and Moral Majority Co-Founder," *New York Times*, June 1, 1995, https://scholar.lib.vt.edu/VA -news/VA-Pilot/issues/1995/vp950601/06010439.htm.

18. *The New Right Report*, November 1979; *Conservative Digest*, January 1980.

19. *Conservative Digest*, August 1979; see also Diamond, BANC MSS98/70c3, Carton 8, Folders 4–6.

20. William Martin, *With God On Our Side: The Rise of the Religious Right in America* (New York: Broadway Books, 1996), 218–219.

21. For more information about the organization and activities of the Moral Majority, see Clyde Wilcox and Carin Robinson, *Onward Christian Soldiers? The Religious Right in American Politics* (New York: Routledge, 2011), 43–44; and Robert C. Liebman and Robert Wuthnow, eds., *The New Christian Right: Mobilization and Legitimation* (New York: Aldine, 1983).

22. See, for example, Charles Kurzman, "Organizational Opportunity and Social Movement Mobilization: A Comparative Analysis of Four Religious Movements," *Mobilization: An International Journal*, 3, no. 1 (1998): 23–49; and J. Craig Jenkins, "Resource Mobilization Theory and the Study of Social Movements," *Annual Review of Sociology* 9 (August 1983): 527–553.

23. William H. Marshner was a Thomistic Catholic theologian who taught at Christendom College, a conservative Catholic college that Weyrich supported through his sponsorship of student internship programs. He also was a regular contributor to reports and publications put out by Weyrich's Free Congress Research and Education Foundation.

24. Dr. William H. Marshner, "The New Creatures and the New Politics," Religious Roundtable, Diamond, Carton 13.

25. *Conservative Digest*, August 1979.

26. Paul M. Weyrich Archive, "Memo from Cope," September 3, 1979, LoC Weyrich, Box 7, Folder 8, Vol. 26.

27. *Time*, August 20, 1979, LoC Weyrich, Box 7, Folder 7, Vol. 25.

28. Quoted in "Is Morality All Right?," *Christianity Today*, November 2, 1979, Diamond, Carton 8.

29. Paul M. Weyrich, "Weyrich from Washington: Building the Moral Majority," *Conservative Digest*, August 1979.

30. Timothy A. Byrnes, *Catholic Bishops in American Politics* (Princeton, NJ: Princeton University Press, 1991), 88.

31. Byrnes, *Catholic Bishops in American Politics*, 88.

32. Connaught Marshner, "Memo to Interested Parties re: Conservative Strategy for WHCC: Arguing the Issues," May 9, 1978, AHC, Box 38, Folder 27.

33. Draft Strategy Letter on the WHCF, AHC, Box 38, Folder 27.

34. "Pro-Family Position Paper," undated but located in a folder dated 1980, AHC, Box 21, Folder 25.

35. John Finnis, *Natural Law and Natural Rights*, 2nd ed. (New York: Oxford University Press, 2011), 146.

36. Lewis Z. Koch, "Family Passages," *Washingtonian*, n.d., AHC, Box 38, Folder 27.

37. Carter Archives, White House Conference on Families: Listening to America's Families, June 1980, White House, Box 104.

38. Koch, "Family Passages."

39. Koch, "Family Passages."

40. JoAnn Gasper, "Building a Conservative Coalition," *Conservative Digest*, January 1980.

41. *The New Right Report*, November 29, 1979.

42. *Conservative Digest*, May-June 1980.

43. Marshner, "Draft Strategy Letter on the WHCF," AHC, Box 38, Folder 27.

44. *Conservative Digest*, October 1980.

45. "America's Pro-Family Conference," Moral Majority Archives online, http://cdm17184.contentdm.oclc.org/cdm/compoundobject/collection/p17184coll1/id/480/rec/3.

46. The introduction to the Voting Index was written by Robert Billings, the executive director of the Moral Majority. This may explain why both documents reproduce the same definition of pro-family and operationalize a similar historical narrative premised. The Voting Index asserts, "Several years ago, the family was considered to be totally beyond the scope of government interference." It continues, "No one then thought of 'defining' the family. It was just there. The relationships were natural and unrehearsed." But voters are told, "Times have changed" as a result of the New Deal and the Great Society. National Christian Action Coalition, 1980, The Christian Voters' Victory Fund's Family Issues Voting Index, AHC, Box 21, Folder 25.

47. "America's Pro-Family Conference," Moral Majority Archives online, http://cdm17184.contentdm.oclc.org/cdm/compoundobject/collection/p17184coll1/id/480/rec/3.

48. Legislative summary, AHC, Box 82, Folder 13.

49. Republican National Committee Platform, July 15, 1980, https://www.presidency.ucsb.edu/documents/republican-party-platform-1980.

50. Family Advisory Board memo, AHC, Box 36, Folder 34.

51. "Memorandum," AHC, Box 19, Folder 13.

52. "Confidential Memorandum; The New Right and the Reagan Campaign—Administration," May 29, 1980, AHC, Box 19, Folder 13. Weyrich wrote, "We should not delude ourselves that a Reagan administration will be a conservative one to our

liking unless it is pushed in that direction. Instead it will lean as far to the left of center as it can without causing outcries from 'regular' country club set Republicans. Why? Because of paranoia about being cast as 'right wingers' and a desire to be accepted by the establishment 'power elite' of the country."

53. *Conservative Digest*, October 1980.

54. *Conservative Digest*, October 1980.

55. While Falwell and others frequently cited the three million number, *Congressional Quarterly* pointed out "it has little factual basis." *Congressional Quarterly*, September 6, 1980, LoC Weyrich, Box 8, Folder 7, Vol. 29.

56. "H.R. 7955 (96th): Family Protection Act," GovTrack, 1980, accessed: January 2, 2017, https://www.govtrack.us/congress/bills/96/hr7955.

57. Memo from Connie Marshner to the Coalition, June 17, 1981, AHC, Folder 13, Box 19. While Marshner claimed the Jepsen-Smith bill was "substantially different," the core principles and aims of the two bills were fundamentally the same.

58. Jan Fowler, "The Family Protection Act," Congressional Research Service, July 20, 1981, WM, Box 79, FPA 81 Notes.

59. Concept Summary, The Family Protection Act—97th Congress, Senator Jepsen's office, AHC, Folder 13, Box 19.

60. Jan Fowler, The Family Protection Act, Congressional Research Service, July 20, 1981, WM, Box 79, FPA 81 Notes.

61. James A. Autry, "'Family Protection Act': Saving Whom from What?," August 2, 1981, WM, Box 79.

62. Connie Marshner, "Memo of Facts, Re: Family Protection Act," AHC, Box 19, Folder 13.

63. Senator Jepsen, Letter to Jack Kilpatrick, February 25, 1981, AHC, Box 19, Folder 13.

64. Handwritten notes, untitled and undated, AHC, Box 21, Folder 25.

65. Cooper, *Family Values*, 62.

66. Phyllis Schlafly, *Conservative Digest*, January 1981.

67. *Conservative Digest*, February 1981.

68. Most notably, the Christian Right scored a significant win with the appointment of C. Everett Koop to the office of Surgeon General. See Wilcox and Robinson, *Onward Christian Soldiers?*, 124.

69. See, for example, the anecdote concerning Falwell's response to Reagan's nomination of Sandra Day O'Connor to the Supreme Court that William Martin recounts in *With God on Our Side*, 228.

70. *Conservative Digest*, November 1980.

71. "Coalition Fires 'Cover-up' Charge," Bend, OR, Bulletin, July 9, 1981, LoC Weyrich, Box 10, Folder 5.

72. Bill Peterson, "For Reagan and the New Right, the Honeymoon Is Over," *Washington Post*, July 21, 1981, LoC Weyrich, Box 10, Folder 5.

73. John B. Judis, "Pop-Con Politics," *New Republic*, n.d., filed along with

September–December 1984 papers, LoC Weyrich, Box 14, Folder 2.

74. Daniel Schlozman, *When Movements Anchor Parties: Electoral Alignments in American History* (Princeton, NJ: Princeton University Press, 2015), 15.

75. Schlozman, *When Movements Anchor Parties*, 3, 15, 81.

76. Schlozman, *When Movements Anchor Parties*, 107.

77. See, for example, Damon Linker, *The Theocons: Secular America under Siege* (New York: Anchor Books, 2007).

78. Gary Gerstle, "The Protean Character of American Liberalism," *American Historical Review* 99, no. 4 (October 1994): 1046.

Epilogue: Who Is It That Overcomes the World?

1. Paul Weyrich, "Cultural Conservatism: Political Trend of the '80s," *Bethlehem Globe-Times*, May 9, 1986, LoC Weyrich, Box 16, Folder 1.

2. William S. Lind and William H. Marshner, *Cultural Conservatism: Toward a New National Agenda* (Washington, DC: Free Congress Foundation, 1987), 9.

3. Lind and Marshner, *Cultural Conservatism*, 80.

4. Lind and Marshner, *Cultural Conservatism*, 83.

5. Lind and Marshner, *Cultural Conservatism*, 83.

6. Lind and Marshner, *Cultural Conservatism*, 87–88.

7. While competing definitions of liberalism and neoliberalism abound, we might understand the former as a system in which the state's principal mandate is the preservation of the rights of individuals, which requires it to, at times, subjugate the market. Neoliberalism inverts this relationship, making the preservation of the market the principal aim of the state, and necessitating the decentralization and devolution of power away from the state to the market, frequently resulting in the subjugation of the individual to the market. Recent scholarship on the Right, such as Melinda Cooper's *Family Values: Between Neoliberalism and the New Social Conservatism* (Princeton, NJ: Zone Books, 2017), and Jason Hackworth's *Faith Based: Religious Neoliberalism and the Politics of Welfare in the United States* (Athens: University of Georgia Press, 2012), has expertly demonstrated the convergence of Christian social conservatism with economic and political neoliberalism.

8. Cooper, *Family Values*, 62.

9. Cooper, *Family Values*, 63.

10. Andrew R. Lewis, *The Rights Turn in Conservative Christian Politics: How Abortion Transformed the Culture Wars* (Cambridge: Cambridge University Press, 2017), 1, 165–166.

11. Patrick J. Deneen, *Why Liberalism Failed* (New Haven, CT: Yale University Press, 2018), 1.

12. 1 John 5:5, New International Version.

13. Andrew Torba and Andrew Isker, *Christian Nationalism: A Biblical Guide for Taking Dominion and Discipling Nations* (N.p.: Gab AI, 2022), 8.

14. Torba and Isker, *Christian Nationalism*, 11.

BIBLIOGRAPHY

Archival Collections Cited and Consulted

Arthur J. Finkelstein Papers at the Library of Congress (referenced as LoC Finkelstein).

Conservative Digest and *The New Right Report* collections at the Rare Book and Manuscript Library at Columbia University and the New York Public Library (referenced by publication name).

Jerry Falwell and Moral Majority Archives at Liberty University (referenced as Moral Majority)

Jimmy Carter Papers at the Jimmy Carter Library (referenced as Carter).

Paul Weyrich Notebooks at the Library of Congress (referenced as LoC Weyrich)

Paul Weyrich Papers at the American Heritage Center at the University of Wyoming, Laramie (referenced as AHC).

Sara Diamond collection on the US Right, BANC MSS 98/70 cz, Bancroft Library, University of California, Berkeley (referenced as Diamond).

William Martin Religious Right collection at the Woodson Research Center at Rice University (referenced as WM).

Works Cited

Alvis, Jason W. "Christianities and the Culture (Wars) of Victimhood: Persecution, Purity, Patience." *Philosophy Today* 65, no. 4 (August 2021): 881–898.

Apostolicam Actuositatem. http://www.vatican.va/archive/hist_councils/ii_vatican_coun cil/documents/vat-ii_decree_19651118_apostolicam-actuositatem_en.html.

Ball, Howard. *The Supreme Court in the Intimate Lives of Americans.* New York: New York University Press, 2002.

Balmer, Randall. *Bad Faith: Race and the Rise of the Religious Right.* Grand Rapids, MI: Wm. B. Eerdmans, 2021.

———. "The Historian's Pickaxe: Uncovering the Racist Origins of the Religious Right." https://www.sas.upenn.edu/andrea-mitchell-center/sites/www.sas.upenn .edu.andrea-mitchell-center/files/Balmer%20-%20Historian%27s%20Pickaxe .pdf.

———. "Jimmy Carter and the Evangelical Divide." *HuffPost.* June 9, 2014. https:// www.huffingtonpost.com/randall-balmer/jimmy-carter-evangelical-_b_5473456 .html.

———. "The Real Origins of the Religious Right." *Politico Magazine*. May 27, 2014. https://politi.co/2JsQoNr.

———. *Thy Kingdom Come: An Evangelical's Lament*. New York: Basic Books, 2006.

Barr, Beth Allison. *The Making of Biblical Womanhood*. Grand Rapids, MI: Brazos, 2021.

Bell, Daniel. *The Radical Right*. Piscataway, NJ: Transaction, 2001.

Berbrier, Mitch. "The Victim Ideology of White Supremacists and White Separatists in the United States." *Sociological Focus* 33, no. 2 (May 2000): 175–191.

Bergh, Katie, and Dottie Rosenbaum. "Debt Ceiling Agreement's SNAP Changes Would Increase Hunger and Poverty for Many Older Low-Income People: New Exemptions Would Help Some Others." Center on Budget and Policy Priorities. May 31, 2023. https://www.cbpp.org/research/food-assistance/debt -ceiling-agreements-snap-changes-would-increase-hunger-and-poverty-for.

Bjork-James, Sophie. "White Sexual Politics: The Patriarchal Family in White Nationalism and the Religious Right." *Transforming Anthropology* 28, no. 1 (March 2020): 58–73.

Boggs, Carl. "Marxism, Prefigurative Communism, and the Problem of Workers' Control." *Radical America* 11 (November 1977): 99–122.

Borter, Gabriella, and Sharon Bernstein. "Factbox: U.S. State Abortion Legislation to Watch in 2023." Reuters. May 3, 2023. https://www.reuters.com/world/us /us-state-abortion-legislation-watch-2023-2023-05-03/.

Braaten, Carl E. "Protestants and Natural Law." *First Things*. January 1992. https:// www.firstthings.com/article/1992/01/protestants-and-natural-law.

Bromley, David G., and Anson Shupe, eds. *New Christian Politics*. Macon, GA: Mercer, 1984.

Bruner, Jason. *Imagining Persecution: Why American Christians Believe There Is a Global War against Their Faith*. New Brunswick, NJ: Rutgers University Press, 2021.

Butler, Anthea. *White Evangelical Racism*. Chapel Hill: University of North Carolina Press, 2021.

Byrnes, Timothy A. *Catholic Bishops in American Politics*. Princeton, NJ: Princeton University Press, 1991.

Cadegan, Una. "Catholic Immigrants Didn't Make It on Their Own. They Shouldn't Expect Others To." *Washington Post*. April 18, 2017. https://www.washingtonpost .com/posteverything/wp/2017/04/18/catholic-immigrants-didnt-make-it-on -their-own-they-shouldnt-expect-others-to/.

Carian, Emily K., Alex DiBranco, and Chelsea Ebin, eds. *Male Supremacism in the United States: From Patriarchal Traditionalism to Misogynist Incels and the Alt-Right*. New York: Routledge, 2022.

Casti Connubii. Encyclical of Pope Pius XI on Christian Marriage. https://w2.vati can.va/content/pius-xi/en/encyclicals/documents/hf_p-xi_enc_19301231_casti -connubii.html.

Catholic Bishops of the United States. "On Racial Harmony." August 23, 1963.

https://www.usccb.org/issues-and-action/cultural-diversity/african-american/resources/upload/On-Racial-Harmony.pdf.

Catholic Bishops of the United States Pastoral Letters. "Discrimination and Christian Conscience." November 14, 1958. https://www.usccb.org/issues-and-action/cultural-diversity/african-american/resources/upload/Discrimination-Christian-Conscience-Nov-14-1958.pdf.

Catholic Traditionalist Manifesto. December 31, 1964. http://www.latinmass-ctm.org/about/charter.htm.

Champagne, Anthony M. "The Segregation Academy and the Law." *Journal of Negro Education* 42, no. 1 (Winter 1973): 58–66.

Clemens, Elisabeth S., and James M. Cook. "Politics and Institutionalism: Explaining Durability and Change." *Annual Review of Sociology* 25 (1999): 441–466.

Cohen, Adam. *Supreme Inequality: The Supreme Court's Fifty-Year Battle for a More Unjust America*. New York: Penguin Books, 2021.

Collier, R. B., and D. Collier. *Shaping the Political Arena: Critical Junctures, the Labor Movement, and Regime Dynamics in Latin America*. 2015. https://escholarship.org/uc/item/8qr1z7gc.

"Congress Fails to Act on School Prayer Amendments." *CQ Almanac 1964*, vol. 20 (Washington, DC: Congressional Quarterly, 1965). http://library.cqpress.com/cqalmanac/cqal64-1304697.

Connelly, Matthew. *Fatal Misconception: The Struggle to Control World Population*. Cambridge, MA: Harvard University Press, 2008.

Cooper, Davina. "At the Expense of Christianity." In Leslie G. Roman and Linda Eyre, eds., *Dangerous Territories* New York: Routledge, 1997.

Cooper, Melinda. *Family Values: Between Neoliberalism and the New Social Conservatism*. Princeton, NJ: Zone Books, 2017.

Cornish, Flora, Jan Haaken, Liora Moskovitz, and Sharon Jackson. "Rethinking Prefigurative Politics: Introduction to the Special Thematic Section." *Journal of Social and Political Psychology* 4 (May 2016): 114–127.

Crawford, Alan. *Thunder on the Right*. New York: Pantheon Books, 1980.

Critchlow, Donald T. *Intended Consequences: Birth Control, Abortion, and the Federal Government in Modern America*. New York: Oxford University Press, 2008.

———. *Phyllis Schlafly and Grassroots Conservatism: A Woman's Crusade*. Princeton, NJ: Princeton University Press, 2008.

CRT Forward. UCLA School of Law. 2023. https://crtforward.law.ucla.edu/.

CSPAN. "Q and A with Paul Weyrich and Brian Lamb." March 22, 2005. http://www.c-span.org/video/transcript/?id=7958.

Cuneo, Michael W. *The Smoke of Satan: Conservative and Traditionalist Dissent in Contemporary American Catholicism*. Baltimore: John Hopkins University Press, 1999.

Dalhouse, Mark Taylor. *An Island in the Lake of Fire: Bob Jones University, Fundamentalism, and the Separatist Movement*. Athens: Georgia University Press, 1996.

Deneen, Patrick J. *Why Liberalism Failed*. New Haven, CT: Yale University Press, 2018.

Devins, Neal. "On Casebooks and Canons, or Why Bob Jones University Will Never Be Part of the Constitutional Law Canon." William and Mary Law School Scholarship Repository Faculty Publications, Paper 363, 2000.

Diamond, Sara. *Not by Politics Alone: The Enduring Influence of the Christian Right*. New York: Guilford Press, 1998.

———. *Spiritual Warfare: The Politics of the Christian Right*. Boston: South End Press, 1989.

Dobson, Ed, Jerry Falwell, and Edward E. Hindson. *The Fundamentalist Phenomenon: The Resurgence of Conservative Christianity*, 2nd ed. Grand Rapids, MI: Baker Book House, 1981.

Domonoske, Camila. "Hate Crimes Rose in 2015, with Religious Bias a Growing Motivation, FBI Data Shows." NPR. November 14, 2016. https://www.npr.org/sections/thetwo-way/2016/11/14/502036699/hate-crimes-rose-in-2015-with-religious-bias-a-growing-motivation-fbi-data-shows.

Duerringer, Christopher. *Crucified Christians, Marked Men, and Wanted Whites: Victimhood and Conservative Counterpublicity*. PhD diss., Arizona State University, 2011.

———. "The 'War on Christianity': Counterpublicity or Hegemonic Containment?" *Southern Communication Journal* 78, no. 4 (September 2013): 311–325.

Ebin, Chelsea. "Tomorrow's Past Today: The Prefigurative Construction of Christian Right Belonging." In Cody Musselman, Erik Kline, Dana Lloyd, and Michael J. Altman, eds., *American Examples: New Conversations about Religion*. Tuscaloosa: University of Alabama Press, 2024.

Edsall, Thomas, and Mary Edsall. *Chain Reaction: The Impact of Race, Rights, and Taxes on American Politics*. New York: W. W. Norton, 1992.

Ethics and Religious Liberty Commission of the Southern Baptist Convention. "5 Facts about the History of the SBC and the Pro-Life Cause." January 17, 2020. https://erlc.com/resource-library/articles/5-facts-about-the-history-of-the-sbc-and-the-pro-life-cause/.

Elifson, Kirk W., and C. Kirk Hadaway. "Prayer in Public Schools: When Church and State Collide." *Public Opinion Quarterly* 49, no. 3 (1985): 317–329.

Equality Maps. Movement Advancement Project. 2023. https://www.lgbtmap.org/equality-maps/.

"Evangelicals and Catholics Together: The Christian Mission in the Third Millennium." *First Things*. May 1994. https://www.firstthings.com/article/1994/05/evangelicals-catholics-together-the-christian-mission-in-the-third-millennium.

Falwell, Jerry. *An Autobiography*. Lynchburg, VA: Liberty House, 1997.

———. *If I Should Die Before I Wake*. Nashville, TN: Thomas Nelson , 1986.

———. *Listen, America!* New York: Doubleday, 1980.

———. *Strength for the Journey: An Autobiography*. New York: Simon & Schuster, 1987.

Farber, David. *The Rise and Fall of Modern American Conservatism: A Short History.* Princeton, NJ: Princeton University Press, 2012.

Farmer, Brian. *American Conservatism: History, Theory and Practice.* Cambridge: Cambridge Scholars Publishing, 2005.

Fetner, Tina. *How the Religious Right Shaped Lesbian and Gay Activism.* Minneapolis: University of Minnesota Press, 2008.

————. "Working Anita Bryant: The Impact of Christian Anti-Gay Activism on Lesbian and Gay Movement Claims." *Social Problems* 48, no. 3 (August 2001): 411–428.

Finnis, John. *Natural Law and Natural Rights,* 2nd ed. New York: Oxford University Press, 2011.

Fiorina, Morris P., and Samuel Abrams. "Americans Aren't Polarized, Just Better Sorted." *Washington Post.* September 4, 2022. https://www.washingtonpost.com /news/monkey-cage/wp/2014/01/21/americans-arent-polarized-just-better-sorted/.

Fitzgerald, Francis. "Jerry Falwell's Christian Army." *New Yorker.* May 16, 2007. https:// www.newyorker.com/magazine/1981/05/18/a-disciplined-charging-army.

Flippen, J. Brooks. *Jimmy Carter, the Politics of Family, and the Rise of the Religious Right.* Athens: University of Georgia Press, 2011.

Frank, Gillian. "'The Civil Rights of Parents': Race and Conservative Politics in Anita Bryant's Campaign against Gay Rights in 1970s Florida." *Journal of the History of Sexuality* 22, no. 1 (January 2013): 126–160.

Furlow, R. Bennett. "Extremism and Victimhood in the U.S. Context." Arizona State University Center for Strategic Communication. Report No. 1204. November 5, 2012.

Gallup. "Gallup Election Polls: Vote by Group 1976–1980." Gallup.com. https://web .archive.org/web/20171010174814/news.gallup.com/poll/9460/election-polls -vote-groups-19761980.aspx.

————. "The Protestant and Catholic Vote." Gallup.com. June 8, 2004. https://news .gallup.com/poll/11911/Protestant-Catholic-Vote.aspx.

Gaston, K. Healan. *Imagining Judeo-Christian America: Religion, Secularism, and the Redefinition of Democracy.* Chicago: University of Chicago Press, 2019.

————. "A Trumped-Up Controversy? School Prayer in Policy, History, and Ethics." Berkley Center for Religion, Peace, and World Affairs. February 13, 2020. https://berkleycenter.georgetown.edu/responses/a-trumped-up-controversy -school-prayer-in-policy-history-and-ethics.

Gelder, Craig Van, Dwight J. Zscheile, and Alan Roxburgh. *The Missional Church in Perspective: Mapping Trends and Shaping the Conversation.* Grand Rapids, MI: Baker Academic, 2011.

Gerstle, Gary. "The Protean Character of American Liberalism." *American Historical Review* 99, no. 4 (October 1994): 1043–1073.

Gilgoff, Dan. *The Jesus Machine.* New York: St. Martin's Griffin, 2007.

Gjerde, Jon. *Catholicism and the Shaping of Nineteenth-Century America.* Edited by S. Deborah Kang. Cambridge: Cambridge University Press, 2012.

Goldberg, Jonah. "Defining Conservatism." *National Review.* June 20, 2015. https://www.nationalreview.com/g-file/conservatism-definition-difficult-produce/.

Goldberg, Michelle. *Kingdom Coming: The Rise of Christian Nationalism.* New York: W. W. Norton, 2006.

Goodwin, Jeff, James M. Jasper, and Francesca Polletta. *Passionate Politics: Emotions and Social Movements.* Chicago: University of Chicago Press, 2009.

Gordon, Linda. *The Moral Property of Women.* Champaign, IL: University of Chicago Press, 2007.

Graetz, Michael J., and Linda Greenhouse. *The Burger Court and the Rise of the Judicial Right.* New York: Simon & Schuster, 2016.

"The 'Great Replacement' Theory, Explained." National Immigration Forum. December 2021. https://immigrationforum.org/wp-content/uploads/2021/12/Replacement-Theory-Explainer-1122.pdf.

Greenhouse, Linda, and Riva B. Siegel. "Before Roe v. Wade: Voices That Shaped the Abortion Debate before the Supreme Court's Ruling." Creative Commons. 2012. https://papers.ssrn.com/sol3/papers.cfm?abstract_id=2131505.

Griffin, Martin I. J. "The Anti-Catholic Spirit of the Revolution." *American Catholic Historical Researches* 6, no. 4 (October 1889): 146–178.

Hackworth, Jason. *Faith Based: Religious Neoliberalism and the Politics of Welfare in the United States.* Athens: University of Georgia Press, 2012.

Hankins, Barry. *Francis Schaeffer and the Shaping of Evangelical America.* Grand Rapids, MI: Williams: B. Eerdmans, 2008.

————. *Jesus and Gin: Evangelicalism, the Roaring Twenties, and Today's Culture Wars.* New York: Palgrave Macmillan, 2010.

Hannon, James T. "The Influence of Catholic Schools on the Desegregation of Public School Systems: A Case Study of White Flight in Boston." *Population Research and Policy Review* 3, no. 3 (October 1984): 219–237.

Harding, Susan Friend. *The Book of Jerry Falwell: Fundamentalist Language and Politics.* Princeton, NJ: Princeton University Press, 2001.

Hedges, Chris. *American Fascists: The Christian Right and the War on America.* New York: Free Press, 2008.

Herdt, Jennifer. "Natural Law in Protestant Christianity." In Tom Angier, ed., *The Cambridge Companion to Natural Law Ethics,* 155–178. Cambridge: Cambridge University Press, 2019.

Herman, Didi. "'Then I Saw a New Heaven and a New Earth': Thoughts on the Christian Right and the Problem of Backlash." In Leslie G. Roman and Linda Eyre, eds., *Dangerous Territories,* 63–74. New York: Routledge, 1997.

Heyer, Kristin E., Mark J. Rozell, and Michael A. Genovese, eds. *Catholics and Politics: The Dynamic Tension between Faith and Power.* Washington, DC: Georgetown University Press, 2008.

"H.R. 7955 (96th): Family Protection Act." *GovTrack.* 1980. Accessed January 2, 2017. https://www.govtrack.us/congress/bills/96/hr7955.

Horwitz, Robert B. *America's Right: Anti-establishment Conservatism from Goldwater to the Tea Party*. Cambridge: Polity Press, 2013.

Hunter, James Davison. *Culture Wars: The Struggle to Define America*. New York: Basic Books, 1991.

International Christian Concern. "Violent Threats and Vandalism: An Attack on Pro-Life Organizations." June 30, 2022. https://www.persecution.org/2022/06/30/violent-threat-and-vandalism/#.

Jenkins, J. Craig. "Resource Mobilization Theory and the Study of Social Movements." *Annual Review of Sociology* 9 (August 1983): 527–553.

Jenkins, J. Craig, and Bert Klandermans, eds. *Politics of Social Protest: Comparative Perspectives on States and Social Movements*. Minneapolis: University of Minnesota Press, 1995.

Johnson, Olatunde C. A. "The Story of Bob Jones University v. the United States: Race, Religion, and Congress' Extraordinary Acquiescence." In William Eskridge, Philip P. Frickey, and Elizabeth Garrett, eds., Columbia Law School Public Law and Legal Theory Working Paper No. 10–229 (2010). https://scholarship.law.columbia.edu/faculty_scholarship/2523/?utm_source=scholarship.law.columbia.edu%2F-faculty_scholarship%2F2523&utm_medium=PDF&utm_campaign=PDFCoverPages.

Jones, Jeffrey M. "Abortion Poised to Be a Bigger Voting Issue Than in Past." Gallup, June 6, 2022. https://news.gallup.com/poll/393263/abortion-poised-bigger-voting-issue-past.aspx.

Kaplan, Esther. *With God on Their Side*. New York: New Press, 2004.

Kirk, Russell. *The Conservative Mind*. Washington, DC: Regnery,

Klatch, Rebecca E. *Women of the New Right*. Philadelphia: Temple University Press, 1987.

Kurlander, David. "'We Want Them Burned': The 1978 IRS Controversy over Discriminatory Schools." *Cafe*. February 17, 2022. https://cafe.com/article/we-want-them-burned-the-1978-irs-controversy-over-discriminatory-schools/.

Kurzman, Charles. "Organizational Opportunity and Social Movement Mobilization: A Comparative Analysis of Four Religious Movements." *Mobilization: An International Journal* 3, no. 1 (1998): 23–49.

Lahr, Angela M. *Millennial Dreams and Apocalyptic Nightmares: The Cold War Origins of Political Evangelicalism*. New York: Oxford University Press, 2007.

Lane, Frederick. *The Court and the Cross: The Religious Right's Crusade to Reshape the Supreme Court*. Boston: Beacon Press, 2009.

Laycock, Douglas. "A Survey of Religious Liberty in the United States." *Ohio State Law Journal* 47, no. 2 (1986): 409–451.

Lewis, Andrew R. *The Rights Turn in Conservative Christian Politics: How Abortion Transformed the Culture Wars*. Cambridge: Cambridge University Press, 2017.

Liebman, Robert, and Robert Wuthnow, eds. *The New Christian Right: Mobilization and Legitimation*. New York: Aldine, 1983.

Lind, William S., and William H. Marshner. *Cultural Conservatism: Toward a New National Agenda.* Washington, DC: Free Congress Foundation, 1987.

Linker, Damon. *The Theocons: Secular America under Siege.* New York: Anchor Books, 2007.

Lowndes, Joseph. *From the New Deal to the New Right.* New Haven, CT: Yale University Press, 2008.

Mansbridge, Jane. *Why We Lost the ERA.* Chicago: University of Chicago Press, 1986.

Mansbridge, Jane, and Shauna L. Shames. "Toward a Theory of Backlash: Dynamic Resistance and the Central Role of Power." *Politics and Gender* 4, no. 4 (December 2008): 623–634.

Manuel, Paul Christopher, Lawrence C. Reardon, and Clyde Wilcox, eds. *The Catholic Church and the Nation-State.* Washington, DC: Georgetown University Press, 2006.

Marsden, George M. *Fundamentalism and American Culture,* 2nd ed. New York: Oxford University Press, 2006.

Martin, William. *With God on Our Side: The Rise of the Religious Right in America.* New York: Broadway Books, 1996.

Martinez HoSang, Daniel. *Racial Propositions: Ballot Initiatives and the Making of Postwar California.* Berkeley: University of California Press, 2010.

Massa, Mark S. J. *The American Catholic Revolution: How the Sixties Changed the Church Forever.* New York: Oxford University Press, 2010.

———. *The Structure of Theological Revolutions.* New York: Oxford University Press, 2018.

Mason, Carol. "Created Equal, but Equal in No Other Respect: Opposing Abortion to Protect Men." In Emily K. Carian, Alex DiBranco, and Chelsea Ebin, eds., *Male Supremacism in the United States: From Patriarchal Traditionalism to Misogynist Incels and the Alt-Right.* Abingdon, UK: God's Right Hand, 2022.

———. *Reading Appalachia from Left to Right: Conservative and the 1974 Kanawha County Textbook Controversy.* Ithaca, NY: Cornell University Press, 2009.

Maxwell, Angie, and Todd Shields. *The Long Southern Strategy: How Chasing White Voters in the South Changed American Politics.* New York: Oxford University Press, 2019.

McAdams, A. James, and Alejandro Castrillon, eds. *Contemporary Far-Right Thinkers and the Future of Liberal Democracy.* New York: Routledge, 2022.

McCarthy, Tom. "Trump's Judges: A Revolution to Create a New Conservative America." *The Guardian.* April 28, 2020. https://www.theguardian.com/us-news/2020/apr/28/donald-trump-judges-create-new-conservative-america-republicans.

McGirr, Lisa. *Suburban Warriors: The Origins of the New American Right.* Princeton, NJ: Princeton University Press, 2002.

McGuire, Kevin T. "Public Schools, Religious Establishments, and the US Supreme Court: An Examination of Policy Compliance." *American Politics Research* 37, no. 1 (January 2009): 50–74.

McIntyre, Thomas J., with John C. Obert. *The Fear Brokers.* Boston: Beacon Press, 1979.

Mead, Frank, Samuel S. Hill, and Craig D. Atwood. *Handbook of Denominations in the United States,* 13th ed. Nashville, TN: Abingdon Press, 2010.

Messerly, Megan. "Thousands Lose Medicaid in Arkansas: Is This America's Future?" *Politico.* June 14, 2023. https://www.politico.com/news/2023/06/13/medicaid-insurance-coverage-arkansas-00101744.

Michels, Robert. *Political Parties.* Translated by Eden and Cedar Paul. Kitchener, Ontario: Batoche Books, 2001.

Miller, Steven P. *Billy Graham and the Rise of the Republican South.* Philadelphia: University of Pennsylvania, 2009.

Minnow, Martha. "Should Religious Groups Be Exempt from Civil Rights Laws?" *Boston College Law Review* 48 (2007): 781–849.

Molina, Natalia. *How Race Is Made in America: Immigration, Citizenship, and the Historical Power of Racial Scripts.* Berkeley: University of California Press, 2014.

Moses, James Charles. "Desegregation in Catholic Schools in the Archdiocese of Chicago, 1964–1974, Including a Case Study of a Catholic High School." PhD diss., Loyola University, 1977. https://ecommons.luc.edu/cgi/viewcontent.cgi?article=2747&context=luc_diss.

Mudde, Cas. *The Far Right Today.* Cambridge: Polity Press, 2019.

Nadler, Anthony, and A. J. Bauer. *News on the Right: Studying Conservative News Cultures.* Oxford: Oxford University Press, 2019.

Nash, George H. *The Conservative Intellectual Movement in America since 1945.* Wilmington, DE: Intercollegiate Studies Institute, 2006.

National Association of Evangelicals. "What Is an Evangelical?" Accessed September 8, 2022. https://www.nae.org/what-is-an-evangelical/.

Nixon, Richard. "387—Veto of the Economic Opportunity Amendments of 1971." December 9, 1971. https://www.presidency.ucsb.edu/documents/veto-the-economic-opportunity-amendments-1971.

Noble, Alan. "Why Do Evangelicals Have a Persecution Complex?" *The Atlantic.* August 4, 2014. https://www.theatlantic.com/national/archive/2014/08/the-evangelical-persecution-complex/375506/.

Nostra Aetate. October 28, 1965. http://www.vatican.va/archive/hist_councils/ii_vatican_council/documents/vat-ii_decl_19651028_nostra-aetate_en.html.

NPR. "How Abortion Became a Mobilizing Issue among the Religious Right." NPR. May 8, 2022. https://www.npr.org/2022/05/08/1097514184/how-abortion-became-a-mobilizing-issue-among-the-religious-right.

O'Brian, Neil A. "Before Reagan: The Development of Abortion's Partisan Divide." *Perspectives on Politics* 18, no. 4 (December 2020): 1031–1047.

Onishi, Bradley. *Preparing for War: The Extremist History of White Nationalism—and What Comes Next.* Minneapolis, MN: Broadleaf Books, 2023.

Orlick, Annelise. *Rethinking American Women's Activism.* New York: Routledge, 2015.

OSHA. "League of Conservation Voters Scorecard." https://scorecard.lcv.org/roll -call-vote/1972-653-osha-exemptions.

Oxx, Katie. *The Nativist Movement in America: Religious Conflict in the 19th Century.* London: Routledge, 2013.

Palin, Sarah. *Going Rogue: An American Life.* New York: Harper, 2009.

Peterson, Kristina. "House Republicans Now Unanimous in Opposing Abortion Rights." *Wall Street Journal.* March 21, 2019. https://www.wsj.com/articles/house -republicans-now-unanimous-in-opposing-abortion-rights-11553172954.

PRB. "Record Number of Women in the U.S. Labor Force." February 1, 2002. https:// www.prb.org/resources/record-number-of-women-in-the-u-s-labor-force/.

Reed, Roy. "Parochial School Desegregation Asked by Catholics in Louisiana." *New York Times.* July 26, 1970. https://www.nytimes.com/1970/07/26/archives/pa rochial-school-desegregation-asked-by-catholics-in-louisiana.html.

Raekstad, Paul. "Revolutionary Practice and Prefigurative Politics: A Clarification and Defense." *Constellations* 25, no. 13 (September 2017): 359–372.

Rensmann, Lars. "The Noisy Counter-Revolution: Understanding the Cultural Conditions and Dynamics of Populist Politics in Europe in the Digital Age." *Politics and Governance* 5, no. 4 (December 2017): 123–135.

Republican National Committee Platform. July 15, 1980. https://www.presidency .ucsb.edu/documents/republican-party-platform-1980.

Ribuffo, Leo P. "Family Policy Past as Prologue: Jimmy Carter, the White House Conference on Families, and the Mobilization of the New Christian Right." *Review of Policy Research* 23, no. 2 (March/April 2006): 311–338.

"Robert Billings, Religious Activist and Moral Majority Co-Founder." *New York Times.* June 1, 1995. https://scholar.lib.vt.edu/VA-news/VA-Pilot/issues/1995 /vp950601/06010439.htm

Robin, Corey. *The Reactionary Mind.* Oxford: Oxford University Press, 2011.

Rokeach, Milton. "Part II: Religious Values and Social Compassion." *Review of Religious Research* 11, no. 1 (Autumn 1969): 24–39.

Rolsky, L. Benjamin. "Producing the Christian Right: Conservative Evangelicalism, Representation, and the Recent Religious Past." *Religions* 12, no. 3:171 (March 2021): 1–17.

Roman, Leslie G., and Linda Eyre, eds. *Dangerous Territories.* New York: Routledge, 1997.

Rosenberg, Gerald. *The Hollow Hope: Can Courts Bring About Social Change?,* 2nd ed. Chicago: University of Chicago Press, 2008.

Ross, Loretta. "White Supremacy in the 1990s." Political Research Associates. http:// www.publiceye.org/eyes/whitsup.html.

Roth, William. "The Politics of Day Care: The Comprehensive Child Development Act of 1971." December 1976. https://www.irp.wisc.edu/publications/dps/pdfs /dp36976.pdf.

Rymph, Catherine. *Republican Women: Feminism and Conservatism from Suffrage through the Rise of the New Right.* Chapel Hill: University of North Carolina Press, 2006.

Saloma, John S. III. *Ominous Politics: The New Conservative Labyrinth.* New York: Hill & Wang, 1984.

Sax, Karl. *Standing Room Only: The Challenge of Over Population.* Boston: Beacon Press, 1955.

Schaeffer, Francis. *Plan for Action: An Action Alternative Handbook for "Whatever Happened to the Human Race?"* Grand Rapids, MI: Fleming H. Revell, 1980.

———. *The Church at the End of the 20th Century.* Westmont, IL: InterVarsity Press, 1970.

Schaeffer, Francis, and Everett C. Koop. *Whatever Happened to the Human Race?* N.p.: L'Abri Publishing, 1979.

Schaeffer, Frank. *Crazy for God.* Philadelphia: De Capo Press, 2007.

Schäfer, Axel. *Countercultural Conservatives.* Madison: University of Wisconsin Press, 2011.

Schickler, Eric. *Racial Realignment: The Transformation of American Liberalism, 1932–1965.* Princeton, NJ: Princeton University Press, 2016.

Schlozman, Daniel. *When Movements Anchor Parties: Electoral Alignments in American History.* Princeton, NJ: Princeton University Press, 2015.

Schmidt, Vivien A. "Britain-out and Trump-in: A Discursive Institutionalist Analysis of the British Referendum on the EU and the US Presidential Election." *Review of International Political Economy* 24, no. 2 (March 2017): 248–269.

———. "Discursive Institutionalism: The Explanatory Power of Ideas and Discourse." *Annual Review of Political Science* 11, no. 1 (June 2008): 303–326.

———. *Handbook of Critical Policy Studies.* Cheltenham, UK: Edward Elgar, 2015.

———. "Taking Ideas and Discourse Seriously: Explaining Change through Discursive Institutionalism as the Fourth 'New Institutionalism.'" *European Political Science Review* 2, no.1 (March 2010): 1–25.

Schreiber, Ronnee. *Righting Feminism: Conservative Women and American Politics.* New York: Oxford University Press, 2008.

Self, Robert O. *All in the Family: The Realignment of American Democracy since the 1960s.* New York: Hill & Wang, 2012.

Shea, Mark. "The Seamless Garment: What It Is and Isn't." *National Catholic Register.* June 14, 2014. https://www.ncregister.com/blog/the-seamless-garment-what-it-is-and-isn-t.

Shea, William M. *The Lion and the Lamb: Evangelicals and Catholics in America.* Oxford: Oxford University Press, 2004.

Sheingate, Adam. "Institutional Dynamics and American Political Development." *Annual Review of Political Science* 17 no. 1 (December 2013): 461–477.

———. "Political Entrepreneurship, Institutional Change, and American Political Development." *Studies in American Political Development* 17, no. 2 (October 2003): 185–203.

Sitomer, Curtis J. "Why Reagan Grabbed the Initiative on School Prayer." *Christian Science Monitor*. May 10, 1982. https://www.csmonitor.com/1982/0510/051005.html.

Smillie, Dirk. *Falwell Inc.* New York: St. Martin's Press, 2008.

Staggenborg, Suzanne. *Social Movements*, 2nd ed. Oxford: Oxford University Press, 2016.

"State Legislation Tracker." Guttmacher Institute. https://www.guttmacher.org/state-legislation-tracker.

Stewart, Katherine. "How the Christian Right Took over the Judiciary and Changed America." *The Guardian*. June 25, 2022. https://www.theguardian.com/world/2022/jun/25/roe-v-wade-abortion-christian-right-america.

———. "Opinion: Christian Nationalists Are Excited About What Comes Next." *New York Times*. July 5, 2022. https://www.nytimes.com/2022/07/05/opinion/dobbs-christian-nationalism.html.

———. *The Power Worshippers*. New York: Bloomsbury, 2020.

Sunstein, Cass R., and John M. Olin. "The Law of Group Polarization." Preliminary. Economics Working Paper, University of Chicago Law School, December 7, 1999. https://chicagounbound.uchicago.edu/cgi/viewcontent.cgi.

Tagliarina, Daniel. "Power, Privilege, and Prayer: Christian Right Identity Politics and Mobilizing for School Prayer." PhD diss., University of Connecticut, 2014. https://opencommons.uconn.edu/dissertations/525/.

Teter, Magda. *Christian Supremacy: Reckoning with the Roots of Antisemitism and Racism*. Princeton, NJ: Princeton University Press, 2023.

Tentler, Leslie Woodcock. *Catholics and Contraception: An American History*. Ithaca, NY: Cornell University Press, 2004.

Tesh, Sylvia. "In Support of 'Single-Issue' Politics." *Political Science Quarterly* 99, no. 1 (Spring 1984): 27–44.

Tezcür, Günes Murat. "The Moderation Theory Revisited." *Party Politics* 16, no. 1 (August 2009): 69–88.

Tønnessen, Alf Tomas. *How Two Political Entrepreneurs Helped Create the American Conservative Movement, 1973–1981*. Lampeter, UK: Edwin Mellen Press, 2009.

Torba, Andrew, and Andrew Isker. *Christian Nationalism: A Biblical Guide for Taking Dominion and Discipling Nations*. N.p.: Gab AI, 2022.

US Department of Commerce/Bureau of the Census. May 7, 1971. "Current Population Reports: Consumer Income." https://www2.census.gov/library/publications/1971/demographics/p60-77.pdf.

Viguerie, Richard A. *The New Right: We're Ready to Lead*, rev. ed. Falls Church, VA: Viguerie Company, 1981.

"Voting Laws Roundup: June 2023." Brennan Center for Justice. 2023. https://www.brennancenter.org/our-work/research-reports/voting-laws-roundup-june-2023?_ga=2.117393990.1560545562.1689609770-2045684559.1689609770&_gac=1.153346634.1689619289.CjwKCAjwsvujBhAXEiwA

_UXnAMr25CY86g680c845K3eXdyQ9_CglusuZUGkBuoMpT4BWdShT 7wZphoCIGAQAvD_BwE.

Waggoner, Michael D. "When the Court Took on Prayer and the Bible in Schools." Religion and Politics. 2012. http://religionandpolitics.org/2012/06/25/when-the -court-took-on-prayer-the-bible-and-public-schools/.

Weaver, Mary Jo, and R. Scott Appleby, eds. *Being Right: Conservative Catholics in America.* Bloomington: Indiana University Press, 1995.

Wenger, Tisa. *Religious Freedom: The Contested History of an American Idea.* Chapel Hill: University of North Carolina Press, 2017. https://uncpress.org/book /9781469634623/religious-freedom/.

"What Anti-Trans Bills Passed in 2023?" Trans Legislation Tracker. https://transleg islation.com/bills/2023/passed.

Whitehead, Andrew L., and Samuel L. Perry. *Taking America Back for God: Christian Nationalism in the United States.* New York: Oxford University Press, 2020.

Wilcox, Clyde. "Popular Backing for the Old Christian Right: Explaining Support for the Christian Anti-Communism Crusade." *Journal of Social History* 21, no. 1 (Autumn 1987): 117–132.

———. "Sources of Support for the Old Right: A Comparison of the John Birch Society and the Christian Anti-Communism Crusade." *Social Science History* 12, no. 4 (Winter 1988): 429–449.

———. "Support for the Christian Right Old and New: A Comparison of Supporters of the Christian Anti-Communism Crusade and the Moral Majority." *Sociological Focus* 22, no. 2 (May 1989): 87–97.

Wilcox, Clyde, and Carin Robinson. *Onward Christian Soldiers?: The Religious Right in American Politics.* New York: Routledge, 2011.

Wilde, Melissa. *Vatican II: A Sociological Analysis of Religious Change.* Princeton, NJ: Princeton University Press, 2007.

Williams, Daniel. *God's Own Party: The Making of the Christian Right,* 1st ed. New York: Oxford University Press, 2010.

Williams, Daniel K. "Jerry Falwell's Sunbelt Politics: The Regional Origins of the Moral Majority." *Journal of Policy History* 22, no. 2 (March 2010): 125–147.

Wills, Garry. *Heart and Head: American Christianities.* New York: Penguin Press, 2007.

———. *Under God: Religion and American Politics.* New York: Simon & Schuster, 1990.

Winsboro, Irvin D. S. "Religion, Culture, and the Cold War: Bishop Fulton J. Sheen and America's Anti-Communist Crusade of the 1950s." *Historian* 71, no. 2 (June 2009): 209–233.

Winters, Michael Sean. *God's Right Hand: How Jerry Falwell Made God a Republican and Baptized the American Right.* New York: HarperOne, 2012.

———. *Left at the Altar: How the Democrats Lost the Catholics and How the Catholics Can Save the Democrats.* New York: Basic Books, 2008.

Wuthnow, Robert. *The Restructuring of American Religion.* Princeton, NJ: Princeton University Press, 1988.

Young, Neil J. *We Gather Together: The Religious Right and the Problem of Interfaith Politics.* New York: Oxford University Press, 2016.

INDEX

definition of, xxv–xxvi; formation of, xv, xvi, 20, 29, 30, 52, 56, 105, 135, 136, 143; growth of, 106, 145; illiberalism of, 5, 15, 17, 167, 168; institutions of, xxiii; key leaders of, 18; mission of, xiii; mobilizing tactics, 12, 17, 20; myth of a "traditional" past, 5, 154; national political agenda, 20–21; as political movement, xiv, 8, 19, 29, 106, 145–146; prefigurative practices of, 8, 13, 15, 21; primary sources about, xv; proactive agenda of, 54; "pro-family" platform, 7–8, 20–21, 147–148, 163; radicalism of, xvii, 12, 21–22, 53; Reagan administration and, xvi, 21, 159, 160; Republican Party and, 161; supremacist politics of, 8, 15–17, 18, 50, 51; victimhood ideology of, xvi–xvii, 5, 8, 10, 32

New Deal, 59, 61, 153, 202n46

New Left, 13

New Right: agenda of, 78; Catholicism and, xxv, 18; "child development" agenda, 98; as civil rights group, 155; coalition politics, 97, 101–102; conservatism of, 80, 86, 87–88, 89, 96–97; coordinative discourse of, 81, 92, 100, 101, 126; definition of, xxv; emphasis on social policy, 87; formation of, xiv–xv, 18–19, 67, 198n31; fragmented nature of, 97–98; fundraising campaigns, 93; goal of, 141; growth of, 92, 93; instrumentalization of "emotional" issues, 101; Nixon's resignation and, 92; organization of, 91–94; political action committees, 19, 80; political influence of, 29; political organizations launched by, 79, 93, 186n3; prefigurative practices of, 13–14; "pro-family" platform, 45, 140, 151, 164; publications of, 144; radicalism of, 12; Reagan administration and, 159, 160–161; Red Flag issues, 36; Republican Party and, 162; single-issue politics of, 91, 94–100, 168; strategies and tactics of, 85, 91; structure of, 81; think tanks network, 138; two right-wing camps within, 87; values of, 77; voter mobilization, 100, 102

Nixon, Richard: abortion issue and, 74; conservative criticism of, xiv, xvi;

laissez-faire economic worldview, 87; nominations of Supreme Court Justices, 29; political agenda of, 85; presidential elections, 79, 138; resignation of, 92; "southern strategy" of, 138; taxation of private religious schools and, 47; veto of the EOE bill, 84

Nostra Aetate declaration, 66

O'Boyle, Patrick, 71, 72
O'Brian, Neil A., 182n62
Occupy Wall Street, 13
O'Connor, Sandra Day, 160
Office of Economic Opportunity, 85
"Old Time Gospel Hour" (TV and radio show), 143, 144
Onishi, Bradley, 12
oral contraception, 137. *See also* birth control pills

Packwood, Robert, 73
Palin, Sarah, *Going Rogue*, xi
parental rights, 17, 99
"Parents' Action Guide," 118, 198n33
Parents Opposed to Sex and Sensitivity Education (POSSE), 119
Parents Opposed to Sex Education (POSE), 119
Paul VI, Pope, 62, 71
People Against Unconstitutional Sex Education (PAUSE), 119
Peripheral Urban Ethnics (PUE), 138
Perry, James, 194n54
Perry, Samuel L., 16
Phillips, Howard: founder of Conservative Caucus, 93, 98, 102, 186n3; New Right and, 144, 160; novel strategies, 56; political activism of, 91, 141; Reagan administration and, 160
Phillips, Kevin, xiv, 79, 97
Pike, James A., 35
Pius XI, Pope, *Casti Connubii* encyclical, 61
Pius XII, Pope, 67
political opportunities, 177n14
population control debates, 69–70, 74–75
postmillennialism, 110, 115
Potter, Gary, 140
Praise The Lord network, 132

www.ingramcontent.com/pod-product-compliance
Lightning Source LLC
Chambersburg PA
CBHW020249150125
20401CB00009B/210/J